DARK
PARADISE

- *NORFOLK ISLAND* -
ISOLATION, SAVAGERY, MYSTERY
AND MURDER

ROBERT MACKLIN

hachette
AUSTRALIA

This is for Aria

First published in Australia and New Zealand in 2013
by Hachette Australia
(an imprint of Hachette Australia Pty Limited)
Level 17, 207 Kent Street, Sydney NSW 2000
www.hachette.com.au

This edition published in 2016

10 9 8 7 6 5 4 3 2 1

Copyright © Robert Macklin 2013

National Library of Australia
Cataloguing-in-Publication data:

Macklin, Robert, 1941–
Dark paradise / Robert Macklin.

978 0 7336 3737 7 (pbk.)

Murder – Norfolk Island.
Murder victims – Norfolk Island.
Norfolk Island – Social conditions.
Norfolk Island – History.

364.1523099482

Cover design by Josh Durham
Cover image courtesy of Lesley McEwan Images/Flickr/Getty Images
Text design and digital production by Bookhouse
Typeset in Bembo by Bookhouse, Sydney
Printed and bound in Australia by McPherson's Printing Group

MIX
Paper | Supporting
responsible forestry
FSC® C001695

The paper this book is printed on is certified against the
Forest Stewardship Council® Standards. McPherson's Printing
Group holds FSC® chain of custody certification SA-COC-005379.
FSC® promotes environmentally responsible, socially beneficial
and economically viable management of the world's forests.

CHAPTER ONE

The uneasy past

All nations lie about their past.

The Japanese, for example, are notorious for the official euphemisms that cloak their atrocities in the Second World War. The Turks threaten their own people with death if they tell the truth about the Armenian genocide. The Israelis justify the savage oppression of their fellow Palestinian Semites with the claim that their God granted them a particular piece of real estate. The Americans attribute demigod status to their Founding Fathers, not least the slave-owning sexual predator Thomas Jefferson, and habitually invoke the blessing of *their* God for the most arrogant of their military adventures. Australians are no better – for 200 years they have denied the very existence of the frontier wars that ripped to pieces the oldest continuous living culture the world has known. But in this they have learned well from their progenitors, the true masters of historical mendacity: the British imperium.

No nation has been so successful in disguising and distorting the reality of its colonial brutality as the British. The fiction that they are to be praised for having brought 'civilisation' to the ignorant and backward masses within the empire is not just an article of faith in Britain today, it has received a general – if impressionistic – acceptance in the Western world and even among its erstwhile victims. The plunder and pillage of vast areas of Africa, for example, is set against the depravity of the Portuguese in Angola or the Belgians in Congo and found to be relatively benign. The crime against humanity that was Britain's attempt to turn an entire nation of Chinese into opium addicts – and to enforce the outrage with Indian militia – has been forgiven, if not forgotten, by a magnanimous China. The Indians themselves have consigned the splitting of their country into two warring states to historical wonderland and prosecuted two wars (with more to come) between the divided states with irrepressible enthusiasm. And even the Americans, who were forced to conduct two separate wars of independence in 1776 and 1812 to escape the British oppressor, now rejoice in a famously 'special' relationship.

The British propaganda campaign has been unremitting and astonishingly successful. The image makers have surpassed all possible expectations. They have created the world's perception of Britain as the mother of democracy despite the fact that it remains a bastion of aristocratic privilege. And in a bewildering paradox the campaigners have even engaged the comic opera of its hereditory monarchy as an earnest example of its commitment to the democratic system.

It has played the underdog brilliantly in two world wars despite its leading role in prosecuting the first and by its vindictiveness at the peace talks in Versailles creating the conditions that gave rise to the second. It has made a soaring international hero of Winston Churchill, whose madcap schemes caused the needless death of 8,000 Australians and many more of his fellow countrymen at Gallipoli and similar disasters in Norway and Dieppe in the second great conflict. Churchill is celebrated as the saviour of democracy, whereas the reality is that the war was won by the overwhelming power and resources of the United States and the Soviet Union.

It helped the image makers' cause that Churchill himself wrote history (which valued sentiment above scholarship) and that his principal antagonist was a homicidal maniac beside whom Churchill's faults seem inconsequential. And of course he was on the side of right.

It was the Second World War that marked the effective end of the British Empire, and victory allowed it to sanitise its centuries of cruel colonial oppression within the sanctimonious narrative that the world has come to accept. It has also helped that humanity's attention span is short and becoming shorter by the decade.

All of which goes some way to explain why one striking element of the narrative has never before been fully explored and understood as the *sine qua non* of the savagery that underpinned the British Empire. And it is to be found in the most unlikely setting: a tropical paradise, an emerald isle in a vast ocean of the deepest blue, surrounded and protected by natural rock walls, a haven for birds on their great migratory journeys, a nesting place free of predators, a perfect climate rarely touched by the great cyclonic swirls that thunder and carve their way across the Pacific to the north and east; a tiny place, less than 9,000 acres (3,600 hectares) of heart-shaped land, forested in parts, park-like in others with clear freshwater streams tumbling from its heights to cascade down a final slope and into the sea.

We know it now as Norfolk Island. And indeed it was the folk from the north – the British in the person of another of their flawed colonial heroes, the Yorkshireman James Cook – who in 1774 discovered and named it for a woman who, unbeknown to him, was already decomposing within an aristocratic tomb. Over the next 200 years it would host all the horrors that man's ingenuity could visit upon his fellows. So terrible have they been that even today a resident would confide to me in an unguarded moment, 'I have to tell you – Satan lives here.'

However, while the actors in the drama to follow are almost invariably British, and engaged in horrific and outrageous excesses against their fellow man, there is no intention to gratuitously traduce British colonial rule. There are wider issues at stake. While my account will, I trust, explode the myth of British benevolence, it is designed only to reveal that there is no justification for the posturing of superiority by any nation. We are all vulnerable to the urgings of the darker angels. We are all capable of the most appalling behaviour. We can never relax our vigilance as governments use ever more effective technology to manipulate sentiment and pervert our inherent sense of natural justice.

What follows is a story like no other, since it incorporates three distinct yet inseparable tales – the convict settlements that plumbed the depths of human malevolence; the mutiny on the *Bounty* and its lurid and little known aftermath; and finally the High Anglican Melanesian Mission in all its arrogance, violence, sexual predation and ultimate futility. Together they boast a cast of characters ranging from the most high-minded to the vilest ever to have walked the earth, all playing their parts in a setting that today is steeped in controversy and at the brink of total collapse. However, there is hope. It is just possible that this cursed isle will at last find redemption.

The obvious place to begin is on the bluff overlooking the seeming infinity of the Pacific Ocean as Captain Cook's converted North Sea collier, the sloop HMS *Resolution*, hoves into view. Cook is on the homeward leg of his three-year expedition to discover the fabled Great South Land – or *Terra Australis Incognita* – as its champion, Alexander Dalrymple, termed it. Sadly for Dalrymple, the first hydrographer of the Admiralty, Cook's search as far south as the Antarctic Circle and then in a giant rough rectangle around the South Pacific had blown the Scottish-born geographer's fancy to the four winds.

Not that Cook was unduly perturbed. Dalrymple was a rival for the Admiralty's favours and had sought to command the expedition himself. In the British hierarchy of the day, he had a head start through his mother's family connections. She was the daughter of the Earl of Haddington while Cook's mother Grace Pace was no one at all, except to the three surviving children of her marriage to his father, also James, a Scottish day labourer who had fled his native land following the Jacobean uprising of 1715.

Cook was that rarest of commodities in the British Navy of the time, having won his preferment largely by merit, although even he depended on the good graces of the immensely wealthy Sir Joseph Banks, whose great grandfather had made the family fortune as a real estate agent for the aristocracy of Lincolnshire. Banks had accompanied him on his first voyage to the Pacific during which he charted the east coast of Australia and claimed it for Britain, despite the obvious presence of a human population already in possession.

Cook first sighted them on the shore at Bawley Point on the far south coast of what would become New South Wales as his HMS *Endeavour* – another converted collier – buffeted its way north. From a distance, Cook wrote, 'They appear'd to be of a very dark or black Colour but whether this was the real colour of their skins or the C[l]othes they might have on I know not.'[1]

Happily for Cook and his masters, it turned out to be the former. This immediately disqualified them from fully human status, much less the right of possession of the land they had transformed over 60,000 years to 'the biggest estate on earth'.[2] However, this was no special failing in Cook's humanitarian perceptions. It had been ingrained in British Government policy since 1562 when a predecessor, Captain John Hawkins, undertook the first of three journeys carrying black slaves from Africa to the Spanish colonies in the Americas.

That was just a foretaste of a massive official enterprise. In the next 250 years, Britain would mount no fewer than 10,000 voyages trading in dark-skinned human beings, most to support their sugar plantations in Barbados and other British West Indian colonies. By 1760, only a decade before Cook's Australian sighting, Britain had clearly overtaken its Portuguese, Spanish and Dutch competitors to become the foremost European slave trader. Of the 85,000 Africans traded each year, 42,000 were carried in British ships and in such appalling conditions that often a quarter of them failed to survive the journey.

But this was of little moment in an economic bonanza that returned £4 million annually to His Majesty's Government's coffers from the plantations compared with only a quarter of that figure from all the other colonies combined. It financed not only the massive and obscenely wasteful mansions of the principals still proudly maintained as British heritage buildings, but also the Industrial Revolution that would extend Britain's imperial primacy for another 100 years.

Industrialisation would in turn create a massive metropolitan underclass in its own society.[3] These restless unfortunates would be held in check by the most draconian code of laws since Draco himself. And if they transgressed – as inevitably they did – those who escaped the frayed and sweat-soaked hangman's noose would be transported in similar conditions to the colonies, albeit with the distant prospect of eventually rejoining the white brotherhood and becoming slave owners themselves.

Cook's first voyage in the *Endeavour* would turn out to be fortuitous after George Washington crossed the Delaware in 1776 and led his American rebels to victory in the Battle of Trenton. With America no longer available as a convict dumping ground, the Great Navigator's discovery would provide a splendid alternative.

But that iconic battle was still two years away when the *Resolution* hove to among the rocky outcrops just off the north-west tip of Norfolk Island. It must have been a rare tranquil day as Cook joined his naturalists, the German Lutheran Pastor Johann Reinhold Forster, his son George and the botanist William Wales in the ship's boat that landed on the pebbled shore in the early afternoon. The Forsters were last-minute substitutes for Banks. He had wanted to bring an entourage and added an additional upper deck and a raised poop deck to the *Resolution* to accommodate them. However, sea trials had revealed the ship to be top heavy, so the Admiralty designed more modest quarters. Banks found them quite unsuitable to his station and withdrew. The substitution of the lesser qualified naturalists would be pivotal to the unfolding horrors ahead.

It appears that the party roamed the island for a single afternoon, but this was long enough for Wales to identify a species of wild flax that they all agreed would provide the raw material for canvas sails. Even better, the great pine trees that abounded in the forested areas would make for magnificent masts and spars. This was a stunning discovery. Until then, both commodities had to be imported to Britain from Riga on Russia's Baltic coast, 1,000 insecure kilometres from Portsmouth and a world away from the colonies in the Far East. As Cook recorded, 'I know of no island in the South Pacifick where a ship could supply herself with a Mast or a Yard, was she everso distress'd for want of one . . . the discovery may be both useful and valuable.'

And with that he sailed away. However, he carried with him in Forster Sr's journal a passage that provides an equally significant thread in the Norfolk tapestry. On their outward journey they had visited Tahiti where Cook was regarded with godlike awe since his initial landing there in the *Endeavour*. When the scores of canoes brought a happy, uninhibited crowd of frolicsome maidens aboard to welcome his return, the stern Lutheran pastor was almost undone. And when they went ashore the carnal delights sent his poor heart into overdrive with sights of the Tahitians and the sailors 'exercising themselves in the grassy fields of sport, wrestling on the yellow sand, others to the left and right feasting on the grass amid a scented grove of laurel, whence the mighty stream of Erydanus rolls through the woodland in the upper world'.

Son George was nowhere to be seen.

Their sister ship HMS *Adventure*, under Commander Tobias Furneaux, would take aboard a splendid young Tahitian, Omai of Ra'iatea, who would spend two years in England – much of it sporting in the beds of fashionable ladies – before Cook himself would return him to his home on his third and fatal voyage.[4] His sailing master on that journey would be one William Bligh.

The *Resolution* reached Portsmouth on 30 July 1775, and Cook was promoted, somewhat belatedly, to captain, and at 47 reluctantly accepted honorary retirement as an officer at Greenwich Hospital. From there he published his journal to great acclaim. He was showered with honours as a member of the Royal Society and awarded the Copley Gold Medal. But he was restless. 'A few months ago,' he wrote to a friend,[5] 'the whole Southern Hemisphere was hardly big enough for me, and now I am to be confined within the limits of Greenwich Hospital, which are far too small for an active mind like mine.'

He resumed married life with Elizabeth, nee Batts, the daughter of a Wapping tavern owner, and produced a sixth child, George, in 1776, but he was restless in spirit and yearned for the open sea, a stout ship and most particularly the omnipotence of command. On land in England, Cook was never allowed to forget his humble birth and mendicant status in the hierarchy. But out there among the elements he was the font of all power, the final unquestioned and unquestionable authority. It was a heady mix and Cook relished it as much as any, and more than most.

But the loneliness of command also had its darker side, and the bluff Yorkshireman was prey to the corruption of power that distorts self-perception and feasts on the generosity of spirit among those it infects. Add the physical hardships and poor diet, and the most debilitating casualty became the consistency and clear-headedness that had earlier marked his relations with those around him.

His use of the lash had been sparing on the *Endeavour*, more frequent on the voyage of the *Resolution*, where almost a fifth of his earlier crew had chosen to sail with him. But it was still no more than the average at a time when many crew members had been unwillingly pressed into service from the taverns and flophouses of Plymouth and Portsmouth. But on this third voyage – also in the refitted *Resolution* with *Discovery* under Captain Charles Clerke as sister ship – Cook became a martinet. And when they reached the Pacific his behaviour became alarmingly erratic.

He was subject to violent outbursts of rage. In Tonga, for example, he broke his own strict rules of earlier visits by meting out floggings of up to six dozen lashes to islanders who stole from his ships. And as a midshipman noted, his punishments became increasingly bizarre, 'cutting off their ears, firing at them with small shot or ball as they were swimming or paddling to the shore; and suffering the [crewmen] to beat them with the oars; and stick the boathook into them wherever they could hit them'.[6] Another wrote, 'I cannot help thinking the man totally destitute of humanity.'[7]

However, when they reached Tahiti's Matavai Bay, the ecstatic welcome from the islanders calmed his ragged spirits as they boarded the ships, 'weeping and slashing themselves, searching for old friends and lovers and embracing them fervently when they found them'.[8] Cook declared a day of festivity. According to the surgeon, David Samwell, when night fell a group of women dressed in short ruffled skirts performed a dance designed to drive the crewmen – Master Bligh among them – wild with desire. The dance, he wrote, 'bespoke an excess of joy and licentiousness . . . most were young women who put themselves into several lascivious postures, clapp'd their hands and repeated a kind of Stanzas. At certain parts they put their garments aside and exposed with seemingly very little sense of shame those parts which most nations have thought it modest to conceal, & a woman of more advanced years stood in front, held her cloaths continually up with one hand and danced with uncommon vigour and effrontery as if to raise in the spectators the most libidinous desires.'

The crewmen, he says, responded with 'a sort of rapture that could only be expressed by the extreme joy that appeared on their countenances'.[9] Well, not quite the only response. In truth, the six-week sojourn was a glorious sensual orgy, a careless delight at the time, but it would have only the most sad and terrible consequences. The crewmen had brought venereal diseases with them and, perhaps unknowingly, had spread them among their various partners. The exuberant sexual expression intrinsic to Tahitian society meant they would eventually take a terrible toll.

The visit would confirm Cook's dangerously inflated perception of himself as a demigod among the Pacific Islanders, and this would lead to his violent death at their hands before his tiny convoy returned to Britain. And it was *ne plus ultra* of Bligh's experience with the Great Navigator. It is highly doubtful whether young William indulged himself sexually. Certainly he made no 'island marriage' as did so many of his fellows. As will be seen, there are indications that he was somewhat ambiguous in his sexuality. But equally, he may well have patterned his behaviour on that of the father figure who had taken the ambitious 22-year-old in hand and tutored him in all the finer arts of navigation and hydrography. (Indeed, he would later represent himself to the Tahitians as James Cook's son.)

Cook seems to have resisted the gentle consolations so freely offered by the Tahitian chieftains and indeed the women themselves. Or if he did indulge, it was within the discreet confines of his Great Cabin on the *Resolution*. Either way, Bligh would have been impressed by the fact that, in spite of his increasingly erratic behaviour, Cook's command at sea would never be questioned, much less challenged, by those who served under him.

Cook's violent demise in Hawaii in February 1779 came as a terrible blow to his young admirer. But worse was in store. Bligh, it seems, was decidedly unpopular with the deputy commander, Captain John Gore, and on publication of the edited journal of the voyage he would be denied any credit for the pioneering hydrographic surveys he had undertaken. That went to his assistant Henry Roberts, whom Gore found a much more congenial character. Worse, Roberts was promoted to lieutenant while Bligh remained in the lower ranks as master. He was deeply humiliated and aggrieved.

His only consolation was his marriage in 1781 to the attractive and modestly well-connected Betsy Betham on the Isle of Man, a match that would endure for 31 years – despite (or perhaps because of) Bligh's frequent absence and wildly turbulent fortune – ending with her utter exhaustion in 1812. The marriage had been a step up the social ladder for Bligh, born on 9 September 1754 in his grandfather's stone farmhouse in Cornwall. His father

Francis worked as a customs officer in Plymouth and helped on the farm. And though there was naval tradition in the family background, by the time William was born there was no relative in the service who could act as his patron.[10]

At only seven, Bligh was enlisted as a captain's servant on the 64-gun warship HMS *Monmouth* – which rarely left its Plymouth moorings – and attended school on shore. At 15 he confirmed his intention to pursue a career in the navy by enlisting as an able-bodied seaman while waiting for a midshipman's berth. It arrived six months later when he was posted to HMS *Crescent*, a 32-gun frigate under the command of Captain James Corner. For three years the *Crescent* patrolled the Leeward Islands of the West Indies and Bligh surveyed and charted parts of the archipelago. Corner was a harsh disciplinarian, and in 1774 on the ship's return to England he had 17 of his crew flogged for attempted desertion. The lessons would not have been lost on the short, balding midshipman.

Bligh transferred to the eight-gun sloop HMS *Ranger* on smuggling patrol in the Irish Sea terminating at the Isle of Man, where Betsy's family boasted an uncle, Duncan Campbell, a wealthy merchant who owned convict hulks on the Thames and a fleet of merchant vessels trading with the slave colonies of the West Indies.

Bligh's progress up the Admiralty ladder was painfully slow, and although he passed his master's examination and completed the six years at sea required for a naval commission, he remained a lowly midshipman. When Cook appointed him the *Resolution*'s master, he remained a senior warrant officer, though the opportunity to work in harness with the Great Navigator was highly prized. When on his return his achievements were overlooked,

Bligh was not just angry and resentful, but he nursed a sense of umbrage and rancour that would bite deep into his personality.

He finally secured an acting commission in September 1781 as a 5th lieutenant on the 74-gun HMS *Berwick* as Britain engaged in yet another battle for maritime dominance, this time against the Dutch. Other minor postings followed in various engagements against French and Spanish squadrons until in 1783, the Americans having finally secured their independence with the signing of the Peace of Paris, the British felt able to reduce their naval expenditure. Bligh was discharged on half pay, a lordly two shillings a day. Penury beckoned. Only Betsy's family stood between the anxious, irascible junior lieutenant and total despair. And of them, only her uncle Duncan provided an avenue of escape. When he offered Bligh a post as captain of the *Lynx*, one of his West Indian traders, at £500 a year the 29-year-old leapt at the chance to be a 'rum and sugar captain' in the merchant marine. Over the next four years he plied the Atlantic as commander of various ships within Campbell's fleet.

During his preparation of the *Britannia* for sea, he received a fateful letter from a well-known Isle of Man family seeking his indulgence. They had 10 children, and two of the sons were sent to Cambridge, but following the death of the head of the house – an attorney – they had fallen on hard times. Despite his excellent record at school, the next eldest son was unable to follow his brothers to university. So the 18-year-old enlisted in the navy as a midshipman and soon rose to the rank of acting lieutenant. Now he too was a victim of the peace and his mother appealed to Bligh to find a place for him.

His name was Fletcher Christian.

At first Bligh resisted. He'd already signed on a full complement of officers. Then came a personal plea from Christian himself. Wages were no object; his sole concern was to pursue his career. 'We Midshipmen are gentlemen,' he wrote. 'We never pull at a rope. I should even be glad to go on one voyage in that situation, for there may be occasions when officers may be called upon to do the duties of a common man.'[11]

Bligh relented and Christian signed on as a gunner. Almost as soon as they met, Bligh was attracted to the tall, handsome, athletic (if bow-legged) 23-year-old. And Christian himself seems to have been proudly adept at gaining the approval and affections of his shipmates.

'It was very easy to make oneself beloved on board a ship,' he wrote to his brother Edward. 'One only has to be ready to obey one's superior officers, and to be kind to the common men.'

It certainly worked with Bligh, whom he described as a 'passionate' man and who urged his officers on the *Britannia* to treat him as one of their own. The chief mate on the ship, Edward Lamb, would later tell Bligh, 'I saw your partiality to the young man. I gave him every advice and information in my power, though he went about every point of duty with a degree of indifference that to me was truly unpleasant; but you were blind to his faults and had him to dine and sup every other day in the cabin; and treated him like a brother in giving him every information.'[12]

Meanwhile, Uncle Duncan's convict hulks – and others like them – were filled to overflowing. In the Thames and in the southern harbours from Plymouth to Portsmouth, the convicts were penned like animals within the decommissioned naval vessels as disease and starvation took their inevitable toll. The shore-based gaols threatened to burst at the seams. Something had to be done.

Transportation was by no means a novel solution. It had been part of government policy since 1620, and both Scottish and Irish prisoners of war had actually been sold as slaves in North America. But the total numbers involved were about 50,000 over almost two centuries. The new policy with Botany Bay as its destination was of a different order of magnitude. Now a whole criminal underclass was to be banished to a destination about which almost nothing was known but for the most fleeting landfalls on the east coast.

When the 47-year-old part-time farmer Captain Arthur Phillip set sail on 13 May 1787 with 772 convicts and their gaolers aboard 11 ships of the First Fleet, he carried with him instructions to establish a second settlement on a much smaller destination — Cook's chance discovery in the 'South Pacifick': Norfolk Island.

CHAPTER TWO

Colonial beginnings

The British Empire came relatively late to the missionary game. While the Portuguese and the Spanish conquistadors brandished a sword in one hand and the Bible in the other, the British overlords showed very little interest in converting their colonies to Christianity until the second half of the 18th century. If their black slaves actually possessed souls – a much debated notion – then they would have to find their own path to a blissful eternity; their owners were much more interested in squeezing the last drop of profit from their corporeal flesh.

As early as 1724, the Colonial divine, Jonathan Edwards, welcomed the possibility of 'gospelising' not just the native Americans but those of *Terra Australis Incognita* and other remote regions of the Pacific 'where', he noted, 'the devil has reigned quietly from the beginning of the world'.[1] But it would be another 70 years before his urgings bore tropical fruit.

When Arthur Phillip landed at Sydney Cove on 26 January 1788, he was accompanied by an Anglican chaplain, Richard Johnson, who had joined the fleet at the insistence of William Wilberforce, a wealthy and influential MP who had undergone a religious conversion during his grand tour of the Continent. But while Wilberforce pursued his Christian vocation and became a leading proponent of the abolition of the slave trade, neither Chaplain Johnson nor Governor Phillip were much interested in 'gospelising' the Australian natives. Indeed, there is no record of any contact between Johnson and the Aboriginal population, and Phillip would spare neither the labour not the materials to build his chaplain a church. It was not until five years later that Johnson finally erected one himself, using £67 from the tidy profit that convict slave labour that had turned on his farm. It burned down in 1798. Johnson departed for England three years later, never to return.

However, his assistant and successor Samuel Marsden was made of sterner stuff. Where Johnson was a well-connected grammar school lad, Marsden was the son of a blacksmith who received a basic education at the village school before being apprenticed to his father. In his late teens, he was much taken with the Methodist revivalists in his native Yorkshire and soon became a prominent lay preacher.

This attracted the attention of one John Milner, the head-master of the same grammar school in Hull that both Johnson and Wilberforce had attended. And although the preacher was by now 24, Milner offered him a place as a student. Marsden accepted, studied hard and Wilberforce sponsored his entry to Magdalene College, Cambridge in 1790. Three years later – again at Wilberforce's initiative – he set forth for the convict colony of New South Wales and its satellite, Norfolk Island. After he unpacked his few belongings and settled his new wife Elizabeth on a small land grant at Parramatta, he set sail for Norfolk, arriving early in 1795.

Much had occurred there in the previous seven years.

Only 18 days after the First Fleet's arrival, Phillip had dispatched his protégé Lieutenant Philip Gidley King to establish a settlement on the island. King was 34 and unmarried. Born in Launceston, Cornwall to a local draper, he had joined the navy at 12 as captain's servant on the HMS *Swallow* in 1770 just as Captain Cook was charting the east coast of *Terra Australis* on the other side of the world.[2] The 60-gun warship would now carry King to the Far East, where as a midshipman over the next five years he would also serve on HMS *Dolphin* and the HMS *Prudent*, showing the flag in Britain's pursuit of naval supremacy.

On the outbreak of war with the American colony, he was posted to the HMS *Liverpool* in American waters then transferred to the HMS *Renown*, where he saw action against the French fleet and secured his lieutenant's commission in 1779. The following year he met the man whose influence would guide the rest of his life – Captain Arthur Phillip, his master and commander on the HMS *Ariadne*. Their mutual attraction and trust would serve both men well. They sailed together for three years and scored victories over the French and American forces. When Phillip was given command of HMS *Europe*[3] for a mission to India in 1784, he arranged King's transfer to the ship.

On their return both men were retired on half pay, and while Phillip had the consolation of a splendid property in Hampshire courtesy of his wife's first husband (a member of the noble

Pembroke line), Lieutenant King was soon in financial straits. So when Phillip responded to the call in 1786 to head the first major disposal of the underclass to the unmapped and largely unknown southern land and called upon King to rejoin him, the 32-year-old Cornishman leapt at the chance.

By now he had acquired many of the attributes that would define his character and conduct for the 18 years remaining to him. His face was fleshy, his figure full, reflecting a predisposition for rich foods and large helpings. He retained his Cornish accent and despite his conservative opinions would never be accepted as 'a gentleman' by his more favoured rivals. His constitution was never robust, and the hard stressful life in the colonies would take a fierce toll of both his health and his temperament.

When he set out for Norfolk from Sydney Cove in HMS *Supply* with his group of 15 convicts – nine male and six female – and seven free men including two marine guards, he was in high spirits. This was his opportunity to stand out from the ruck and if, as expected, the flax and pines could be converted to sails, masts and spars for the British Fleet, there was a triumph in the making.

The rest of his company cannot have entertained such cheerful expectations. If transportation to New South Wales[4] was comparable in the 18th century to a journey to the dark side of the Moon, the additional voyage was to a barely glimpsed asteroid in the infinity of space. Shortly after they sailed through the Heads they were struck by a storm with winds so powerful that the experienced King confided to his journal, 'I often thought it was a critical situation.'

The tough little 175 ton *Supply* under the command of Lieutenant Henry Ball survived the onslaught and the next few days were plain sailing. However, the strange and forbidding nature of their journey was confirmed two days out when passengers and crew were treated to a dreadful sight – a huge thresher shark leapt from the water like some vengeful monster from the deep to attack a whale each time it rose to breathe. After more than an hour of unremitting struggle the seagoing mammal surrendered its life to the predator.

They reached the island on leap day – February 29 – but then spent five days in the ship's boat searching for a passage through reef and rocks to a safe landing. Finally, at noon on 5 March, the *Supply*'s master David Blackburn went out alone and discovered a channel through the reef at what would become Sydney Bay, where tents, stores and the 23 souls who would remain could be disembarked.

This was completed by late afternoon, and King and Ball assembled their people on the shore for a much beloved British ritual to mark their ownership of the tiny territory. They raised the colours on a flagpole imported for the occasion and drank the health of His Majesty King George III – at the time foaming at the mouth in the grip of porphyria at Cheltenham Spa; the Queen, formerly Princess Charlotte of Mecklenburg-Strelitz, who met her husband-to-be on their wedding day; and the Prince of Wales, their eldest son, a scandalous voluptuary who during his 10-year reign as George IV would earn the contempt of the entire nation.

But despite the Royal auguries, there was no doubting King's enthusiasm for the task ahead as he led the party in three ragged cheers on the alien shore. He already had his eye on one of the convict women, Ann Inett, a 30-year-old dressmaker condemned to death by hanging for the theft of clothing from one of her customers, later commuted to seven years transportation. She would bear him the first child native to the island, a boy he would name – somewhat literally – Norfolk.

Her five convict sisters, who were also expected to join the cheering (and the mating), were Elizabeth Hipsley, also a dressmaker convicted of the theft of a few miserable possessions of another; Olivia Gaskin, found guilty of robbery of less than £15 and condemned to hang; Elizabeth Colley, the recipient of a stolen gown and cloak; Susannah Gough who had been on the game in London's back streets; and Elizabeth Lee, a 24-year-old cook who had played a part in the theft of the liquor store of her employer, one Thomas King.[5]

The nine male convicts had also been tried for non-violent crimes and all had been selected on the advice of the First Fleet's surgeon, Arthur Bowes Smyth. However, while most were able-bodied, he unaccountably included the 72-year-old thief Richard Widdicombe and a 14-year-old cutpurse, Charles McLellan. Bowes, as he was known in New South Wales, also recommended the seven free men to join the party – two surgeon's mates, Thomas Jamison and John Altree, the master's mate on the HMS *Sirius*, James Cunningham, as well as seamen Roger Morley and William Westbrook, skilled in weaving and woodwork respectively; and marine guards John Batchelor and Charles Kerridge.

As the *Supply* set sail and disappeared behind the dark silhouette of Phillip Island to the south-east, the small gathering could be forgiven for thinking themselves more the victims of a marooning than as colonial pioneers. For it must have seemed that no humans had ever before ventured upon this speck in the vast Pacific Ocean, much less settled there.

Until the late 20th century when Australian archeologists discovered clear evidence of their presence, no one was aware that Norfolk Island had been first settled by a small community – estimated between 20 and 50 – of East Polynesian seafarers either from the Kermadec Islands or from the North Island of New Zealand.[6] They arrived by double canoe in the 13th to 15th centuries, and survived for several generations before disappearing, whether from voluntary abandonment or the kind of internal violence that, as we shall see, is endemic to a small, isolated community with a serious imbalance of the sexes. Their main village site has been excavated at Emily Bay, just 500 metres from the spot where King and his band raised their flag.

They built a communal house and a religious *marae* or shrine, and lived on a varied diet of fish, birds, shellfish and the occasional seal before disappearing into the mists of pre-history. But they left behind two elements of the utmost significance to the British settlers. One was the *harakeke* (*Phormium tenax*), or New Zealand flax plant, which had so attracted the Admiralty. In fact, it is no relation to European flax but at the time this disparity seemed to matter little to Cook's naturalists or the naval hierarchy.

The other was more insidious – the Polynesian rat had either travelled undetected in the Maori longboats or been deliberately imported for its protein. Either way it had secured a foothold in the predator-free environment then spread across the island. Now its numerous descendants were joined by some stowaways from the *Supply*'s bilges: their British cousins. They had scampered into the thick undergrowth and would glory in this true paradise for their kind. They would mate and multiply exponentially. Soon they would threaten the very existence of the micro-colony.

Unaware of his lurking adversary, King set his party to work at dawn the next day. 'I began to clear a piece of ground for sowing some seeds,' he wrote. 'We found a very fine rivulet of water which ran close to the back of the settlement.' However, he was aware of his limitations. 'As I had only 12 men, exclusive of the mate and surgeon, my progress for some time must of course be slow.'[7]

He oversaw the planting of the grain and its tending by the female convicts. He put the sawyer, William Westbrook, in charge of a party of men to cut down the pines for building log huts. They proved adequate for the purpose. But unfortunately for King and his Admiralty commanders they were much too brittle for masts or spars. This was a fearful blow. Another was to follow; at first King was unable to find any evidence of the flax that had so excited Cook and his naturalists. But then what he'd taken for 'a kind of iris'[8] growing in abundance all around them was identified by Surgeon Jamison as the New Zealand flax plant.

His seaman–weaver Roger Morley was unfamiliar with it and was unsure how to process the plant into cloth. He knew that the first step was 'retting', where the inner stalk was rotted away leaving the outer fibres intact. Once the straw within the fibres was extracted by breaking it into short lengths, the remaining fibres would be available for the next stage in the process. Morley soaked the stalks in the rivulet and in time made a reasonable fist of the retting. However, that was the limit of his knowledge and he could proceed no further.

King reported this progress in his journal and noted the need for additional expertise, perhaps from New Zealand, which was then regarded as part of New South Wales. Until that could be secured he turned his attention to more pressing matters. The timber cutters were continually in need of treatment for serious cuts and broken limbs. Then a previously unknown species of conifer spurted sap that blinded one man and left others in excruciating pain. Surgeon Jamison and his assistant, the eponymous John Altree, tended their complaints with only the most basic medicaments.

More troubling was the morale of some key members of the party. The early enthusiasm of the tiny band had quickly dissipated. Sexual tension replaced it. Men outnumbered women by three to one. The disparity was exacerbated when Olivia Gaskin and Susannah Gough paired up with two of their fellow convicts and Surgeon Jamison solemnised the unions with what passed for a marriage service on the island. With Ann Inett already claimed by King that left only three, all named Elizabeth – Hipsley the seamstress, Colley the servant girl and Lee the cook – available for 13 lusty males (not counting the 72-year-old Richard Widdicombe) through the long, soft, tropical nights.

The result was predictable: arguments, fights and a resort to hard liquor. It reached a crisis when King caught John Batchelor, one of the two marines sent to maintain order, stealing rum from his tent. King reacted swiftly and decisively. 'In the afternoon,' he confided to his journal, 'I assembled the settlement and punished the offender with 36 lashes, causing him to be led by a halter to the place of punishment.'[9]

If King believed that the public thrashing would discourage others, he was soon disappointed. Only three days later the libidinous 15-year-old Charles McLellan was caught red-handed rifling rum from Surgeon Jamison's billet. 'I ordered him to be punished with 100 lashes which I hope will have good effect,' he wrote.

For the moment, it seems to have ended the pilfering of liquor, and King took the opportunity to codify his own set of island laws into 11 commandments and to proclaim them on the noticeboard on 18 April. They began with a nod in the direction of his Mosaic predecessor with the demand that all attend divine service 'in the commandant's house' every Sunday morning at 11 o'clock 'and behave themselves devoutly'. Thereafter they dealt with the daily work schedule – daylight to sunset with breaks for breakfast (7.30 to 8.30) and lunch (11.30 to 2.00); Saturday to be devoted to the cultivation of their private gardens. Throughout the week the women would cook and clean, and on Fridays they would collect the men's dirty linen and return it washed and mended on Sunday morning. The men were responsible for the maintenance of their tools and either handed them in to the storekeeper or guarded them in their tents.

The commandments included several idiosyncratic taboos. Some were easily understandable. For example, they were forbidden from cleaning fish near the houses; this had to be done by the seashore for obvious hygiene reasons. And they were banned from chopping down any banana trees (another legacy of the fleeting Polynesian settlement).

Less clear was the injunction against exchanging items of clothing with each other, since all clothing and bedding was the property of the crown. However, the most serious prohibition was for anyone to stray in or near Turtle Bay. 'Every person is strictly forbid [sic] going near,' he wrote. 'Those who are found in it, or going there, will be instantly and severely punished.'

The reasons for the prohibition are not immediately obvious. Turtle Bay – later renamed Emily Bay – is a sandy beach leading to still water. Perhaps the island's skiff or fishing boat was anchored there.

Finally, King's commandments offered a carrot and stick. Those who showed a willing disposition to work and be honest and obliging to each other would find favour with 'those in power' – that is, himself. However, the dishonest and idle 'will be totally excluded from any present or future indulgences and will also be chastised, either by corporal punishment on the island or be sent to Port Jackson to be tried in a criminal court'.

Whether or not his admonitions worked with the settlers, the island itself brought forces to play that were quite beyond his power to command. Hot winds combined with the rats to devastate the grain shoots. Any plants that survived the initial assault fell victim to a particularly ravenous species of caterpillar grub. King organised a counterattack. He devised rat traps using empty casks and caught 'upwards of 1,000'; as well, Surgeon Jamison concocted a mixture of oatmeal and ground glass that put paid to many of those who avoided the traps. The women were enlisted to hand-pick the grubs and caterpillars but despite their best efforts they barely dented the underground population.

They had greater success with the rich red soil of their private corn and vegetable patches around their tents and huts. And as they specialised, a rough system of barter encouraged the producers to greater efforts. However, King realised that more hands were needed if the micro-colony were to become self-sufficient and able to export its surplus to the mainland, where Phillip's settlement was in desperate straits.

King's problems were exacerbated when in April John Batchelor, the first man on the island to feel the lash, drowned – either by accident or design – when on a solitary fishing expedition in a small boat. Fish were plentiful, though the convict palates favoured salt beef and pork. King, by contrast, relished the local seafood. 'There are fish in great quantities and of delicious flavour and large size about half a mile from land,' he wrote. 'Streams contain a number of eels, larger and finer than any I saw in England.'[10] Despite his best efforts he secured few converts. Indeed, substitution of fish for meat would soon become the trigger for Norfolk's first attempted mutiny.

Three other men were lost in August when their boat smashed into rocks as they unloaded stores and tools from the visiting *Supply*. This meant a fifth of his scarce manpower had been claimed by the sea in less than six months. When the HMS *Golden Grove* arrived shortly afterwards with a further 20 male and female convicts, the new additions would cause as many problems as their numbers would solve.

King put them to work on a second attempt to grow grain, and this time he was more successful. His optimistic reports to Phillip encouraged the governor to send more convicts, and with them an increasing number of freemen together with half a dozen marine guards. However, this meant the loss of King's personalised relationship with the original members and the resumption of the inherent conflict between the prisoners and their gaolers. Eleven months from the first comic opera ceremonial on Norfolk's shore, the convict ringleaders headed by one William Francis devised a plot to capture and kill the authority figures on the island.

They knew that King indulged himself on Saturdays with a visit to the now heavily pregnant Ann Inett, whom he'd established on a little farm in the area he'd named Arthur's Vale after his beloved patron. To get there he had to pass through a forest, and there they would lie in wait.

They also knew that the marines occupied themselves on Saturdays in another part of the forest collecting the sweet red berries of the cabbage palms. So if their timing was right, they would first capture King then send to the surgeon's house to report he'd been injured in a fall and say they needed both him and his colleague, John Altree. They in turn would be 'dealt with'. Then, when the marines returned down the same path from their foraging, the mutineers would be waiting to overpower them. That would put them in effective command of the settlement.

The second phase of the plan was more problematic. When the next ship arrived from Port Jackson (or elsewhere), they would capture and conceal the first boat party to reach the shore. Then three convicts – one dressed as an officer – would row out in their own small skiff and report that the boat had struck rocks and was badly damaged. So a second lighter would be employed to bring stores and (with a little luck) the captain and his top wardroom colleagues to dine at the commandant's invitation. They would suffer the same fate. Now with two big boats at their disposal – together with their own craft – the mutineers would row out after dark and overpower the remaining officers and crew. With the ship safely secured, the convicts would bring their comrades aboard and set sail for Tahiti leaving the island to the survivors – if indeed they spared any to tell the tale.

It was a bold, if bloodthirsty, plan and soon the overwhelming majority had signed on to it. However, with so many 'in the know' it was bound to leak to the authorities. And it did so through the agency of a gardener, Robert Webb. His paramour, Elizabeth Anderson, was eager for him to sign up, but Webb resisted and finally told King.

The commandant was flabbergasted and at first refused to believe it. But then the only other male convicts who had declined to join – a rope-maker, John Rice, and two carpenters, Nathaniel Lucas and the ageing Richard Widdicombe, all 'originals' – confirmed the allegation.

King acted swiftly and soon had William Francis, 'a troublesome wretch . . . of the most villainous kind', in heavy chains. He was appalled to discover that 26 of the 29 male convicts had joined the plot. It was a fatal blow to his naive ambitions for the colony as some kind of benevolent commune. He sent Francis in chains back to Port Jackson with a request to Phillip that if he were to be hanged – King's preferred punishment – then he should be returned to Norfolk for his dispatch 'so that an example may be made'.

In the event, the mutineer was spared on a technicality: no insurrection had actually taken place so neither did the trial. Instead he served his time with 'hard labour' and his subsequent fate is unknown. King was not pleased. But he determined to do his best to ensure there would be no repetition.

Lieutenant David Collins, the deputy judge advocate of the colony in New South Wales, later wrote, 'Mr King had . . . treated them with [the] kind attentions which a good family meets with at the hands of a humane master; but now he saw them in their true colours.'[11] He withdrew from their company. He had them clear the trees from around the settlement to reduce their capacity to gather in private. As it happened, this probably saved many lives, since almost immediately afterwards a fierce hurricane struck the island, bringing huge pines crashing down in the area surrounding the tents and flimsy huts.

But while King would have rejoiced that his actions saved lives, he expected (and received) no thanks from the convicts. As 1789 drew to a close, the new regime of the colony had taken on all the insidious characteristics of a gaol with conflict simmering just beneath the surface.

Governor Phillip added vinegar to the mix by deciding to use Norfolk as the dumping ground for some of his more intransigent villains while warning King, 'No confidence can be placed in the convicts whatever.' However, he sugared his decision with a personal blessing, 'I assure you every part of your conduct meets my warmest approbation.'[12]

CHAPTER THREE

Mutiny

While King was asserting his command over a recalcitrant rabble seduced by the charms of escape to Tahiti, another principal in the drama was similarly beset in the fabled isle itself. Captain William Bligh in his converted collier HMS *Bounty* reached Tahiti on 26 October 1788 and sailed up the east coast in brilliant sunshine, tacked around the aptly named Point Venus into Matavai Bay and a delirious welcome from the islanders.

Though he would disguise it in euphemisms and outright lies to the Tahitians, his mission was in support of his empire's slave colonies. The brainchild of Sir Joseph Banks, the island's native breadfruit plants were to be dug up and transported to the West Indies to feed the sugar industry's human chattels. The plants would be an excellent substitute for bread made from grain since it 'is procurd [*sic*] with no more trouble than that of climbing a tree and bringing it down'.[1]

Bounty, with its figurehead of an aristocratic young lady in a green riding habit, was only 84 feet (25.6 metres) long and had been specially fitted to store the hundreds of plants required for transplantation. This involved one alteration that would prove highly significant in the dramatic events to follow. The Great Cabin, the most spacious and handsome chamber aboard, was the captain's exclusive domain in naval vessels, and added dignity and gravitas to its occupant. This was a valuable asset at a time when a ship's master exercised the power of life and death over a crew. However, on the *Bounty* it was remodelled to accommodate the breadfruit plants. The diminutive Lieutenant William Bligh – still smarting for having been denied promotion to captain – was forced to live cheek by jowl with the crew in much reduced quarters. The commander's tiny cabin was set amidships on the lower deck, opposite the sailing master's quarters on the port side. Between them was the captain's cramped dining room and pantry. The effect was not only to strip away the lofty authority of the commander, but also to exacerbate Bligh's own inferiority complex.

This was particularly so in his turbulent relationship with the athletic young man he had chosen as his master's mate, Fletcher Christian. By now they had become more than usually close. When the *Bounty* had been anchored off the Isle of Wight waiting final orders to depart for the South Seas, Bligh's wife Betsy and his daughters travelled there to be near him. Bligh took Christian with him several times to meet his family. He also lent him a sum of money.

Christian's brother Charles also took the opportunity to visit Fletcher on the island and was much taken with his youthful vigour. He could leap from a standing start in one ship's barrel to its neighbour without touching the sides of either. When he bared his arm Charles was amazed at its brawniness. Fletcher laughed. 'This has been acquired by hard labour,' he said. 'I delight to set the men an example. I not only can do every part of a common sailor's duty but am on a par with a principal part of the officers.'[2]

Though he was only a midshipman on the *Bounty*, shortly after they sailed on 23 December 1787 Bligh promoted him to acting lieutenant over the master, John Fryer, and put him in charge of the third watch. But at the same time he constantly found fault with Christian's seamanship and harped on the debt he had yet to repay. His unpredictable and 'passionate rages' were invariably directed at his protégé and he threatened to write to his brother demanding repayment with interest.

Christian reacted with equal passion. According to a shipmate, he was 'excessively annoyed at the share of the blame which repeatedly fell to his lot [and] could ill endure the additional taunt of private obligations'.[3] The latent homosexual nature of the relationship would seem to leap from the textbook, and indeed the tradition of a service that a First Lord, Winston Churchill, would characterise as 'rum, sodomy, prayers and the lash'.[4] It is unlikely that the attraction was ever consummated; had that occurred it would undoubtedly have emerged during the mutineers' trial. But Bligh's obsession with the man's physicality is nicely demonstrated in his written description of him as 'five feet nine inches high, blackish or very dark complexion; strong made; a star tattooed on his left breast . . . his knees stand out a little and he may be called rather bow-legged . . . he is subject to violent perspirations, and particularly in his hands, so that he soils anything he handles.'[5]

Then there is the unusual observation that the young man is 'tattoed on his backside'. It is perfectly possible that in the crowded intimacy of the ship in tropical climes the captain would have had opportunities to observe his protégé naked. If so, the tattoo obviously seared itself into his memory.

The rest of the crew — 44 petty officers and seamen in total — lived in greater discomfort than their master and commander. The petty officers shared quarters for'ard, the midshipmen amidships, and the 13 seamen slung their hammocks beside the smells and snorts of the livestock (pigs, sheep and goats) to be slaughtered along the way.

The outward voyage had been relatively frictionless. Bligh followed the precepts of his mentor James Cook in ensuring his men received a hot breakfast and a change of dry clothes when they went below. Like Cook, he conducted 'dancing' on deck as exercise and also took his lead in combating scurvy. In the first five months, he recorded no instance of it, nor of flux or fever.

He was also proud of the discipline aboard, which in the early weeks he achieved without the usual recourse to the lash. In fact, it was more than two months before he had a sailor stripped to the waist and spread-eagled against the deck grating for two dozen lashes. The charge, levelled by sailing master Fryer, was 'insolence and contempt'. The offender was an able seaman, Matthew Quintal, and the punishment was no doubt well deserved. Quintal was a thug and his subsequent actions would reveal few if any redeeming features.

Bligh steered his ship south and west to the coast of South America, then attempted to round the Horn. But the fierce winds were against him and he finally turned away — to the cheers of his crew — and made for the Cape of Good Hope.

There he repaired and restocked the *Bounty* and set sail before the Roaring Forties for Tasmania, arriving at Adventure Bay on Bruny Island off the south-west coast on 21 August 1788.

In the days following, they took firewood aboard and Bligh had his first serious contretemps with his petty officers, exhibiting one of the 'violent tornadoes' of temper that disfigured his captaincy and his character. He accused his carpenter William Purcell of cutting the logs too long for easy storage and put him on short rations for several days.

Soon afterwards he clashed with his surgeon, Thomas Huggan – notoriously fund of rum – over the death of an able-bodied seaman, James Valentine, from an infected wound. He then found himself in conflict with master Fryer whom he forced to countersign 'good behaviour' reports of some of his colleagues, much against Fryer's inclinations.

But it was his hot-and-cold relationship with Fletcher Christian that disrupted the harmony of the ship's company as the *Bounty* headed to what Bligh called 'the Paradise of the World'. And when the captain ordered David Nelson, the gardener–botanist who had been with Cook on his final voyage and spoke Tahitian reasonably well, to tell the welcoming chieftains that he was actually Cook's son, Christian joined with the other petty officers in laughing up his sleeve.

By contrast, the effect on the islanders was profound. If Cook was a god, his son was at least a demigod, and that meant he and his men were welcome to all the Tahitians had to offer. And over the next two months they grabbed it with both hands. Bligh revelled in his exalted role, while the rest of the ship's company – Christian prominent among them – gloried in the sensual gifts of the island women. He and the other midshipmen – Thomas Haywood, the sallow-skinned Edward Young from the West Indies and George Stewart from the Orkneys – enjoyed a marathon of sexual extravagance. From time to time they were joined in their adventures by the master at arms Corporal Charles Churchill, gunner's mate John Mills, bosun's mate James Morrison, and another midshipman, Peter Heywood.

They had known nothing like it in the straight-laced society of Britain with its furtive couplings in the dark. Nor had they experienced such unabashed admiration and acceptance from the opposite sex. They marked their membership of this glorious club by having a star tattooed on the left of their chests. Little wonder that when a total of 774 breadfruit pots were squeezed into the Great Cabin by Christmas Eve 1788 they were dismayed that this golden idyll was soon to end.

But then a series of events delayed their departure. First came a fearsome cyclone that kept them at anchor sheltering behind the mound of Venus for several days. When the weather cleared on 5 January, three of their number – Churchill, John Millward and William Muspratt – deserted the ship. Bligh postponed the sailing date until they were recaptured. One of Christian's followers, Thomas Hayward, had been on watch at the time and his excuse – that he'd fallen asleep – sent Bligh into a rage. He ordered Hayward clapped in irons and threatened him with the full force of the law. He was even more furious when he discovered the deserters had fled in the ship's cutter and taken with them an arms chest of eight muskets and ammunition.

He sent John Fryer after them, and with the help of some Tahitians he retrieved the cutter. However, Fryer reported that the men had probably been offered sanctuary by tribal chieftains who valued their firepower in the endless hostilities between island tribes. Bligh searched the men's quarters and discovered in Churchill's sea chest a list of names, including Christian's and Peter Heywood's, whom he took to be plotting against him since it was customary when mutiny was afoot for the organisers to insist that each man commit himself on paper before the act as a precaution against backsliding on the day. According to historian Anne Salmond, 'It is likely that Christian, Stewart and Morrison, and perhaps others, had made some kind of pact during their time on the island . . . but this does not mean that they had decided to desert the ship or mutiny against their captain.'[6]

It took the Tahitians several days to track the deserters down, and Bligh himself came ashore to direct their seizure. As it happened, he found the three men waiting for him in willing surrender. Unimpressed, he had them clapped in irons, severely lashed with the cat o' nine tails and remanded for 'further punishment'. He then assembled the crew and read sections of the Articles of War in a fiery lecture on 'Desertion and Entertaining Deserters', which mandated a death sentence for offenders. He believed it had a salutary effect; and he reinforced it with a further public lashing of the deserters on 4 February.

The swaying palms and languorous lifestyle ashore were so at odds with the order and routine of naval tradition that Bligh, caught in the middle, found it increasingly difficult to take the strain. For example, when the spare sails were unfurled and laid on the beach to air prior to departure, the canvas was found to be mildewed and rotten at the seams. Bligh exploded. He raged against Fryer and bosun William Cole and belayed them with his viperous tongue before the seamen. In his journal he accused them of 'criminality', and would have sacked them on the spot if there were any who could replace them. Alas, there were none who could meet his exacting standards.

On 2 March, a Tahitian stole an azimuth compass from the shore tent, and this time Bligh singled out George Stewart who was duty officer at the time. Moreover, when the Tahitians delivered the culprit, he lost all sense of proportion and had the native clapped in irons and flogged with 100 lashes. It was as though Cook's disease in his final voyage had re-emerged in the man who had falsely claimed filial descent. 'I have such a neglectful set about me,' he wrote, 'that I believe nothing but condign punishment can alter their conduct.' He consoled himself with a series of elaborate farewells, replete with feasts and flattery from the Tahitians.

At last, on 4 April 1789 the ship's boats towed the *Bounty* out to sea with an escort of weeping Tahitians in their canoes. Once clear of the reefs, the sailors hauled the boats on deck and the captain set course for Huahine, another of the Society Islands. He ordered a double ration of rum for the men, a gesture that in his eyes compensated for any perceived injustices on his part and ruled a line beneath the dissension that had marked their time on the island. Christian and the other recipients of his vituperation were not so easily won over. The ship seethed with discontent.

The reason for Bligh's detour to Huahine was his desire for a reunion with the Tahitian Omai, who had returned there with Cook on the *Resolution*. However, when they arrived the islanders paddled out to the ship with the news that Omai had died only 18 months after his return. So after he and the crewmen had bought some taro, yams and coconuts to supplement their rations,

Bligh pressed on in a roundabout course for his Caribbean destination. He sailed west towards Tonga, chief among the ironically named Friendly Islands group where cannibalism still flourished.

The winds were favourable and they reached the natural harbour of Annamooka at sundown on 23 April. By morning the ship was surrounded by canoes and Bligh invited the chieftain aboard. He sent two parties ashore, one led by Fletcher Christian, to collect water and firewood. They were soon confronted by hostile natives. Some began pelting Christian's party with stones, while a chief threatened him with a feathered spear. According to James Morrison, the bosun's mate who kept his own log on the voyage, 'The islanders [were] so troublesome that Mr Christian found it difficult to carry on his duty.'

When he returned with only a few gallons of water, Bligh called him 'a cowardly rascal fearful of a set of naked savages' despite being armed with guns and cutlasses. Christian struck back: 'The arms are no use while your orders prevent them from being used.'[7] Bligh repeated his disgust and contempt at Christian's inability to carry out his orders. He noted in the ship's log, 'I [never] feel myself safe in the few instances I trust to [him].' The conflict between them was becoming so vicious and personal that it was inescapable for the entire ship's company.

They departed Tonga on 26 April and the following afternoon found themselves approaching Tofua where an active volcano lit the seas with a spectacular display of pyrotechnics and gouts of flame. Bligh paced the deck, where both officers and crew had stacked their individual stores of coconuts between the guns. Suddenly he stopped at his own pile. Some were missing. He was seized by an eruption of rage and ordered all officers and crew on deck. Christian had kept the morning watch and was sleeping in his hammock. When he reached the deck Bligh was almost hysterical. He demanded to know how many coconuts he had brought aboard and how many he had eaten. Christian responded, 'I do not know, Sir, but I hope you don't think me so mean as to be guilty of stealing yours.'

According to Morrison, this caused Bligh to lose total control. 'Yes, you damned hound,' he screamed, 'I do. You must have stolen them from me or you would give a better account of them. God damn you, you scoundrels, you are all thieves alike, and combine with the men to rob me. I suppose you'll steal my yams next. But I'll sweat you for it, you rascals; I'll make half of you jump overboard before you get through Endeavour's Straits.'[8] He stopped their rum ration and confiscated all their coconuts. Then, in an outburst of spite, he ordered Christian to take the morning watch from 4 a.m. to 8 a.m. once again. This was quite contrary to standard practice, which allowed for only one in three turns at the least welcome period on duty. But in typical Bligh fashion he followed this with an invitation to dine with him that evening. Christian sent his regrets through Thomas Hayward, whom Bligh had excoriated for sleeping on duty. Christian was feeling poorly, he said. Bligh then asked the messenger to join him for the evening meal and a bemused Hayward accepted.

By now Christian was in a state of mental and emotional turmoil. He approached the carpenter William Purcell, a warrant officer some 10 years his senior, 'with tears running from his eyes in big drops'. Purcell could do no more than assure him that he need endure the captain for only 'a short time longer'. It was little comfort. Christian spoke of taking the captain in his arms and jumping overboard with him to escape the 'hell' the ship had become.

Alone once more, he decided to make a raft and abandon the *Bounty* that night. He went to his cabin and tore up his personal papers then threw overboard the 'curiosities' he had acquired during the voyage. He sought out George Stewart and Peter Heywood, told them of his plans and secured their help in gathering materials for the raft and supplies for the journey to Tofua. Then he set to and lashed a pair of masts from the ship's launch to a broad plank to make a rudimentary craft before returning to collapse in his hammock. It is clear from subsequent events that as Christian slept Stewart and others sounded out selected crew members about the possibility of taking over the ship.

Stewart woke him at 4 a.m. with the news that 'the people are ripe for anything'. This was the moment Christian made the decision that would echo down the years: mutiny. At one level it would be the stuff of legend, the source material for a library of books, documentaries and feature films. It would embed itself in Western consciousness as a rollicking tale, a psychological case study, a *casus belli* between rival camps of Bligh and Christian supporters. But at another level it would have the most painful and disgraceful consequences for those most vulnerable among the mutineers' descendants. And it would plague the dark paradise of Norfolk Island.

Fletcher Christian and his small coterie spread themselves furtively through the cramped and darkened corridors of the *Bounty* gathering support for their insurrection. On deck, the watch under Thomas Haywood, Bligh's dinner guest, was diverted by a huge shark that was alternately swimming in the wake and surfacing at the side of the vessel like some omen of impending disaster aboard. It was less than an hour in arriving.

Christian demanded the keys to the arms chest from the armourer, Joseph Coleman, claiming he planned to shoot the shark. Coleman, who would reluctantly find himself numbered with the mutineers, passed them over, but when he reached the arms chest Christian found Midshipman John Hallett (who should have been at his post on deck) asleep on the chest. Christian ordered him back to his watch, and when the youngster was out of the way he was joined by three of the most eager recruits to the mutiny – Churchill, Isaac Martin and the egregious Matthew Quintal, followed by another group led by John Adams, alias Alexander Smith.

Adams, 32, had been born in Middlesex but little is known of his parentage, and his own accounts of his life are often contradictory. Like most of his fellow mutineers he was damaged goods – brutal, angry and uneducated. He and the others took the firearms as Christian handed them out, then they swarmed up the companionway and on to the deck. Thomas Hayward later described their arrival. 'To my unutterable surprise,' he says, 'I saw Fletcher Christian, Charles Churchill, Thomas Burkett, John Sumner, Matthew Quintal, William McKoy, [the American] Isaac Martin, Henry Hilbrandt and Alexander Smith [Adams] coming aft, armed with muskets and bayonets. I asked Fletcher Christian the cause of such an act and he told me to hold my tongue.'9

Leaving Isaac Martin on deck to guard the watch, Christian and the others went below to seize Bligh and prevent the loyalists from staging a counter-coup. Christian himself burst into Bligh's cabin and roughly jolted him awake. As Bligh screamed,

'Murder!' a wild-eyed Christian held a cutlass at his throat. By now Christian had a lead weight tied around his own throat. If the mutiny failed he would throw himself overboard and drown. Bligh's scream wakened Fryer and others, but the crewmen were onto them before they could respond. Quintal roughed up Fryer, telling him, 'You are a prisoner.'

The other petty officers were similarly neutralised. Only midshipmen Peter Heywood, 17, Stewart, 23, and the West Indian-born Ned Young, 27, with his mouthful of rotten teeth, would break ranks with the officer class to join the mutineers, whereas 14 of the 18 seamen would number themselves among the rebels. According to Hayward on deck, 'Soon after, I saw Lieutenant Bligh brought up upon the Quarter Deck with his hands bound behind him; he was surrounded by most of those who came last on deck. Now some of the officers were permitted to come on deck, and Christian ordered us to hoist the cutter out.

'We remonstrated against it, she being too small and very leaky to contain us, and he gave us the launch, and as soon as the launch was out Christian ordered Mr. John Samuel, the clerk, Mr. John Hallet, Midshipman, and myself into her.

'We requested time sufficient to collect a few clothes before we disembarked, which being granted, I repaired to the main hatchway, but was prevented from descending at first by Matthew Thompson, who was armed with a cutlass. Gaining his consent, I descended with Mr. Hallet, and perceived Peter Heywood in his berth; I told him to go into the boat, but in my hurry do not remember to have received any answer.'

Meantime, on deck a barefoot Bligh clad only in his nightshirt with his hands bound had his backside exposed to the night air. He continued to remonstrate with Christian, and when Fryer was brought up he too pleaded with the leader to change course even then. Christian shouted him down: 'Hold your tongue, Sir. It is too late!' And to Bligh he cried, 'Mamoo [Tahitian for 'quiet'], not another word or you are dead this instant!' Then to the world he loosed his infamous lament, 'I have been in hell this past fortnight and am determined to bear it no longer . . . I have been used like a dog all the voyage.'

When Hayward returned to the deck, most of the 18 loyalists were already in the 23-foot launch. Hayward joined them. 'Lieutenant Bligh was then forced in,' he says, 'and we were veered astern, the mutineers saying they would give us a tow towards the land [Tofua].'

Bligh declined the offer.

'In this situation astern of the ship,' Hayward says, 'we prayed much for arms, ammunition and more provisions. We received four cutlasses and a small addition of pork. Numbers of the mutineers had collected themselves at the taffrail, [including] Richard Skinner, Matthew Quintal, John Millward, Henry Hilbrandt, Thomas Ellison, Alexander Smith [Adams] and William Brown, who publicly insulted Lieutenant Bligh. Richard Skinner would have shot into the boat, but was prevented by others of the mutineers. John Millward jeered us saying, "Go and see if you can live upon a quarter of a lb. of yams per day." '

Concerned that the more vicious of the mutineers among the 25 who remained aboard might be working themselves up to let loose a volley of musket balls, Bosun William Cole gave the order to pull away from the ship. Bligh shouted to the armourer Coleman and carpenter's mates Charles Norman and Thomas McIntosh, who were forced to remain aboard, 'Never fear, my lads, you can't all go with me . . . I'll do you justice if ever I reach England.'

As the distance lengthened between the two vessels, Bligh turned the crowded launch towards Tofua. Christian threw off the iron weight, broke open the rum and set a haphazard course for Tahiti.

CHAPTER FOUR

To Pitcairn

The natives on Tofua were hostile. Had Christian succeeded in his initial plan to flee there by raft he would undoubtedly have been murdered and probably eaten. Bligh and his party landed and collected some water and coconuts but it soon became apparent they were in mortal danger. As they beat a hasty retreat from a volley of sling-stones the lumbering quartermaster, 36-year-old John Norton, was seized and beaten to death. The rest escaped with cuts and bruises.

At first Bligh was inclined to head back to Tahiti but Fryer counselled against it. That was almost certainly where the mutineers were headed and they would have no compunction about blasting the frail launch out of the water with the *Bounty*'s four-pounder guns. The prevailing south-east trade winds made it almost impossible to reach the settlement at Botany Bay, so Bligh opted for Timor, almost directly west of their position, via the coast of northern Australia, a distance of almost 3,600 nautical miles. He had no way of knowing that a refuge awaited less than a third of that distance away and only a few points south of due west. By June 1789 King was boasting to Governor Phillip that his Norfolk Island colony was thriving.

That month Phillip sent a unit of 14 marines to the island led by Lieutenant John Cresswell, who would take control of the colony should King be killed or otherwise disabled. King's exaggerated reports of the island's fertility had encouraged Phillip to send increasing numbers of convicts – men, women and children – to serve their sentences there and help supply desperately needed food to the Port Jackson settlement. But he also included some of the most intractable troublemakers and this caused growing division and dissension.

By now King and had become frustrated in the quest for a viable flax industry. But he had cleared 17 acres of ground for wheat and corn, and a combination of private and communal vegetable plots was producing enough to feed the colony. He built a road from the Sydney Bay (later Kingston) settlement across the island to Cascade Bay, which would become an alternative landing stage for boats bringing supplies.

The area around Cascade, so named for the waterfall that spilled over a rich green precipice into a fertile valley, was soon settled and producing rich crops and groaning fruit trees. The stream itself harboured a plentiful supply of eels and where it reached the sea there was good fishing to be had. Indeed, the bays and reefs all around the island were an angler's delight.

Then came another discovery that would have far-reaching consequences. A party of convicts seeking timber on Mt Pitt, the high point of the island, stumbled across hundreds of birds' nests dug into the soft earth. They belonged to a species of mutton bird otherwise known as Solander's Petrel after the naturalist who had travelled with Cook on the *Endeavour*. The colonists were soon collecting their eggs by the hundreds.

King, whose mistress Ann Inett was about to give birth to their second son (to be given the equally geographical label, Sydney) had attempted to introduce some of the accoutrements of civilisation with the erection of a small schoolhouse, but was frustrated in his attempts to discover a suitable teacher. Some of the convicts could read and write but none had the slightest inclination towards public pedagogy.

In the second half of 1789, Phillip recommended him for naval promotion, but this raised difficulties because of King's lack of seniority. So the secretary of state, the Duke of Leeds, announced in December that King would be appointed lieutenant-governor of Norfolk Island at a salary of £250. However, before this news reached New South Wales, King would sail for England in March 1790 on Phillip's orders to report on the difficulties of the whole settlement. He was also suffering from gout and needed rest from the travails of 'his' colony.

His home leave would allow Phillip to rid himself of one of the most objectionable and recalcitrant characters in New South Wales – his own lieutenant-governor and commander of the marines, Major Robert Ross. Born in Scotland, Ross was an embittered, stiff-necked 46-year-old when he arrived at Norfolk Island on the *Sirius* in March 1790 just prior to King's departure. He had joined the marines as a second lieutenant in 1756, and had served on the losing side in the American War of Independence and later against the French in the Mediterranean and the West Indies. He was appointed lieutenant-governor to Phillip in 1786, but from the moment he arrived in New South

Wales he detested the place with a passion. 'I do not scruple to pronounce that in the whole world there is not a worse country than what we have yet seen of this,' he wrote. 'All that is contiguous to us is so very barren and forbidding that it may with truth be said, here Nature is reversed.'

It only went downhill from there.

He engendered hatred among his colleagues in the administration and was frequently at odds with his own officers. But he reserved his greatest contempt for his convict charges and afforded his soldiers *carte blanche* in their treatment of them. Phillip's sigh of relief in ridding himself of his troublesome deputy was no doubt sufficient to power the *Sirius* halfway across the Pacific. That ship and the accompanying *Supply* carried two companies of marines and more than a hundred convicts together with as much food and other provisions as Phillip could afford. But while the little *Supply* was able to berth safely in Cascade Bay and both ships were able to unload most of their marines and convicts, it was necessary for the master of the *Sirius*, Captain Hunter – who would later succeed Phillip as governor – to take his ship around to the deeper anchorage of Sydney Bay to unload the provisions and the last of the convicts. What followed was an unmitigated disaster.

King watched in horror from the shore as the tenders leaving *Sirius* with the precious provisions were lost in a sudden raging sea and the *Sirius* was driven on to a coral reef. Water rushed into the hold and the captain ordered the masts cut away. Sailors and convicts alike dragged what they could from the hold onto the deck, then threw the stores into the sea, hoping they would float ashore.

Some did, only to be appropriated by the convicts and secreted in their hovels or hastily buried nearby despite the thin blue line of marines on watch for pilferers. Meantime, the crew of *Sirius* were able to float a rope to shore, and soon a hawser was attached to allow most of the remaining officers and men to make their perilous way to safety. Two convicts volunteered to return to the ship to continue the process, but when they reached it they discovered the rum and got roaring drunk. Over the next five days some of the stores were retrieved before *Sirius* sank forever beneath the waves.

By then, King had departed on the *Supply* and Major Ross had declared martial law over the 498 reluctant residents of the colony. He marked the occasion with a ceremony on the beach in which everyone was forced to pass beneath the British flag and doff their hats in submission to imperial rule. The Norfolk horror was about to begin.

Meantime, Fletcher Christian was having second thoughts about his impetuous insurrection. Indeed, as the *Bounty* turned tail to the east he offered the captaincy to George Stewart who at 27 was his senior by a year. However, Stewart was too much the Scottish martinet for the mutineers' taste and they howled the idea down. Christian was at first unwilling to return to Tahiti, which was becoming a favoured destination for British and foreign vessels, and set course for Tubuai, some 400 miles (644 kilometres) south. It was sufficiently isolated to provide a hideaway, but still part of the Polynesian group with – he hoped – the same welcoming attitudes to visitors from another world.

He was to be fatally disappointed. When on 28 May 1789 they arrived off the entrancing isle with its green-clad hills rising from white sand beaches and protected by a ring of coral, Christian sent Stewart off in the cutter to seek out a channel through the reef. He was unaware that during Cook's last voyage two crewmen had deserted when the *Resolution* berthed at a nearby island and had finished up on Tubuai, where they had been the catalyst for fatal clashes with islanders sent to recapture them.

Stewart found passage through the reef and although a war canoe attacked and wounded two of his men, the next morning Christian edged the *Bounty* into the lagoon. He was met by a swarm of hostile Tubuaians in canoes. This was followed by an attempt to board the vessel from behind as, on the other side, the sailors slavered over a deliberately provocative performance from 18 island sirens. Undeterred, Christian went ashore with two armed boats and selected an area for eventual settlement. Again there was a clash with the islanders, this time resulting in the death of 11 Tubaian men and one woman. Although the total population was only about 3,000, it was fiercely tribalised and some groups sided with the newcomers. Their chieftains offered the mutineers a permanent home.

However, some of the crewmen lusted after their women on Tahiti, and after a couple of days Christian bowed to their wishes and sailed the *Bounty* cautiously back to Matavai Bay, where he planned to gather livestock – and women – for his new settlement. The Tahatian leaders were more than a little surprised at the arrival of the *Bounty* without Captain Bligh and half the crew. In explanation, Christian lied, as Bligh had done, telling them that they had discovered Captain Cook alive and well on distant Aitutaki where Mr Bligh now remained with him. Christian said Cook had sent them back to Tahiti to collect pigs, goats and chickens. The Tahitian supreme chief couldn't understand why Cook himself hadn't come along, and Christian's lies became ever more elaborate and finally dismissive. They were, after all, only 'Indians'.

Ten days later on 16 June, they departed with almost 500 pigs and other livestock together with nine Tahitian women, eight men, seven boys and one little girl. Christian had become infatuated with a tall and striking woman, 'Isabella' (whom his men called Mainmast), while Stewart had paired up with 'Peggy', John Adams with 'Jenny' and William McCoy with 'Mary'.

Welcomed back to Tubuai by two of the chieftains, they were granted land where Christian planned a stockade, which they named Fort George after the king, and armed it with cannon and swivel guns. The islanders refused to allow their women to stay at the mutineers' camp, or to become wives, although they didn't mind if the sailors had sex with them in their houses during the day. But the Englishmen were not to be denied their pleasures where and how they wanted them, and soon armed parties of mutineers started burning houses and desecrating shrines to obtain women. More battles ensued and more natives were killed. One mutineer, the heavily tattooed Thomas Burkett (who was later hanged in England) was speared in the side and after only two months order threatened to break down in the English camp. Christian decided to abandon Tubuai and they sailed the *Bounty* back to Tahiti.

When they reached Bligh's 'Paradise of the world' on 22 September 1789, they were startled to learn that a British privateer, *Mercury*, had been and gone less than three weeks earlier. Indeed, it had passed almost within hailing distance of Tubuai at night and its lookout had reported fires on the beaches. This confirmed Christian's decision to stay no longer than necessary. By now, however, 16 of the mutineers had decided they'd had enough of the peripatetic life with their brutal and ungovernable shipmates. It was the more mature and better educated seamen who opted for Tahiti, notably George Stewart and Peter Heywood. Others included the three deserters – Churchill, Millward and Muspratt – together with the diarist James Morrison.

The remaining eight Christian loyalists were the West Indian midshipman Ned Young, who was well liked by some of the Tahitian women; gunner's mate John Mills (and his Tahitian 'Prudence'); and an assistant gardener, William Brown. The rest were brawny seamen – thuggish Matthew Quintal, William McCoy (and 'Mary' with her daughter from an unknown father), John Mills from Guernsey and the American, Isaac Martin. By now, it seems, Adams had parted with his 'Jenny' and Quintal too was unaccompanied. Altogether they were the very definition of a motley crew.

Also aboard and bound to Christian were the high ranking islander Tetahiti and his (male) attendant, Oha. However, by now discipline on the *Bounty* was lax and no watch was kept. So when Christian decided after a grog-soaked dinner to clear out immediately, there were 18 Tahitian women and four island men on the ship, as well as the armourer Joseph Coleman who promptly dived overboard (as did one of the Tahitian women). Next day when he sobered up Christian permitted six of the older Tahitian women to depart in a canoe, leaving a total ship's complement of 26 – of whom only 12 were women. The disparity of the sexes would prove a fatal flaw.

In his search for a permanent redoubt, Christian rifled through Bligh's voluminous charts as he sailed the *Bounty* west to the Cook Islands, where at Raratonga they were joined aboard by an islander whom he permitted to try on his beaded midshipman's jacket. But the visit was cut short when one of the drunken mutineers shot him dead.

Next they tried the Tongan islands but without success. Then they discovered a reference to a remote island by Captain Philip Carteret, commander of the British sloop *Swallow*, who in 1767 happened upon it and named it after the midshipman who spotted it on the horizon: Robert Pitcairn. Carteret charted it incorrectly by about three degrees of latitude, so in 1773 Cook was unable to locate it during his second voyage. But Carteret's description of its inviting topography and fresh water excited the mutineers and they set a course to the south-east.

Two months later – on 12 January 1790 – they finally reached the forbidding cliffs of Pitcairn Island and in rough seas were able to circumnavigate the island. It was three days before they were able to land and when they did Christian led a party of six armed men. They discovered evidence of earlier habitation but now it was quite deserted. As they explored it they realised it had everything they could possibly have hoped for – fertile soil, fresh water, tropical fruits, difficult access and remoteness from everything the civilised world held dear.

They returned to the ship and manoeuvred it into a rough inlet they named Bounty Bay, where they stripped it of everything useful and began the process of settlement. The ship itself was a bone of contention. Some wanted to retain it as a possible means of return to Tahiti; others feared its masts might be visible and give them away; still others that its destruction would signal the end of any possible escape to the wider world. Matthew

Quintal settled the matter decisively. At night he returned to the hulk and set it alight. It burned to the waterline.

—

By then William Bligh had completed his celebrated 47-day journey via the north Queensland coast, through the Torres Straits to Kupang, a Dutch settlement in what is now Indonesian West Timor. There were several Dutch ships in the harbour, and the local governor, Van Este, arranged for the captain and all 17 survivors to be well looked after. However, the torments of the voyage in the open boat had so weakened them that Bligh and some of the men fell ill and the botanist David Nelson succumbed to fever.

Bligh returned home to the Isle of Wight on 13 March 1790 and immediately began a campaign to justify his actions and vilify the mutineers as pirates 'of the blackest dye'. At the formal court martial he was acquitted of all blame, and in December 1790 he was promoted to post-captain on half pay awaiting his next command. By then the Admiralty had commissioned one of the vilest creatures in the service, Captain Edward Edwards, to take the 24-gun, 500 ton frigate HMS *Pandora* on a hunting expedition for the mutineers in the South Seas.

Edwards, at 48, was cruel to the point of savagery. According to Sir Basil Thomson, a colonial administrator in the South Seas, he was 'a cold, hard man, devoid of sympathy and imagination, and of every interest beyond the straitened limits of his profession. Edwards in the eye of posterity was almost the worst man that could have been chosen.' His record confirms it. In 1782, he had provoked then mercilessly scuppered an attempted mutiny aboard his HMS *Narcissus*. Six sailors were killed in the uprising, five were later hanged and 14 flogged so fiercely that one died and others never fully recovered.

The Admiralty arranged for two of Bligh's survivors from the *Bounty*, midshipmen Thomas Hayward and John Hallett, to sail with him, and they reached Tahiti on 23 March 1791. Even before they dropped anchor, Joseph Coleman, who had leapt from the *Bounty* as Christian took flight, swam out to the ship and clambered aboard. He happily revealed the whereabouts of the others on the island and shortly afterwards Peter Heywood and George Stewart also presented themselves to the captain.

Edwards clapped them all in irons and as the remainder were rounded up they too were imprisoned under the half deck while the ship's carpenter built a locked enclosure three metres by five with restricted ventilation and open tubs for their urine and excrement. Into this hellhole Edwards forced the 14 surviving crewmen from the *Bounty*, including three – McIntosh, Norman and Coleman – whom Bligh had specifically exonerated during the court martial. Sweating and groaning in endless pain from the tight handcuffs and leg irons, they watched helplessly through the cracks of their prison as wives, children and lovers in nearby canoes wailed and cut themselves until the sea was red with their blood.

Edwards banned further family visits, while he and his officers took full measure of the sensual delights of Tahitian hospitality. Finally sated and sanguine, they raised anchor on 9 May and sailed away with the captives naked and half-demented in their 'Pandora's box'. His orders were to check out three other islands for Christian and his cohorts if they were not found in Tahiti, and Edwards did his duty. He made enquiries at Huahine and Aitutaki but could find no trace so headed home taking roughly the same route as Bligh had pioneered in the *Bounty*'s launch. But Edwards was not only vicious, he was incompetent. He lost six men in the ship's yacht when they separated from the mother ship, and when he reached the well-charted Endeavour reef he lost the *Pandora* itself.

The ship smashed into the reef at night. Edwards staggered on deck as all hands manned the pumps. He even released the three prisoners Bligh had declared innocent and put them to work until two of the pumps broke down. By now there was 3 metres of seawater in the hold and the other prisoners were screaming for mercy. They had been madly trying to loosen their shackles and with adrenalin raging through their veins they finally freed themselves and began to bang on the stout timber trapdoor that held them captive. As soon as he realised they were no longer fettered, Edwards ordered the trapdoor bolted with armed guards at the ready. When it seemed they might loosen the trapdoor, the master-of-arms ordered, 'Fire upon the buggers.' Morrison the diarist pleaded with them not to shoot and just then a wave crashed into one of the boats on deck, sweeping it away. The moment passed. They stayed penned as the water rose.

The storm was unrelenting and as dawn broke the *Pandora*'s mainmast split and crashed onto the deck, killing one sailor and seriously injuring another. With all hope gone Edwards gave the order to abandon ship just as she heeled over and the cannons broke their bonds and careered across the decks. Edwards and his officers took to the remaining boats. The armourer's mate Joseph Hodges finally opened the trapdoor and released some of the prisoners before leaping into a boat himself.

When George Stewart emerged he was struck by a falling spar and killed outright, others fell into the sea and were drowned, dragged under by the chains around their wrists and ankles. But the *Bounty* men had a well-honed survival instinct and 10 of the 14 survived while 31 of the *Pandora*'s crew perished.

They were able to rescue four boats from the ship and, on the hot and sandy shore, after doling out provisions salvaged from *Pandora*, the small flotilla made its way, in freakish repetition of Bligh's epic, to Kupang. The new governor, Mr Wanjon, had been deputy to Van Este when Bligh arrived. His reaction to this bizarre British encore is not recorded. In Batavia (now Jakarta), Edwards and the prisoners embarked on the Dutch ship *Vreedenbergh* for the Cape of Good Hope, arriving back in Portsmouth on 19 June 1792. Three months later, the mutineers were tried by court martial. The men whom Bligh had exonerated were acquitted. Peter Heywood and James Morrison were found guilty but pardoned, and another reprieved on a legal technicality. Then on 29 October 1792 at 11.26 a.m. Able Seamen Thomas Burkett, John Millward and Thomas Ellison were hanged from the yardarm of HMS *Brunswick* in Portsmouth harbour. The bodies were left to hang in the rain for two hours.

—

Philip Gidley King had returned to Norfolk Island on the HMS *Atlantic* in November 1791 to discover a colony seething with discontent among the administrators, and festering hatred among the convicts. Major Ross abused his authority among his marines, and his lieutenant quartermaster Ralph Clark wrote, 'I wish to be away from this place for a great many of my fellow officers are jealous of me because I am greatly in favour with Major Ross.'

The convicts' complaints were much more fundamental. They were prey to the soldiers' whims and appetites; and each day they suffered a gruesome tally of punishments neatly recorded in Clarke's journal. Ross ruled with the cat o' nine tails, and neither age nor gender prevented the convicts from being mercilessly flogged, imprisoned, bolted in stocks or literally 'chained to the grindstone' in the primitive mill that stands today as a wretched reminder.

But most debilitating was Ross's mad scheme, as stores ran low, to cut their rations progressively and force them to make up the difference with their own production on allotments of roughly an acre each. The few among them with farming experience scraped by, but for most it was a regime of gradual but certain starvation. The ration was little enough to begin with – 3 pounds (1.4 kilograms) of flour per week, 1½ pounds (700 grams) of salt beef or 17 ounces of pork; and 1 pound (454 grams) of rice. Children received half. But when, after three months it was cut by a quarter, after six by a half and after 12 disappeared altogether, disaster loomed.

The only saving grace – and the religious motif could hardly be more apt – was the arrival of a mass migration of the Birds of Providence. They settled on their Mt Pitt breeding grounds in their tens of thousands and while Ross attempted to regulate their capture, the half-starved convicts risked his fierce punishments to sate their hunger. Clark's journal became a litany of pain: 'John Lovell, convict, taken out of his hut after Tattoo having sack with 68 Mt Pitt birds in it. 50 lashes . . . Punished W Rainor, convict, for theft. Ordered 100 but only able to bear 16 . . . W. MacNamara ordered to be punished for disobedience but when stripping [for the lash] attempted to stab himself. The knife being blunt he did not effect it and instead of 50 lashes ordered to be chained to the grindstone . . .'[1]

Ross ordered the clear felling of the Long Ridge area to the north-west of the settlement and the convicts slaved in the tropical heat under Clark's supervision. He had clashed with Ross on the mainland, but eagerly adapted to his draconian regime on Norfolk. He ordered a convict carpenter, Leonard Deyer, 150 lashes for daring to strike a marine guarding a house while a colleague had his pleasure with Deyer's woman inside. 'After 75,' Clark noted, 'he could not bear anymore. I could not forgive that . . . damned rascal of a convict to strike a soldier.' The surgeon intervened to send the man to the foetid hut of a hospital.

King was appalled by the condition of his colony and immediately countermanded Ross's mad rationing scheme. It appears they almost came to blows before Ross and his marines departed a few days later on the transport HMS *Queen*. John Easty, a member of the New South Wales Corps under Captain Paterson who replaced them, was shocked by the conditions the convicts had endured. Norfolk, he wrote, was 'a poor miserable place [where] all manner of cruelties and oppression were used by the [commandant], flogging and beating the people almost to death'. It was almost better, he said, 'for the poor unhappy creatures to be hanged' than to suffer the tortures of Ross and his gang. The commandant, he said, behaved 'more like a madman than a man trusted with the government of an island belonging to Great Britain'.[2]

There was worse to come.

CHAPTER FIVE

Lieutenant-Governor King

Now officially invested as lieutenant-governor, King was accompanied by his new wife, Anna Josepha Coombe, a second cousin who on arrival was already heavily pregnant. They had reached Sydney five weeks earlier where his mistress Ann Inett, who had borne Sydney, his second child, had now taken up with a fellow emancipated convict, Joseph Robinson. King – with wife Anna's agreement – took young Norfolk with him back to the island of his birth. Sydney would later sail to England to be raised in the household of King's mother. The boys never saw their natural mother again.

Before taking ship, King had farewelled his great patron Arthur Phillip, who would depart on the *Atlantic* the following month. The government of the colony would then pass to the 34-year-old Major Francis Grose, commander of the New South Wales Corps, which he helped to raise. Grose's father had been jeweller to King George II, and the son was as foolish as he was fat. He would quickly fall under the sway of his gimlet-eyed fellow officer Lieutenant John Macarthur, and the rule of the infamous Rum Corps would soon be under way.

Also in King's entourage was a slim and lively young man, 18-year-old Willie Neate Chapman, who would be an entertaining companion for Mrs King and a consolation to his patron. But perhaps the most remarkable member of the party was the stay-at-home Chaplain Richard Johnson, still without a church in New South Wales, who reluctantly bestirred himself from his farm to solemnise various unions and conduct baptismal rites before returning on the next available ship.

Captain William Paterson, the commander of King's military force, was Major Grose's second in command. He had a lifetime's interest in botany, but was a prodigious drinker and remained a relatively junior officer at 37 despite connections to Sir Joseph Banks. Elizabeth, his English wife of four years, declined to share the rigours of Norfolk and remained on their generous land grant near Parramatta. Despite his frequently erratic behaviour, Paterson was just as determined as Major Ross had been to assert the rights of his soldiers over the convicts, whom they treated as little more than white slaves to be lashed for the merest infractions.

During the 20 months of King's absence the population had grown to more than 700, including a number of free settlers from the ranks of the military and civilians who had been employed in the building trades. They too were in desperate straits. Violence and thievery were commonplace; and there was still no criminal court on the island. King wrote to the under-secretary of the Home Office in London, Evan Nepean, that he was surrounded by 'discord and strife on every person's countenance'. And now he was faced with 'everything to begin all over again'.[1] He hastily issued a series of regulations designed to bring some semblance of order to a community on the verge of anarchy. He was only partially successful.

New strains appeared when the HMS *Surprize*, one of the hellships of the Second Fleet, arrived in August 1792 with yet another batch of convicts and officials. On the long journey from England, conditions on the ships were appalling. Of the 1,026 prisoners who had embarked on six vessels in London and Portsmouth, 256 men and 11 women were starved and beaten to death during the voyage. And soon after they arrived in Port Jackson a further 124 died from the treatment they had received.

Reverend Johnson was shaken by the spectacle as he stepped aboard from the wharf. 'I beheld a sight truly shocking to the feelings of humanity,' he wrote. 'The misery I saw amongst them is indescribable . . . their heads, bodies, clothes, blankets, were all full of lice. They were wretched, naked, filthy, dirty, lousy, and many of them utterly unable to stand, to creep, or even to stir hand or foot. A great number of them [were] laying nearly naked, without either bed or bedding, unable to turn or help themselves. I spoke to them as I passed along but the smell was so offensive I could scarcely bear it.'[2]

The worst ship in the vile convoy was the HMS *Neptune*, on which there were 154 deaths during the voyage. However, among its complement – now transferred to the cleaned and repaired *Surprize* – was the tall, dashing, blue-eyed figure of assistant surgeon D'Arcy Wentworth, who with surgeon William Balmain would become one of King's more effective allies in attempting to restore a sense of humanity to the harsh and soulless penitentiary in its vast isolation.

Wentworth had departed England one step ahead of his third charge for highway robbery and during the voyage he took a mistress, Catherine Crowley. Their baby son, William Charles, would one day organise the first white expedition with his friends Gregory Blaxland and William Lawson to cross the Blue Mountains. After the horror of the *Neptune*, Norfolk would have seemed almost Elysian. Several of the original convicts had by now served their sentences and King granted them blocks of land. Others, like the now 76-year-old Richard Widdicombe, chose to return to England.

The varied topography of Norfolk Island meant that while the convict barracks were concentrated in the Sydney Bay area, outlying settlements at Cascade, Long Ridge and the newly named Phillipsburg and Queensboro in the north boasted small communities of settlers. By 1792 they were producing wheat and corn as well as a great variety of tropical and temperate fruits, from bananas to pears, oranges and strawberries.

Flax was also thriving but they were no further advanced in processing it to canvas. However, during his visit to England King had persuaded the government to order Captain George Vancouver, who was about to leave for the Pacific, to bring native flax-dressers from New Zealand. Vancouver, another martinet with a love of the lash, duly kidnapped two Maoris — Toogee and Hoodoo — but when they arrived it was found that they knew nothing and cared less about flax-dressing, which was 'women's work'. King treated them well, allowing them to stay in his own home. But they pined for their families and he had no choice but to send them back. This would involve a decision that brought into stark relief the major impediment to progress and due process on the island: the shameless behaviour of the thugs and sluggards of the New South Wales Corps towards the convicts. They were 'living in their huts, eating, drinking and gambling with them and perpetually enticing the women to leave the men they were married to or those they lived with'.[3] And when enticement failed bullying succeeded.

Coincidentally, the trading vessel *Britannia* – once captained by William Bligh accompanied by his then protégé, Fletcher Christian – called by the island. Aboard was Nicholas Nepean, a captain in the corps and the brother of Evan, the Home Office under-secretary. Nicholas, a man of rare decency in the unit, was returning home after clashing repeatedly with fat Francis Grose and his *éminence grise*, John Macarthur.

King's corps commander Captain Paterson had recently returned to Sydney and was now trying in vain to find a way over the Blue Mountains. The most senior soldier remaining was the Canadian-born Lieutenant Edward Abbott; so King asked Nepean if he would take charge of the colony while he accompanied the Maoris back to New Zealand on the *Britannia*. Nepean was happy to oblige. King completed the mission in only 10 days. But when Grose heard of this he became apoplectic. He sent a 'rocket' to King by the first available ship and followed it with an official complaint to London. Lieutenant Abbott, Grose wrote, would have been 'perfectly justified' in refusing to accept Nepean's appointment and ignoring his orders. King attempted to smooth the waters with an apology but Grose remained obdurate. And worse was to follow.

It made no difference to the Rum Corps whether or not the convicts had served their time. All were fair game to the bully boys. Typical was the case of emancipist Henry Dring, who complained bitterly that whenever he left home a certain soldier pestered his wife into having sex; and on one occasion when he caught them at it Dring laid him out.

When the case was brought before the lieutenant-governor, the corps demanded 100 lashes for striking a soldier. King merely fined the aggrieved husband 20 shillings and exhorted both sides to 'improve their behaviour'. The next night, a gang of soldiers set upon Dring and battered him half to death. The following night, four of them headed to his farm with lighted torches, intent on burning his corn. And when a fellow emancipist intercepted them, one of the soldiers, Private Downey, thrust his torch in the man's face, burning him severely.

King sentenced Downey to 100 lashes. But then he attempted to mediate by ordering soldiers and emancipists to resolve their problems over a gallon of rum. It was an act of perfect futility. By January 1794 the soldiers were not only raping the convict women and harassing the emancipists and their wives; they were also plotting mutiny against their upstart naval commander. They had taken an oath 'not to suffer any of [their] comrades to be punished for an offence against a convict any more'. They decided the first act in the drama would be to kill Dring. However, their timing would be overtaken by a more histrionic event.

At King's suggestion, surgeon Balmain had organised a monthly performance of a stage play in an elongated hut in the Sydney Bay settlement. On 18 January 1794, King invited his officers and their ladies to a small reception in his home before proceeding to the playhouse. There they discovered an inebriated soldier – one Bannister – arguing with an emancipist over the former convict's reserved seat. King seized Bannister by the shoulder and ordered him confined to the guardhouse. Bannister threw punches at civilians, struggled with his guards and loudly challenged King to a duel. Other soldiers came running to his support and once Bannister was imprisoned Lieutenant Abbott ordered them to lay down their arms. They refused and demanded Abbott release Bannister and relay their demands to the governor. But Abbott had the weight of numbers and was able to force the 10 leading mutineers into the guardhouse with their drunken comrade-at-arms.

It was a long night. Settlers and convicts alike made preparations to defend themselves. King was facing the horrific prospect of 'seven hundred inhabitants opposing themselves to sixty-five armed soldiers'.[4]

Fortunately Lieutenant Abbott himself remained loyal to the governor, and the following morning he and King devised a plan to scatter the unit, sending a detachment to Phillip Island 'to gather feathers' and others to various settlements. While they were away Abbott enlisted 19-year-old Ensign John Piper (whose name would one day grace a delightful part of Sydney Harbour) and a civilian surveyor and head constable, Charles Grimes, to confiscate their rifles. When they returned that evening, King announced that the imprisoned mutineers would be sent to Sydney for trial. Until further notice the colony would be policed by a civilian militia under his personal command. It would consist of 44 former marines and seamen settlers.

By chance the colonial schooner *Francis* arrived on 23 January, and the mutineers – with an appropriate guard – headed back to Port Jackson on the tide. King also sent a full account of the mutiny and his subsequent actions to Francis Grose. Apoplexy was too mild a description for Grose's response to this latest act of sacrilege towards his beloved corps. His 18th century prolixity was no impediment to the venomous outrage that dripped from his trembling quill. Having questioned the corpsmen, he wrote 'The necessity of disarming the detachment I cannot discover; although we all too plainly perceive that *if* the soldiers have been refractory, the insults they have received from the convicts were sufficient to provoke the most obedient to outrage.'

As to King's actions, 'The militia you have ordered to assemble are immediately to be disembodied and their arms are to be sent in the [*Francis*] for the purpose of being served out to those persons who are settled in the Hawkesbury.'

Then came the real kick in the tail: 'Any convict, whether the term of his transportation is expired or not, who shall be accused of striking a soldier, is immediately to be given up to the commanding officer of the detachment who is himself to investigate the matter. And if it appears to him that the soldier has been struck, he will immediately order the offender to be punished with 100 lashes by the drummers of his detachment. *No provocation that a soldier can give is ever to be admitted as an excuse for the convicts striking the soldier.*'[5]

In other words, the soldiers could do as they pleased with the convicts and the emancipists. And to any complaints they would be their own judge and jury. It was the philosophy of the Rum Corps laid bare for the first time – the smoking musket – and it offended every precept of natural justice with breathtaking arrogance and baleful inhumanity.

But it was a gross error of judgement. While the *de facto* regime had been tolerated by the corps' colonial masters in London, its articulation in an official document was quite unacceptable. King immediately recognised his opponent's mistake and stood his ground. He then appealed directly to Secretary of State Lord Portland, and no doubt with the backing of Evan Nepean (after whom he had named a rocky atoll half a kilometre offshore), Whitehall came down on his side.

Grose was forced to apologise, but in doing so delivered a bureaucratic slap, strongly suggesting that Norfolk Island should be closed as a penal colony, since it was too expensive to maintain a military unit there. Instead, he said, it might well be opened for free settlers.

The suggestion was less statesmanlike than it might appear. In an enclosure to his original letter to King, Grose went over the lieutenant-governor's head and granted more than 85 acres of prime land on the island to members of the corps. If the convicts were removed, land values would boom and the corps would reap the windfall. His recommendation was ignored. And later that year his self-indulgence exacted its toll. Nauseated and flatulent, he departed for England and a life of indolence punctuated by occasional forays to Ireland and Gibraltar, postings that kept him well away from the battlefields of the day. In 1808, he made a desultory attempt to gain appointment as governor of New South Wales. But it was occupied at the time by a very different – although hardly more attractive – character: William Bligh.

While King had been struggling against the odds to create a viable penal colony, Bligh had regained his health after a serious attack of malaria, which he had contracted in Batavia. And despite a vigorous campaign by the families of Midshipman Peter Heywood and Fletcher Christian – together with Christian's famous school friend William Wordsworth – he had retained the confidence of the Admiralty. So when Sir Joseph Banks resuscitated his breadfruit scheme, they turned first to the man who had failed so signally to accomplish it the first time around.

Bligh was thrilled at the prospect and haunted the coastal shipyards until he found two vessels suitable for the task − a three-deck West Indiaman more than twice the size of the *Bounty* to be his flagship and a much smaller brig with a crew of 30 that would allow him to chart the shallows of the Endeavour Straits. The Admiralty approved and bought them both, renaming them the HMS *Providence* and the HMS *Assistant* respectively. Bligh took his time selecting his crews, settling on an American, Lieutenant Nathaniel Portlock, as skipper of the *Assistant* and his own nephew, Francis Bond, as his first lieutenant aboard the *Providence*.

He ensured he would be well protected with the recruitment of 20 marines from the Chatham Division and was fortunate to acquire a brace of talented midshipmen in George Tobin, who could write and draw entertainingly, and the 17-year-old Matthew Flinders, already showing a special aptitude for navigation and cartography. Banks appointed two botanists from Kew Gardens, James Wiles and Christopher Smith, to oversee the breadfruit operation. He also asked the Admiralty if Bligh could call by Norfolk Island to take pines from there to the differing soils around Port Jackson. And while he was in the area perhaps he could induce some New Zealanders to travel to the island and solve the flax problem. The Admiralty was equivocal, so Banks sought out Bligh himself to assure him his orders would be 'as flexible as possible' to allow plenty of leeway for the Norfolk detour.

Bligh promised to do his best, and on 2 August 1791 the little flotilla headed out of Portsmouth for his triumphant return to the South Seas. However, soon after they set sail the malaria returned and Bligh was forced to remain in his cabin for several weeks almost blinded by headaches and delirious with fever. It was not until they reached the Cape of Good Hope in December that he was well enough to resume personal command and was soon causing the seemingly inevitable anger and resentment among his officers by his fault-finding and squalls of temper.

He followed the *Bounty*'s course to Adventure Bay on Tasmania's south coast, reaching the sheltered cove on 9 February 1792. After a few days rest – and a brief encounter with an Aboriginal party fascinated by their hats – they headed north-east for the fabled isle of Tahiti. Their course took them within a mere 170 leagues of Pitcairn Island. Bligh had not the slightest hint of its role as the mutineers' redoubt. Nor did he know that since his departure Captain Edwards was returning to England with some of the mutineers for a trial by court martial. His overriding concern was to fulfil his interrupted breadfruit mission.

However, when he arrived back at Matavai Bay in the shelter of Point Venus on 9 April 1792 he quickly learned the details of Edwards' visit and the earlier departure in haste of Christian and his small band of outlaws in the *Bounty*. Unfortunately there was still no word of Christian's whereabouts, nor that of the islanders who had joined the crew. He would certainly be on the lookout during the next phase of his mission. Meantime, his welcome from the island chieftains was tempered by their knowledge that he had lied to them about the fate of Captain Cook and his filial relationship with the great man. For his part, Bligh was appalled by the ravages to the islanders' health and demeanour from the disease-laden British crews they had welcomed so enthusiastically since his last visit.

Venereal disease was rife. Traditional social mores were breaking down. 'Our friends here have benefitted little from their intercourse with Europeans,' he wrote in his journal. 'Our countrymen have taught them such vile expression as are in the mouth of every Tahitian. I declare that I would rather forfeit anything than to have been in the list of ships that have touched here since April 1789.' The chieftains had developed a taste for rum and the natives no longer seemed to care for their appearance or bearing. 'They wear such rags as truly disgust us,' he wrote. 'They are no longer clean Tahitians but in appearance a set of ragamuffins with whom it is necessary to observe great caution.'[6]

Nevertheless, he had arrived at the peak season for breadfruit and the Tahitians were more than willing to part with the 2,000 plants that the *Providence* was fitted to receive in exchange for a few trade goods. Despite the return of a series of debilitating headaches, Bligh was able to oversee the transaction and the two ships weighed anchor on 19 July 1792. Once clear of the reefs they set a rough course west and north, wandering through the island chains in the general direction of Torres Strait. Bligh wanted desperately to discover the remaining mutineers, whom he no doubt imagined as living in sensual splendour on some peaceful, sunbaked isle of tumbling surf and gentle breezes. He travelled from one idyllic archipelago to another but both word or glimpse of his quarry eluded him and every puff of wind took him further from Fletcher Christian and his band of outlaws. Finally he abandoned the search. He was now well behind his mission's timetable. So he broke his promise to Banks to call at Norfolk Island.

Had he known Christian's real circumstance, Bligh would have chortled his way back to England; for the reality on Pitcairn could hardly have been more different from his imaginings. In the nearly three years since they arrived on its rocky shore, the mutineers and their Tahitian companions had torn themselves apart. At first, as they built their houses on the plateau above Bounty Bay, relations between them were relatively congenial. They settled in, divided or shared the livestock – pigs, chickens and goats – and established a regular routine. Christian was generally accepted as the leader and the other white men asserted their racial mastery over the Tahitians. While the whites took a woman each, the six Tahitian men were required to share the remaining three.

Christian lived with the formidable Isabella, and on a Thursday in October 1790 she bore him a son whom they named after his birth date. And while she would produce two more little Christians, life with Fletcher was increasingly difficult. He discovered a cave above the settlement facing the uninterrupted vastness of the ocean, a limitless cordon between the great world and the shabby crew with whom he was destined to spend the rest of his days. He would sit there alone for hours in silent regret. And when he returned his depressive silences would be broken only by sharp words and angry scowls.

The others made arrangements of varying formality and duration. John Adams, for example, had paired with Jenny on the *Bounty*, but during the voyage she had transferred her affections to the tall, bearded Philadelphian, Isaac Martin. Adams claimed the accommodating Puarai, one of the Tahitians they had kidnapped. She would live to regret it. Edward Young bedded Susannah and for a time they lived together. But the well-endowed Young's popularity with the female sex meant he shared his favours wherever and whenever the opportunity presented itself.

John Mills, at 40, had been one of the oldest men on the *Bounty*. He was no friend of Christian's. He objected to his plan to settle on Tubuai and while Christian was ashore had tried to rouse those on board to make sail for Tahiti and leave him to his fate. He called his Tahitian mistress Prudence and constantly abused her. He knocked about with Matthew Quintal whose behaviour towards his woman, Sarah, was even more violent. He regularly thrashed her and eventually – when she returned empty handed from a fishing trip – would bite her ear off in a drunken rage.

McCoy, a stocky Scot with light brown hair, a heavy beard and a scar in the belly from a knife wound, had been employed in a distillery in his native land, and in time would put his knowledge to terrible effect. His bed partner on arrival was Mary who brought with her a Tahitian child from an earlier liaison. He teamed with Mills and Quintal as a trio of sullen troublemakers in the small community.

William Brown, was terribly scarred by scrofula, a tubercular infection of the lymph nodes of the neck. It ravaged one cheek, contracted his eyelid and ran all the way to his throat. Brown kept to himself and lived quietly with his woman. Unlike most of the others, they produced no children.

John Williams, a French-speaking native of Guernsey, was a short, slender figure and carried a visible scar at the back of his head. He took up with Pashotu and became the community's blacksmith and sawyer. He was the nearest thing the settlers had to a skilled mechanic and when Pashotu died of a throat disease he became deeply depressed, even threatening to leave the island in one of the two remaining cutters from the *Bounty*. The mutineers – probably led by Quintal – responded by burning the boats.

Among the islanders, the high-born Tararo was married to To'ofaiti. Two of the others – the Tabuaians, Titahiti and Oha (uncle and nephew) – now shared Prudence while the remaining three – Menalee, Timoa and Nehow – were left with the only other woman, Mareva.

It was by no means an ideal arrangement. However, it was workable until Adams lost Paurai after she fell from a cliff and he demanded one of the Tahitian women. Christian and the other whites reluctantly concurred. They then decided that Williams too should be given one of the three women being shared by the six Tahitian men.

They drew lots and Adams took Prudence from the uncle and nephew while Williams claimed To'ofaiti, the wife of the high-born Tararo. Now the situation was untenable and the murderous consequences were not long arriving.

The true story will never be fully known since the only accounts come from John Adams, a proven liar who gave several conflicting versions, and the Tahitian Jenny, the mistress of William McCoy who related what she remembered to a ship's captain, Peter Dillon, more than 30 years later. However, it is undisputed that Tararo, bereft of his bride, ran off into the forest and began secretly plotting with the two related Tubuaians to kill the white men and retrieve their women. But there was one immediate problem – To'ofaiti, it appears, was perfectly happy to have exchanged lovers and was content to live with the relatively benign blacksmith John Williams. Indeed, it was

she who signalled in gentle song from her garden to Christian's
Isabella:

Why do natives sharpen axes?
To kill white men.
Why do natives sharpen axes?
To kill white men.[7]

Isabella took the hint and hurried to Christian, who grabbed
his musket and sought out the Tubuaians. When he confronted
them they bolted for the hills to join Tararo. Christian alerted the
other whites and they rounded up the three other Polynesians –
who shared Mareva – and clapped them in irons. Then suddenly
To'ofaiti disappeared, probably captured by Tataro when Williams
was away at his forge. Confusion reigned. The hobbled Tahitians
protested their loyalty to the whites, who were divided about
what to do with them. The three thugs – Mills, Quintal and
McCoy – would no doubt have murdered them at a stroke. But
Christian, Young and Brown would have wanted to avoid the
effect of such savagery to the community, to maintain at least
the semblance of decency in the tiny settlement. So when one of
the Tahitians, Menalee, volunteered to take out after the rebels,
they compromised. They released him from his bonds and set
him off to track them down. He soon returned with the news
that the younger Tabuaian, Oha, was alone in the south; his
uncle Titahiti was with Tataro and To'ofaiti in the west. This
convinced the whites he was trustworthy, so they gave him a
pistol and sent him back to kill Tartaro.

Menalee was as persuasive as he was deceitful. He inveigled
Tartato to join him by claiming that his own 'wife', Mareva,
had also run away from the whites, and that they should join

forces. Tartaro took the lead along the track to her supposed hideout; Menalee pulled out his pistol, dug it into Tartato's back and pulled the trigger. Happily for the Tabuaian royal, it misfired and he turned on his attacker. However, his reprieve was only temporary. As he and Menalee struggled, To'ofaiti joined in, grabbed a rock and bashed her husband's head in.

They returned to the settlement, where To'ofaiti reunited tearfully with her blacksmith paramour. The Tabuaian uncle and nephew, Titahiti and Ofa, surrendered. But Ofa was not so easily forgiven. Menalee, the great pretender, offered to comb his hair in the time-honoured Polynesian gesture of reconciliation. Ofa submitted. Menalee cut his throat.

The settlement returned to its normal routine, although the bonds of trust between the men had been frayed beyond repair. Soon they would part completely.

Meantime, Captain Bligh made his triumphal entrance to the harbour at Barbados on 22 January 1793 with his precious breadfruit plants. Hailed as a hero by the slave owners, he was presented with an official citation and 100 guineas worth of silver plate. Overcome with modesty, he wrote to Banks, 'Posterity will ever remember *you* for being the means of transmitting to them such an inestimable jewel.' Unfortunately, the slaves found them to be utterly unpalatable in whatever form they were served. The entire imperial enterprise had been for nought.

CHAPTER SIX

Turbulent days

On Norfolk Island King's health began to break down. His gout returned and a chronic bronchial ailment left him gasping after the mildest exertions. Nevertheless, he was able to enforce a tolerable restraint on the Rum Corps' behaviour towards the convicts. In 1794, his former military commandant, Captain William Paterson, had succeeded Grose as acting governor on the mainland, but relations with Government House were not much improved.

By now the great majority of the island's prisoners lived in huts outside the Sydney Bay settlement. They included 293 females and their 90 children usually residing with their legal or *de facto* partners. The gaol was reserved for those who had committed felonies while on Norfolk itself, although King was angered by Paterson's continuing practice of sending some of the more recalcitrant convicts from Sydney. Officers of the corps also lived independently, often with their wives and families, while some of the single men were housed in the garrison or in official accommodation in the distant settlements. There was an inherent tension between convict and guard, but King's experience and demeanour kept it within bounds.

On Pitcairn, by contrast, the two years following the murders in late 1791 were marked by a rising tide of dissent and conflict, particularly between the mutineers and the Tahitian men, but also among the whites themselves. Christian increasingly withdrew and spent much of each day either in his cave or walking alone around the cliff tops. Quintal and McCoy treated the Tahitians as slaves and lashed them mercilessly for any slight, real or imagined. Adams's behaviour was little better. The former midshipman, Ned Young, and the mild mannered William Brown held the thugs in contempt but neither they nor John Williams and Isaac Martin were prepared to stand up to them. Indeed, by general agreement among the whites the Tahitian men were not allowed any land of their own. It was one of the few areas of common cause.

The Tahitian women, it seems, were thoroughly unimpressed with the way in which their countrymen accepted their servile status. And when Menalee appropriated one of McCoy's pigs, the mutineer's woman Mary identified the thief, who received a thrashing from the Europeans. Timoa also felt the cat across his back when he took yams from a white man's patch.

In time, the mutineers became so accustomed to their dominion over the islanders that they allowed them to use their firearms to hunt wildfowl and pigs that had escaped and become feral. They seem to have been unaware of the depth of resentment and rage building in the men whose lives in their native land had been so free from the oppression they now endured. In September 1793, they revolted. According to Young's account, the settlers were about their normal routine, either working their gardens in the village or in the yam patches on higher ground. Some of the women were away collecting sea birds' eggs on the cliffs. Timoa, Titahiti and Nehow armed themselves with guns freely given by their masters for a hunting expedition.

When a shot rang out, Isaac Martin was working in his garden. Thinking they had bagged a pig, he exclaimed, 'Well done. We'll have a glorious feast today.' In fact, they had shot and killed John Williams as he worked on a fence around his vegetable plot. Mills and McCoy were overseeing Menalee, who was tilling their patch, when Titahiti ran up, asking if the Tahitian could be freed to help him carry the pig. They agreed and now the four rebels banded together and planned their assault. Their first target was Fletcher Christian, and they found him clearing ground to extend his holding. According to Young, 'While he was . . . carrying away some roots they went behind him and shot him between the shoulders. He fell. They then disfigured him with an axe about the head and left him for dead on the ground.' Although mortally wounded, he was still alive and McCoy heard his groans. But when he mentioned it to Mills, the former gunner's mate reassured him: it was only Mainmast calling their kids to the midday meal. (By now the first-born Thursday October had two younger siblings.)

The Polynesians conferred. Two down, seven to go.

Since their muskets were notoriously unreliable, they hesitated to attack Mills and McCoy together. So Titahiti ran up to the pair and told McCoy he'd just seen Timoa and Nehow stealing from his house. McCoy swallowed the bait and raced to defend his property. As he rushed into the house they were waiting. Both fired their muskets – and missed. As he backed out Menalee jumped him from behind. But McCoy was now desperate. He managed to throw the islander off his back and into a pigsty before his assassins could reload.

Mills's response was remarkable. When McCoy reached him, Mills in his racial hubris refused to take the threat to his own life seriously. McCoy didn't stop to argue, and ran off to warn Christian. Mills's confidence was misplaced. As the Polynesians approached, they levelled their guns and fired. He staggered into his house where they followed and bashed his head in.

Three dead, six to go.

Isaac Martin the lanky Philadelphian and scar-faced William Brown were working separately in their plots. The rebels went first to the American and shot him. According to Jenny Young, 'He did not fall immediately but ran to Brown's house which was not far off. He was there shot a second time. When he fell they beat him on the head with a hammer until he was quite dead.'[1]

They knocked Brown unconscious with stones and left him for dead. But as they departed he came to and made the fatal mistake of staggering away too soon. 'One of them pursued and overtook him,' she says. 'He begged hard for mercy or that they would not kill him until he had seen his wife. They promised they would spare his life; however, one with a musket got behind him and shot him dead.'

Five down, four to go.

Meanwhile, McCoy had reached Christian's house to discover the mutineer's body. The next plot was owned by Matthew Quintal, who had heard the shooting and armed himself. When McCoy shouted to him, the Tahitians were on the rampage he sent his long-suffering Sarah to warn the others and prepared to flee. Sarah went first to John Adams's place but when she suggested he return with her to Quintal's place he suspected she might be leading him into a trap, especially when he spied the four Polynesians heading his way. Adams took to his heels for the scrub.

But then, it seems, the normally placid Polynesians' lust for revenge was waning. They made no real attempt to kill Ned Young, who in any case was protected by the women with whom he had shared his affections so liberally. And when Adams sneaked back to his yam plot for an armload of vegetables they wounded him but restrained themselves from the *coup de grace*, though two of the four urged the others to finish him off.

Despite the horrors of the day, that evening Young moved into Christian's house, which was a little grander than the others, as befitted the leader. He also took a willing Isabella to his bed along with the late William Brown's woman. On his orders, Adams's wounds were treated. The ball had entered his right shoulder and passed out through his throat.

There was now a moment to take stock. The killings meant that there had been a rebalancing of the sexes. Young's former bedmate Susannah was now available for the other Tahitians and Timoa laid claim to her. But with Quintal and McCoy still alive in the forest, their women were not willing to lower their status by accepting Titahiti and Menalee as bedfellows. Menalee clearly felt his role in the uprising was going unrewarded and as the days passed resentment turned to high dudgeon. One evening as Timoa wooed Susannah by playing his flute, Menalee sprang from the undergrowth and shot his rival dead. Titahiti protested and Menalee threatened to kill him too.

Now the women caucused. Menalee was out of control. They threatened that if he didn't get out they would deal with him. Young backed them with his firearms, and the remaining Polynesians − Nehow and Titahiti, little more than teenagers − were happy to see him go. Once in the forest he hung about with the wounded McCoy and Quintal, who made intermittent attacks on the village, shooting at the Polynesian men from higher ground.

Again the women met. The situation had to be resolved. According to Jenny Young, they sent Quintal's woman, Sarah, and Jenny herself to meet up with the white men in the forest. '[We] strongly advised them to kill [Menalee],' she says. 'That was done that night.' Unaware of the women's changing allegiances, Nehow and Titahiti set out to kill Quintal, and McCoy then returned to Young's house to claim they had again wounded McCoy. It was not true, and the women, who had remained in touch with the outlanders, knew it. Nevertheless, they pretended to go along and arranged for a discussion at Young's house the following day.

The young Tahitian men had no idea they were about to die. Indeed, the next day they were so relaxed that at noon one of them was lying on his back on the floor of the house and the other sitting quietly just outside when Isabella gave Young the nod. Simultaneously, the West Indian shot the man sitting outside and Susannah split the skull of her recumbent countryman with a hatchet. The tables had turned completely: Tahitian men nought, whites four.

Quintal and McCoy returned to the settlement, and Adams recovered from his wounds in about a month. By then the women had cut off the heads of those killed and buried the bodies. The skulls of the five white men remained above ground at the wives' insistence, grisly reminders of a ghastly episode, but of some spiritual significance to the women.

While the white men had disposed of the threat from their Tahitian underlings, they soon faced a thoroughly unexpected consequence. The four survivors were now outnumbered by nine women who had shown themselves willing and able to wield a murderous axe when the occasion arose. Of the four men, only Young was regarded with any real affection, and even he fell from favour when he tried to insist they bury the skulls.

Jenny, who had been briefly attached to both Adams and Young, now led a group of women in a quixotic enterprise to build a boat that would return them to Tahiti. They demanded the men assist and Jenny tore down her own house – which had been built from the *Bounty*'s planks – to provide the frame. As expected, it was an exercise in futility. According to Young, when launched it foundered at the second or third breaker that struck it broadside. All stores were lost but the women were at least able to swim back to shore.

The women, Young says, remained 'much dissatisfied with their condition; probably not without some reason as they were kept in great subordination and were frequently beaten by McCoy and Quintal'. The latter seems by now to have been verging on insanity. In his dealings with the women, Young says, he proposed 'not to laugh, joke, or give anything to any of the girls'.[2]

On 3 October 1794, the men held a dinner to celebrate the first anniversary of their victory over the Polynesian men. By now McCoy was employing his skills garnered from the Scottish distillery to make alcoholic liquor from sugar cane, but he was having little success. Nevertheless, they toasted themselves with the pallid results at dinner and resolved to live in a new spirit of harmony. A month later, however, Young learned (probably from Isabella) that there was a plan afoot to murder all the men while they slept. They hastily convened a meeting and resolved to stop their overt violence towards the women. Young says, 'We did not forget their conduct; and it was agreed among us that the first female who misbehaved should be put to death; and this punishment was to be repeated on each offence until we could discover the real intentions of the women.'

Now the battle of the sexes entered a new phase. Some of the women left the settlement and lived in other parts of the island. They also took muskets and other weapons. However, with a growing band of at least a dozen children to care for, the situation was untenable, and gradually they returned, some living with the men, others ostensibly alone but prepared to have sex when the mood was upon them. It was a workable arrangement and would remain so for the next four years. But in 1798 all that would change when William McCoy's experiments with the roots of the native ti-tree finally bore fruit. In April of that year, he produced his first bottle of fully distilled spirituous liquor.

—

Phillip Gidley King on Norfolk and his naval colleague John Hunter, the new governor of New South Wales from September 1795, were also bedevilled by the demon drink. The Rum Corps had spread their contagion through the colony, making it the principal currency. When Hunter took over officially from William Paterson on the 11th day of that month, he found a penal colony of 3211 people, of whom just over 1900 were convicts. The rest were almost all military and administrative personnel, a small minority of emancipists and only a dozen free settlers.

King himself had lobbied for the vice-regal appointment and his candidacy had been enthusiastically supported by Governor Phillip. However, Hunter, despite his propensity for losing his ships – his career tally would be four including the *Sirius* – enjoyed the patronage of Admiral Lord Howe, the First Lord of the Admiralty. Moreover, Hunter had been designated Phillip's dormant successor on the First Fleet should some tragedy befall the governor.

King was consoled by the fact that Hunter, his senior by more than two decades, understood the Norfolk situation well. After the sinking of the *Sirius* he had spent 11 months on the island and had designed the landing area at Cascade. In any case, King's ill health would not have permitted him to carry out his more exacting duties in New South Wales. His gout had returned with a vengeance and he suffered 'an almost fixed compression of the lungs and breast'. He was also tortured by constant stomach pains. Indeed, four months after Hunter arrived, King applied for sick leave back in England. The governor was sympathetic and he departed in October 1796. Until his expected return, Hunter appointed 37-year-old Captain John Townson of the Rum Corps as acting lieutenant-governor of the Norfolk colony. In fact, King would never see the island again.

Unlike his brother officers, Townson avoided the rum trade. He was partially deaf and the condition worsened while he was on the island. He seems to have been an enthusiastic Freemason and during his regime the first Masonic temple in either element of the New South Wales colony was established in the settlement.

His one great achievement was building the sloop *Norfolk* by the lagoon at Emily Bay. Matthew Flinders would use it in 1789 to circumnavigate Van Diemen's Land.

Relations between Townson and Hunter quickly deteriorated and he complained over the governor's head to Lord Portland, one of the three secretaries of state, about Hunter's dilatoriness. In fact, the same charge could have been made of Townson. He lacked King's personal commitment to the colony, and under his command it gradually deteriorated. Administration was lax, thievery became commonplace and the soldiers exploited their dominance of the convicts. King had discovered a schoolteacher, Thomas McQueen, from among the convicts, built him a schoolhouse and actively supported his work. Townson, a single man, neglected the school and McQueen soon took to the rum bottle. Discipline collapsed. The school would close when Townson departed.

But that would be the least of Norfolk's problems when his successor arrived in 1800. Indeed, its people would look back on the King and Townson regimes as a comparative existential bliss. Nothing had prepared them for their first taste of the empire's colonial sadists, the execrable Joseph Foveaux.

In Pitcairn also, a new regime would be installed by the turn of the century. But the transfer of power there would be of a very different order. It really began on that fateful day in April 1798 when McCoy perfected the distillation of his ti-tree 'jungle juice'. Henceforth he, Adams and Quintal rarely drew a sober breath. And while Young joined them only occasionally – and then, he says, in moderation – some of the women also took to the booze and let themselves go. They neglected their children and lost every inhibition in a public marathon of sexual excess.

They fought naked and in rags. They cast off all decorum and rutted where and when they pleased. Quintal raged and demanded sex with all the women whether drunk or sober. He lashed out when denied; tortured and bashed indiscriminately and even bit the ear off Sarah, the mother of his children and his favourite victim.

McCoy became even more unhinged. In the tiny speck of rock set in the eternal solitude of a vast ocean, whipped by random gales, lashed by storms, forever distant from all that the human species and come to learn and know, the half-literate Scottish distiller drowned his senses in alcohol. Then, according to Adams, he quite deliberately drowned himself by leaping from a cliff face into the sea, having first tied his hands and feet and weighted them with a rock. Adams, however, was thoroughly self-serving in his accounts and it is just as likely that McCoy was murdered by some combination of his fellows, most probably Adams and Quintal, since by then Young was weakened by tuberculosis.

Quintal's woman Sarah also plunged to her death from a cliff. According to Young she was collecting eggs at the time. Either way, it brought an end to her torture. Quintal then demanded Susannah, the younger and prettier of Young's two women, as a replacement despite the fact that there were at least five unattached alternatives. Indeed, it may well be that Susannah was one of the women caught up in the drunken orgies since she was pregnant at the time and would later call the child Edward Quintal. Young refused, as did Adams when Quintal next demanded his woman.

Quintal threatened to kill them both if he didn't get his way. And by now Young's health was failing. He knew he was no match for the burly Quintal, so he and Adams decided to do away with him. The result was so horrific that the memory was seared forever into the nightmares of the children who witnessed the screams and the bloody aftermath. Adams and Young lured him into Adams's house, plied him with liquor then when the moment presented itself produced two hatchets and swung them at his head and neck. Quintal struggled to stay alive, rising, screaming and flailing as the axes sliced into his limbs and scalp, blood spattering the walls until finally he succumbed in a crimson pool leaking through the roughcast floorboards of the *Bounty*.

Edward Young did not survive long thereafter. Tuberculosis claimed him in the early days of 1800. Now only one man remained on the island: John Adams, formerly Able Seaman Alexander Smith. With him were nine women and 20 children, all of whom were fathered by the mutineers Christian, Mills, McCoy, Young, Quintal and Adams himself. The children were named for their presumed fathers but given the free-ranging nature of their sexual mores there could be no certainty about their paternity. This then was the gene pool of a community that would multiply on Pitcairn and would today determine the unique characteristics of the population of Norfolk Island.

CHAPTER SEVEN

Major Foveaux

Phillip Gidley King, fully recovered from his gout and bronchial complaints, returned triumphant to Sydney in early 1800 carrying orders for Hunter's return and his own installation as governor of New South Wales. However, Hunter was somewhat reluctant to vacate the office and King did not assume his vice-regal duties until September. Relations between the two naval men became frosty. Nevertheless, King enthusiastically recommended the appointment of Hunter's nephew, Captain William Kent, who had sailed with him on the First Fleet, as lieutenant-governor of Norfolk Island. Unfortunately Kent's urgent duties as captain of the supply ship HMS *Buffalo* prevented his appointment and the naval officers were obliged to accept Major Foveaux as acting commander of the island colony. At the time, Foveaux, who had arrived with the corps in 1792, had become the biggest landowner in New South Wales with more than 1,000 sheep on his 2,020 acres (817 hectares).

King appears to have been surprisingly sanguine about Foveaux's transfer despite his reputation as a fierce wielder of the lash among the 100 convicts who slaved on his property. And at first blush it is difficult to understand Foveaux's willingness to volunteer for the post since it entailed his selling his grazing interests to John Macarthur. The 33-year-old Foveaux might have seen the posting as a speedy passage to promotion. Moreover, the island retained its reputation as a fertile prospect for development. Grose's suggestion that the convicts be removed and the corps granted the best land could well have regained currency at this time.

Whatever the underlying motives, one element of Foveaux's character would come to overshadow all else in his occupation of the post: his sadistic lust to humiliate and inflict untold agony on the men and women under his control. The source of this compulsion is no doubt to be found in some combination of his background, which is shady at best. He took his name from his legal father, a French cook employed in the household of John FitzPatrick, the Earl of Upper Ossory – an Irish peerage – who at the time of Foveaux's birth in 1767 was a rakish member of the House of Commons for Bedfordshire. FitzPatrick would marry Anne Liddell, who had been divorced from the then prime minister, Augustus Fitzroy, two years later. Whether he was the boy's natural father can only be guessed at, but alone among the five children of Foveaux's mother, the pretty Elizabeth Wheeler, young Joseph was favoured with the Earl's active patronage.

He joined the Bedfordshire's 60th regiment and – remarkable for the son of a servant – was able to purchase a commission in the New South Wales Corps in July 1789. He was promoted to captain two years later and attained his majority in 1796, a meteoric rise that could only have resulted from the continuing interest of his patron. Similarly, his dealing in livestock in the colony required substantial financial backing. However, while such patronage would have been welcome, it brought with it an acute awareness that he was forever denied membership of that strata of society from which it flowed. The corrosive effect on the personality of men caught between the rigid boundaries of the British class system is well documented. In Foveaux's case, it appears to have reached its most egregious expression.

When he arrived on Norfolk in July 1800, Captain Townson had been replaced temporarily by the dunderheaded Captain Thomas Rowley, who was barely able to string a misspelled sentence together. Rowley's one contribution to the settlement was to close down the stills operated by several of the settlers who supplied the convicts with some temporary relief from their travails. King's instructions to Foveaux were principally to cultivate the crown land and distribute the convicts across the island in a manner that would feed, clothe and maintain the inhabitants at the least possible expense to the public purse. He also ordered him to establish a civil court, but concentrated its full authority in the person of the lieutenant-governor, in effect giving Foveaux absolute dictatorial powers if he chose to exercise them.

He seized the invitation. From the moment he landed, he initiated a regime of shocking cruelty. And once he told King he had discovered 'a most disorderly state of things' he kept his reign of terror absolutely secret from the governor, confining his reports to the progress of his building plans and the relocation of administrative personnel. He also censored all mail. According to historian Margaret Hazzard, '[King] was not to realise then, if ever, the sadistic punishments, the bestiality and the terror that would occur on the island.'

He chose the bare Nepean Island as a site where convicts who transgressed would be exiled for extended periods. They worked under a pitiless sun boiling down seawater for salt and were only occasionally visited by boats over the treacherous narrows from the mainland. A merchant captain who visited soon after Foveaux's arrival reported just how hazardous the waters were: 'The surgeon of the island was drowned in his return visit to a ship in the bay,' he says. 'Another officer at the same time was dragged almost lifeless to the shore, the boat dashed to pieces and the greater part of the crew dreadfully maimed.

'Crossing the passage with a cargo of hogs another boat was swallowed up and with the exception of one man, the whole crew to the number of eight were lost.'[1]

The more distant Phillip Island was the *sine qua non* of punishment. Individual 'troublemakers' were banished there for up to four months with no shelter and few stores. Someone from Norfolk would sail there every few weeks to see if the exile were still alive and to replenish his supplies.

Foveaux also quickly recruited a network of informers among the convicts, an operation greatly facilitated by the appalling severity of the corporal punishments meted out to both men and women prisoners. The master carpenter Robert 'Buckey' Jones, an emancipated convict who would become chief gaoler on the island, wrote that Foveaux 'was one of them hard men who believe more in the lash than the Bible'. And the man he chose to wield it – one Richards – shared his sadistic streak. According to Jones he was a 'very powerful man' from Ireland's

County Clare who delighted in ripping 'another half pound [of] meat off the beggar's ribs'.

Where King had reluctantly sentenced serious offenders to 50 strokes, Foveaux regarded 200 as a 'feeler' and at its conclusion the half-dead victim received a bucket of searing salt water across the back. 'Many were relieved by death from this treatment,' Jones wrote. Foveaux insisted on witnessing the lashings himself, he says. 'He would show his satisfactions by smiling an encouragement to the flogger [and] would sometimes order the victim to be brought before him with these words: "Hulloa you damned scoundrel, how do you like it?" and order him to put on his coat and return to work.'

Lashings were only one of Foveaux's instruments of torment. Another favourite, says Jones, was 'to make the leg irons more small each month so they would pinch the flesh', causing infections in the island's tropical humidity. But perhaps the most feared was the tiny isolation cell set in a pit of water where prisoners would be locked naked and in total darkness for the longest 48 hours of their lives, unable to sleep or even crouch for fear of drowning.

Little wonder that Foveaux was able to spread his informer network like a contagion through the convict population who would seek any means to avoid the lash or the chains. It had the added benefit to the gaoler that it spread distrust and fear among the prisoners, who could exact revenge or pursue a grudge against a fellow captive. Writing on his deathbed, Jones says, '[Foveaux's] treatment of the women convicts was most brutal. They were looked upon as slaves and sold openly to the free settlers and convicts alike, the prices often being as high as £10 for young and good-looking girls.'

By now D'Arcy Wentworth had become visiting chief surgeon on the island and he intervened whenever he could. But Foveaux's word was law and he had allies in debauchery, not least the chief constable, Ted Kimberley, whose specialty was the degradation of the women convicts. 'Women in his estimation were born for the convenience of men,' writes Jones.[2] He would organise regular 'amusements' for the officers in their barracks on Thursday nights. After dinner 'all the women would join in the *dances of the mermaids*, each one being naked with a number painted on her back so as to be recognised by their admirers, who would then clap their hands on seeing their favourite perform some grotesque action. And with a gallon or two of rum would end their night's amusement in a drunken state.'[3]

The hellhole claimed even the most worthy newcomers, not least William Mitchell who arrived as a missionary and, according to Jones, 'gave up that profession as there was more money in trading'. He took up with 'a beautiful young woman named Liza McCann who was as cunning as himself [and] who could drink more rum than most of the hardened soldiers'. Mitchell willingly gave himself to the devil and the food he provided the store at inflated prices was rotten. 'The pork supplied to the prisoners,' says Jones, 'was so soft that you could put your finger through it.'

Late in 1801, King appointed Henry Fulton to become Norfolk's official Protestant clergyman despite his having been convicted on charges of sedition. He had been educated at Trinity College, Dublin, and worked for his father in India for two years before returning to marry his childhood sweetheart Ann Walker, joining the Church of Ireland as an ordained minister and being posted to a parish in Galway on the west coast. However, he was caught up in the troubles of 1798, tried and sentenced to transportation for life. His wife and two children accompanied him after her aunt paid 120 guineas for their passage on the HMS *Minerva* and they landed with 180 other 'politicals' on 11 January 1800.

Fulton joined with Wentworth and others in attempts to moderate Foveaux's behaviour but with little effect. The commandant took his pick of the females – including the convicts – but finally settled on Mrs Sherwin, the wife of one of his sergeants after having first confined the soldier to gaol. Sherwin had served in the stores where an extra portion could bring dutiful satisfaction of any sexual proclivity. The sergeant left the island shortly afterwards and set up a grocery in Parramatta.

Yet there remained a spark in the human spirit that defied the most brutal assault from the commandant and his lackeys. Two young Irishmen, Peter MacLean and John Wollaghan, who had been transported to New South Wales after uprisings in the 1790s, worked among their fellows to organise a mutiny. Their weapons would be timber pikes, which they secretly cut, sharpened and tempered with fire then hid in the thick undergrowth. They planned to use them initially to force a captive officer to open the armoury. They would then capture or kill Foveaux and take charge of the colony. Their planning went no further than the initial rush, but somehow they were determined to break the hated shackles or die in the attempt

They had fashioned a hundred pikes and had even enlisted at least four of the soldiers who had also felt the sting of Foveaux's sadistic discipline. By 14 December 1800 they were almost ready to give the signal when a convicted rapist, Henry Gready, saw his chance to curry favour and reported them to Foveaux. He instantly called out the guard, found the two leaders and clapped them in irons. Gready led the soldiers to a cache of 30 pikes. That was evidence enough. Foveaux hastily convened a 'court' of four officers and without any attempt at trial condemned them to be hanged forthwith. Perhaps his resentment against his Irish progenitor was at work behind the raging countenance. Either way, he assembled the entire colony to witness the execution the next day, a Sunday. But that was just a foretaste. A further 22 convicts were, in his words, 'severely punished'.

When he learned the identity of the four soldiers involved, he drummed them out of the regiment and flogged one with no fewer than 500 lashes. This was the one act of 'discipline' that he could not conceal from the authorities, and although Governor King as a naval officer made no protest, Major Paterson, who now commanded the Rum Corps, was affronted by his daring to convict and punish his soldiers without a proper court martial.

This resulted in an increasingly sharp exchange of correspondence and finally Foveaux was forced to take leave in England to protect his position. On Norfolk, prisoners and soldiers alike celebrated. Ann Sherwin, whom they called his 'fancy woman', travelled with him. Whether she accompanied him to the seat of his patron at Amptill Park, Bedfordshire is not known. But the visit was certainly successful from Foveaux's standpoint, since he was actually promoted to lieutenant-colonel and returned to the island confirmed as lieutenant-governor in 1802.

In his absence, King had offered this post to the Rum Corps' Major Johnston, but his commander William Paterson declined on his behalf and Captain Ralph Wilson, who was already on the island, stepped in. Wilson lived with his Irish-born wife, and under his steady hand the colony regained a measure of humanity. The wife of the captain of a visiting ship, Mrs Eliza Kent, spoke kindly of the hospitality of the Wilsons. They gave her a splendid bed and breakfast and accompanied her in walks to some of the nearby settlements.

When Foveaux and his mistress returned he set in train a building program that would drive the convicts to utter exhaustion and many to early graves. All structures were to be made from local stone and his own 'Government House', according to Mrs Kent, was to be 'a large house, pleasantly situated on a general eminence commanding a view of the town of [Kingston], Turtle Bay and the Nepean and Phillip Islands'. Each convict was required to break five barrow loads of stone every day using gimcrack tools that were constantly in need of repair. If a shaft snapped or a pickhead flew off, the convict was whipped then ordered back in his blood-soaked rags to complete his shift.

Foveaux's use of the lash became ever more frantic. According to Jones, 'Many were the unspoken regrets at the return of the Major. How they must have wished they could have been at home and tell the truth. For without a doubt he was guilty and it is I who could tell them so. Murder, simply murder is what I call it. God forgets and forgives but I never can.'

The flogging of one Charles Maher almost brought about another mutiny. 'Poor wretch,' says Jones, 'he received 250 lashes and on receiving 200 Kimberley refused to count, meaning that the punishment was enough. His back was quite bare of skin and flesh.' Foveaux backed down. But on another occasion when one of the convict women insulted Ann Sherwin and he ordered 250 lashes, the flogger Richards said he was 'too sick' to carry out the sentence. Kimberley was ordered to take the whip but he refused, crying out that he didn't flog women. Foveaux flew into a rage and demanded one of the soldiers, Private Mick Kelly, take over. Kelly complied but was so restrained that not a single mark was made on her back. According to Jones, 'This made the Major so wild that he ordered the woman placed in a dark cell for a fortnight.'

New convict arrivals were often given 25 lashes 'to shew authority', and his practice of selling women convicts was institutionalised. 'In every case the women were treated as slaves,' Jones says, 'good stock to trade with and a convict having a good chance to possess one [by thievery] did not want much encouragement to do so.' Inevitably, some prisoners tried to escape on rough rafts but were either drowned or forced back by the waves. 'One man made an attempt to get away on a door after boring two holes in it for his legs but did not get more than ten miles,' he says. 'One of his toes was bitten off.' Others ate sand or drank large quantities of salt water to make themselves ill; the most desperate hacked off a hand or foot in the hope of being sent to the mainland to recover.

But most disgraceful practice of all was the standing order from the British Government that if foreign ships were sighted, the Irish convicts were to be herded instantly into a timber building to prevent them joining an effort to overthrow the administration. And if the foreigners landed, it was to be set alight. It was a command that played on Jones's mind in his last days. 'My orders were to murder all the prisoners under my care should any foreign national bear down upon us,' he wrote. It gave the lie to the claim that the prisoners were under King George's protection. 'Protection be damned,' said Jones.

At the same time that Foveaux was building for posterity on the island, he was pursuing a campaign to transform the nature of the colony by removing the penal element to Van Diemen's Land. His ambitions were now quite clear: he wanted Norfolk as his own fiefdom, cleared and planted by government labour and appointed with magnificent stone buildings designed and built to his own specifications. And to work it he would retain enough convict slaves and administrative staff to labour beneath his dictatorial hand. He would, in effect, become a South Sea monarch of all he surveyed.

Alas for his grand design, the island would not so easily submit to the hubris of 'King Joseph I'. The native foliage combined with the climate to produce asthmatic attacks that left him breathless and eventually threatened his life. In desperation, he left for the mainland in September 1803. The sea voyage and the dry heat of the Parramatta hinterland, which was in drought at the time, helped him recover, and he returned much improved in January the following year. But in a few weeks the asthma was back and, although he struggled to overcome it, by August 1804 he was forced to admit that only a much longer sea voyage would provide the relief he craved. So on 9 September he embarked for England, once more accompanied by his paramour who, according to Jones, 'was looking very old and careworn'.

If he retained his dreams of an island kingdom once he'd recovered his health in Bedfordshire, he was to be sorely disappointed. In a delicious irony, his calls to the Secretary of State for War and the Colonies, Robert Hobart, the 4th Earl of Buckinghamshire, to abandon the penal settlement succeeded too well. While he was travelling to London the British Government took the decision to abandon the island completely.

When he arrived he was faced with a fait accompli – orders had already been sent to Governor King to begin the evacuation of prisoners to Port Dalrymple (later Launceston), on the northern coast of Van Diemen's Land. Foveaux's plans were thrown into disarray. The sea voyage had worked its magic and he was on the mend. His dream kingdom was evaporating. He sought appointments with the bureaucrats and politicians. Pitt the Younger succeeded Lord Liverpool as prime minister and appointed Charles Pratt, the First Lord Camden as Hobart's successor.

Foveaux presented Camden his plans, formulated on Norfolk and refined at sea, for a more 'measured' arrangement that would permit private settlement of the island. The panjandrums listened, somewhat surprised at the turnabout but willing to respond to his first-hand experience. Foveaux then wrote to Governor King seeking his support, while he continued to lobby for his preferred option. Months passed as letters and recommendations crossed the world. And, not surprisingly, King was persuaded that 'his' colony should be preserved in some fashion.

Meanwhile back at Norfolk, administration had passed into the more cultivated hands of Captain John Piper, who had previously served two years on the island under King between 1793 and 1795. The son of a Scottish doctor, the slim and cheery Piper had obtained his commission as an ensign in the New South Wales Corps through the influence of his uncle and sailed for Port Jackson on the HMS *Pitt*, which also carried the new, corpulent commander of the corps, Francis Grose. Young Piper was only 19 at the time but exhibited the all mannerly charm that would endear him to a generation of colonial ladies and most of their husbands.

When he took over as commandant he was only 31, and while at Port Jackson had fathered a child, Sarah, whom he would later acknowledge and celebrate with a lavish wedding to a free settler. But in Norfolk he soon deflowered Mary Ann, the 15-year-old daughter of the emancipists James and Mary Shears, and moved her into the splendid Government House. They would have two sons in quick succession.

Orders from London via Governor King were confusing and contradictory. The government was blaming the costs of maintaining the settlement for its decision, yet under Piper Norfolk was producing bumper crops of vegetables and grain. Moreover, he was sending supply ships to the mainland loaded to the gunwales with salted pork.

The trafficking of convicts was just as puzzling. For every boatload he sent to Port Dalrymple he seemed to receive an equivalent cargo of Irish politicals from Governor King. This leapt into sharp relief when on 7 November 1805 his lookouts spotted no fewer than nine large sailing ships bearing down on the island. Piper immediately followed standing orders and assembled the Irish convicts. However, he declined Foveaux's barbarity and gathered them into the gaol yard, where he posted the full complement of civilian constables to stand guard. As he later told Governor King, 'After receiving information that the Fleet were standing around Cascade Bay, I ordered a Sergeant and 20 men to join the party on duty there; at the same time sent over one of the great guns and immediately followed myself.' He discovered that they flew the British ensign, but when they fired a gun and signalled for the shore party to send out a boat Piper and his officers feared a trap. He sent for the entire military detachment to come to Cascade at the double.

After a five-hour standoff, the flagship dispatched a boat, which landed under the cover of Piper's musketry. Happily for the defenders, the officer in charge turned out to be Lieutenant

Little from Britain's China Fleet under the command of Captain Francis Fayerman. They had been attempting to bluff the Chinese Government into opening their ports to British trade, a process that would lead to the first Opium War in 1842. For the moment, however, Fayerman could make no progress, and was now embarked on a secret mission to detect and record the presence of enemy ships (particularly French or Russian) cruising in the East Indies.

Apparently it was an urgent mission. According to Piper, 'Not withstanding that they were much in want of refreshment, Captain Fayerman was determined to proceed on his passage that evening.'

Finally, in December 1807, Foveaux accepted his orders to return to Norfolk and resume command provided 'sufficient inhabitants remained there'. If not, he was to proceed to Port Jackson to act as lieutenant-governor whenever William Paterson was absent. However, events in the larger colony would put paid forever to his grandiose scheme. When Governor King arrived back in London a month before Foveaux was due to sail, the governor was a broken man. He would die within a year. The Rum Corps had run amok. The half-mad Macarthur was fighting duels with his commander Paterson, and the colony was in a state of anarchy and insurrection. When Foveaux arrived at Port Jackson prior to his intended destination of Norfolk Island he discovered that Major George Johnston was in command, Paterson was in Van Diemen's Land, and the governor – one William Bligh – was under arrest.

CHAPTER EIGHT

Governor Bligh

In the wake of his futile breadfruit saga and the passions aroused against him by the families of Fletcher Christian and Peter Heywood, Bligh found himself out of favour with the naval establishment. It was not until 1795, three years after he delivered the tasteless Tahitian staple to the West Indian slavers, that he received his next command.

It had taken the appointment of Evan Nepean to the post of Secretary of the Navy to change his fortunes. Nepean had a mutually beneficial association with Duncan Campbell when he was organising the transport of convicts to New South Wales from Duncan's vile prison hulks in the Thames and at Portsmouth. Through his influence, Bligh gained command of the 24-gun HMS *Calcutta*, which was engaged in blockading the Dutch coast. There the French were assembling a fleet to invade Britain after the English had seized their West Indian colonies of Tobago and Santa Lucia.

He acquitted himself well in action and over the next seven years fought in several skirmishes, including the battle of Copenhagen in 1801, where as captain of the HMS *Glatton* he earned the praise of Nelson himself for his ability to manoeuvre his ship in combat. But Bligh's career chopped and changed as unpredictably as the seas he sailed. He fell foul of a subordinate in 1804 when surveying the Dutch coast. He had ordered one of his lieutenants arrested after the man claimed, with some justice, that an injury prevented him from standing his watch. The officer was acquitted and then accused Bligh of having 'grossly insulted and ill-treated' him. It was a familiar tale, and the court martial found the charge 'in-part proved', reprimanded the captain and ordered him to be 'more correct in his language'. The admonition had little or no effect. Nevertheless, he retained the all-important favour of Sir Joseph Banks, and a month later on 15 March 1805 after a conversation with Lord Camden, the famous botanist offered to obtain him the governorship of New South Wales to succeed Philip Gidley King. And to spice the deal he would receive a salary of £2,000, exactly double that of the incumbent.

Bligh hesitated. His wife Betsy had a morbid fear of the sea and was most unwilling to leave England while their younger daughters were still unmarried. However, it was a career opportunity that both were most unwilling to pass up. Finally they compromised. Betsy would remain behind, but their eldest daughter Mary would accompany him together with her husband, the naval Lieutenant John Putland.

The Admiralty gave command of the convoy to Captain Joseph Short in the store ship HMS *Porpoise* with Putland as his master and commander. Bligh and Mary travelled on a smaller transport, although he was nominally Short's superior. This was a recipe for disaster, since the temper of the eponymous Captain Short was of the same hair-trigger variety as Bligh's. At one stage during the journey when Bligh altered the course of his transport without prior warning, Short ordered Lieutenant Putland to fire two shots, one across her bows and the other astern. When that had no effect, he ordered the panic-stricken son-in-law to load a third, which according to Mary, 'if we did not bear down immediately he was to fire right into us.'

Bligh responded by boarding the *Porpoise* and seizing control of the convoy. And when they arrived in Sydney he held a kangaroo court into Short's behaviour and sent him back to England to be court martialled. He was honourably acquitted, with the court finding that Bligh had treated him unjustly. However, by then the new governor was himself under rapid fire from the Rum Corps, roused to rebellion by the haughty bravado of John Macarthur.

Governor King had summed Macarthur up neatly in a letter to Nepean in 1803: 'His employment during the eleven years he has been here has been that of making a large fortune, helping his brother officers make small ones (mostly at the public expense) and sowing discord and strife . . . many instances of his diabolical spirit had shown itself before Govr. Phillip left this colony, and since, altho' in many instances he has been the master worker of the puppets he has set in motion.'[1]

By now the Rum Corps controlled virtually all commerce in the colony. New South Wales, like many British territories at the time, was short of coin, and rum became the medium of trade. 'Fat Francis' Grose had relaxed Phillip's prohibition on the trading of rum, mostly from Bengal, but including other spirits, usually made from wheat. The officers of the corps were able to use their position and wealth to buy up all the imported stock and then exchange it for goods and labour at very favourable rates. By 1805 stills had been imported, and grain was diverted to make 'rum' instead of feeding the population. While Macarthur had formally left the corps in 1796, he remained the *éminence grise*, calling the shots to his foot soldiers in the front line.

At first Macarthur had welcomed the newcomer in fulsome strains on behalf of the free settlers and Bligh was suitably flattered. However, it could be no more than a passing fancy. Bligh carried orders to stop the rum trade, the source of Macarthur's power and influence within the corps. And the smallholders among the settlers were outraged by the way he and the corps exploited them. More than 350 signed a letter to Bligh rejecting Macarthur's right to speak for them and blaming him for withholding sheep from the market to raise the price of mutton.

Bligh sided with the smallholders. But in typical fashion he responded with a blizzard of abuse to Macarthur that would have felled another man in his tracks. Not so the gimlet-eyed grazier. As Bligh ranted that he would rip out Macarthur's land grants – and his livestock – from under him, the master of Camden Park (cleverly named for his English patron) stood his ground. It was not long before he was telling his friends that the governor 'will perhaps get another voyage in his launch'.[2]

Norfolk Island played only a small part in Bligh's concerns. His orders to Captain Piper were to keep draining the settlement of its prisoners while maintaining a skeleton administration on the island. The task should be completed by 1809, when Piper himself would return to the mainland. The slim and sprightly commandant willingly complied. Apart from the occasional fright when suspiciously foreign sails appeared on the horizon, life was pleasant enough in Government House surrounded by Ann and their growing brood; but it was no substitute for the social whirl that he enjoyed so much in Sydney.

By the time the rebellion there struck in December 1807, Bligh had managed to alienate many elements of the colony. He had dismissed the popular D'Arcy Wentworth from his position as assistant surgeon for the colony without explanation; so too the clever surgeon-general, Thomas Jamieson, from his seat on the magistracy. And he had sentenced three merchants to a month's imprisonment and a fine for writing a letter he found offensive. Once again the furies had conspired to produce a communal cataclysm with Bligh at its epicentre.

The trigger for the uprising was the decision of six corps officers to abort Macarthur's trial on a civil matter of little consequence. Bligh accused the officers of mutiny and summoned Major George Johnston to deal with the matter. Johnston begged off, claiming he was in no condition to respond, having wrecked his gig while driving home to Annandale after dining in the officers' mess. When he recovered, Johnston sided with Macarthur, released him from gaol and watched as he drafted a petition calling for Johnston to arrest Bligh for 'crimes that render you unfit to exercise the supreme authority another moment in this colony'. Once his fellow officers had signed it, he led the corps, with a full band and colours flying, in a march on Government House, where they claimed to have found Bligh hiding under a bed.

This is unlikely. Bligh had many faults but cowardice was not among them. He said he was hiding official papers prior to an attempted escape. Whatever the truth of the matter, he would defy the mutineers' demands that he decamp for England for more than a year. Instead he would spend the next 15 months confined to Government House while Johnston took command and appointed Macarthur colonial secretary to run the colony's business affairs. This was the situation confronting Lieutenant-Colonel Foveaux on his arrival in Port Jackson on 28 July 1808. As the senior officer he was faced with the decision to support Johnston, reinstate Bligh or take command himself. The last wisps of fantasy for his Norfolk monarchy dissolved in favour of the opportunity to posture on a much bigger stage. He opted to take personal command of New South Wales.

Good living in Britain free from the devil's brew of asthma and bellyaches that had plagued him on Norfolk meant that Foveaux had become 'very corpulent', according to a contemporary. But now he was all business. He sacked Macarthur, attacked the rum trade and encouraged the smallholders to feed their excess corn to pigs. He tried to persuade Bligh to depart, but the embattled governor would have none of it and unsurprisingly they fell out badly.

However, his reign was cut short by the return of Colonel William Paterson on the *Porpoise* from Port Dalrymple, where as lieutenant-governor since 1804 he had been developing the new outpost and laying the foundations for Launceston. He had also taken to drink and was rarely sober. Nevertheless, he insisted on taking over from Foveaux, who had to content himself with the role of deputy. Paterson also insisted that Bligh depart the scene, and finally the governor relented in February 1809 and boarded the *Porpoise* for the journey home for yet another round of judicial hearings. However, once on board he changed his mind and ordered the ship to the Derwent, hoping for the support of Lieutenant-Governor David Collins. When he exhausted his hospitality there, he returned to Port Jackson in early 1810 before finally departing for England in May.

Meanwhile, as Bligh had languished in his vice-regal prison two years earlier, there was an astonishing development among the progeny of his earlier band of mutineers. On Saturday 6 February 1808, the American sealer *Topaz* under Captain Mayhew Folger from Nantucket, Massachusetts was steering south-west in light airs across the broad Pacific when the lookout spotted the island first discovered by Carteret in the *Swallow* in 1767. Folger wrote in his log, 'Steered for land with a light breeze at the east, the said land being Pitcairn Island . . . at 6 a.m. put off with two boats to explore and look for seals.[3]

'On approaching the shore [we] saw a smoke on the land, at which I was very much surprised, it being represented by Captain Carteret as destitute of inhabitants. On approaching still nearer the land, I discovered a boat paddling towards me with three men in her. They hailed me in the English language, asking who was the captain of the ship, and offered me a number of cocoanuts which they had brought off as a present, and requested I would land, there being, as they said, a white man on shore.

'I went on shore and found there an Englishman by the name of Alexander Smith, the only person remaining out of nine that escaped on board the ship *Bounty* . . . under the command of that arch-mutineer, Christian.'

For Folger's benefit, Adams used the name under which he signed up on the *Bounty* (and by which he was known on the island). He then regaled the visitor with his first version of the events following the mutiny. It was a thoroughly self-serving tale that pictured Adams as a shocked onlooker and victim in the murderous rampages of the 1790s. Then, reported Folger, after the death of Ned Young from natural causes, 'he immediately went to work tilling the ground so that it produces plenty for them all, and he lives very comfortably as commander-in-chief of Pitcairn's [*sic*] Island.'

Folger remained only 10 hours and swallowed the mutineer's story whole. 'All the children of the deceased mutineers speak tolerable English; some of them are grown to the size of men and women; and to do them justice, I think them a very humane and hospitable people; and whatever may have been the errors or crimes of Smith the mutineer in times back, he is at present a worthy man, and may be useful to navigators who traverse this immense ocean.'

When Young had died in 1800, the eldest girl was 11 years old, the oldest boy 10; a dozen were six or younger. The real tillers of the soil were the nine remaining women. While Adams would claim that following Young's death he experienced an epiphany that would turn him to the Good Book he saved from the *Bounty*, he well knew that if he misbehaved the women were perfectly capable of dispensing with him by hatchet or musket. This was more than sufficient motive for him to change his ways. And while he claimed that as part of his rehabilitation he destroyed McCoy's jungle juice still, it is much more likely that the women took that initiative.

Nevertheless, Adams did cooperate and was well rewarded. By 1807 he was 40, having been born the year Pitcairn was discovered, and was able to take his pick among the women, most of whom were warm-hearted and vigorous bedfellows. As the only one who could read and write (although neither well), he became the font of knowledge and authority among the children, whom he taught to read from the Bible. Whether he began the practice of 'breaking-in' the adolescent girls sexually is unproven, although a century later it would be claimed that it had 'always happened'[4] among Pitcairners.

In the 21st century world of instant communication, it would be natural to assume that the discovery of the mutineers' hideaway would soon be relayed to the farthest corners of the civilised world. In fact, it would be years before it reached the decision makers at the British Admiralty. As a parting gift, Adams presented Folger with the *Bounty*'s azimuth compass and the Kendall chronometer, which had served Bligh – and later Christian – so well. Folger sailed eastward to Juan Fernandez (Robinson Crusoe's Island) where the compass and the chronometer were both, for some unexplained reason, confiscated by the Spanish governor. The governor then threw Folger and his crew in gaol until some months later a new governor arrived and set the Americans free.

When Folger finally arrived in Valparaiso, the popular stopping-off port in Chile for ships travelling from the Atlantic to the Pacific, he reported his momentous discovery to Lieutenant William Fitzmaurice of the Royal Navy, who was serving on the naval station there. Fitzmaurice forwarded the news, together with an extract of the log of the *Topaz*, to the commander of the British naval station in Brazil on 10 October 1808. But the Admiralty didn't receive the report until 14 May 1809 and the general public didn't learn of it until March 1810 when an article based upon it appeared in the English *Quarterly Review*. The extract of the logbook of the *Topaz* appeared in the *Sydney Gazette* for 27 October 1810, two days after Bligh arrived back in England.

The Lords of the Admiralty were unimpressed by the claims of a mere American sealer. A frustrated Folger wrote to Rear Admiral Hotham on 1 March 1813, and gave a more detailed report of his visit to Pitcairn and added, 'I am sending you the azimuth compass which I received from Alex. Smith. I repaired and made use of it on my homeward passage. I now forward it to your lordship.' Hotham also dismissed the report. It was not until 1814 when two British warships, HMS *Briton* and HMS *Tagus*, commanded by Captains Staines and Pipon respectively, passed near the island that reality struck home. The ships were returning to Valparaiso from a cruise to the Marquesas when the watch noticed what seemed to be houses and regular plots of farmland. As they nosed closer, a canoe was seen paddling towards the *Briton* with two young men aboard. When it came within hailing distance one of the men called, 'Won't you heave us a rope now?'

The sailors were dumbfounded. When they climbed aboard, the well-built, dark-skinned young Pitcairners introduced themselves as Thursday October Christian and George Young. Christian was 24, Young 18, and both were dressed in waist-cloths and straw hats decorated with cocks' feathers. Staines, who had lost an arm in a sea battle, invited them below for a meal then went ashore, where he discovered Adams even more firmly entrenched as the patriarch than reported by Folger.

Staines later wrote to Vice-Admiral Manley Dixon, 'A venerable old man, named John Adams, is the only surviving Englishman of those who last quitted Otaheite in [the *Bounty*], and whose exemplary conduct, and fatherly care of the whole little colony, could not but command admiration. The pious manner in which all those born on the island have been reared, the correct sense of religion which has been instilled into their young minds by this old man, has given him the pre-eminence over the whole of them, to whom they look up as the father of the whole, and one family.'

Since Adams was only 47 – and would live for another 15 years – it seems remarkable that he could be described in such elderly terms. But since he was unquestionably a mutineer and Staines' undoubted duty was to arrest him and return him to Britain for trial, it would be understandable if the penitent chose to emphasise his frailties. Moreover, he'd had plenty of time to refine his tale of the mutiny and its aftermath, to present himself in the best possible light and conceal the fact that he had caused the bloodshed on the island by stealing another man's wife. Staines chose to depart without him, much to the relief, he says, of the small community.

By then the principal protagonist in the mutiny, William Bligh, had left the sea forever. In July 1814, he was promoted to vice-admiral with a pension that ensured his material comfort in the three years left to him. His wife Betsy had died in 1812 but he was often visited by his daughters in his comfortable cottage in Faringham, Kent. Also in 1814, Joseph Foveaux was reaching a fork in his road through life. After abandoning his extravagant colonial ambitions, he had returned to England and devoted himself to his advancement within the military. In June, he was promoted to major-general and he capped the year on 17 November at All Saints, Derby when he finally married his 'fancy woman', Mrs Sherwin.

Back on Norfolk, John Piper had escaped any involvement in the Bligh–Macarthur imbroglio and by 1810 had completed his task of emptying the island except for a few of the older settlers, convicts and a small military detachment. Early that year a vessel arrived to return him and Mary Ann together with their two sons and his horses, cattle and grain to the mainland. Once he arrived in Port Jackson Piper established himself in a grand home overlooking the harbour. By then the New South Wales Corps had been disbanded and the new governor, Lachlan Macquarie, was firmly in charge.

Piper was given the opportunity to transfer to the new 102nd Regiment but decided to resign his commission and devote himself to the great opportunities afforded by colonial life. He and the governor's lady were old friends and Mrs Macquarie had often written to him on Norfolk Island. In 1811, he sailed for England with his family to settle his affairs, buy a splendid new wardrobe and reunite with his daughter Sarah, whom he had sent there for her education. All returned together in 1814, and on the voyage Sarah had a shipboard romance with an adventurous young settler, John Thrupp. Their marriage later that year was a highlight of the social season. Piper himself would finally marry Mary Ann two years later.

However, when he left Norfolk there were still a few hard-heads among the emancipated convicts who were most reluctant to abandon a relatively prosperous farming life they had worked so long to achieve. Macquarie appointed Lieutenant Thomas Crane to oversee the final evacuation. Crane worked with the former convict William Hutchinson who had been emancipated and had risen to become chief superintendent of convicts. On 15 February 1813 the *Minstrel* and the *Lady Nelson* arrived to carry the settlers, stock and military to either Sydney or Van Diemen's Land. When they departed, only Hutchinson remained with a small band of trusted convicts. Their task was to destroy everything.

The stone buildings that had confined so many convicts would be razed to the ground. The remaining livestock – goats, sheep, pigs and old sway-backed horses – would be slaughtered and salted down. The watermills would be smashed to pieces and the dam on Watermill Creek breached to destroy itself. Nothing would remain to tempt the escaping convict or any foreign power to regard it as either a haven or a base for hostilities. And to be quite sure no living mammal survived, they left behind 12 fierce dogs. Once they accounted for any remaining livestock they would rip and tear their own kind to death. Said Hutchinson, 'They'll kill when they're hungry enough.'[5]

On 15 February 1814, exactly a year after the destroyers accepted their assignment, the *Kangaroo* appeared in the bay to take them aboard. They loosed the dogs. They rowed their boats to the ship's side, leaving a devastated island in their wake, a place where screams of agony had so often rent the air, where the veneer of civilisation had been ripped away and vile practice became the norm, where humanity under the guise of imperial righteousness sank to its lowest depths.

Hutchinson reported to Macquarie, 'I have much pleasure in assuring Your Excellency that there remains no inducement for human beings of any kind to visit that place.'

CHAPTER NINE

Imperial righteousness

Imperial righteousness was certainly the guiding star of Samuel Marsden, the leading trumpeter of the London Missionary Society who in 1814 abandoned his somewhat desultory attempts to convert the heathen Aborigines and set course for the South Pacific. Of the Australian natives, he wrote, 'The want of reflection upon their past, present and future, which is so strikingly apparent in the whole of the conduct of the Aborigines, opposes in my mind the strongest barrier to the work of a Missionary.' However, more fertile fields, he believed, awaited the Anglican enthusiast across the seas.

By now Marsden was well versed in fertile fields. He had acquired more than 3,000 acres of the finest grain and pasture land in the colony and his convict slave labour had turned it into a colonial showplace. Successive governors had appointed him to the magistracy and he dispensed justice with scant regard for his Redeemer's injunction to welcome sinners back to the fold. The self-styled 'General' Joseph Holt, one of the few Irish convicts to have departed Norfolk Island (courtesy of John Piper) without falling victim to Foveaux's sadism, witnessed Marsden's version of the golden rule towards one of his countrymen when Holt returned to the mainland in 1810.

'The unfortunate man,' he wrote later, 'had his arms extended round a tree, his two wrists tied with cords, and his breast pressed closely to the tree, so that flinching from the blow was out of the question, for it was impossible for him to stir . . . Two men were appointed to flog, namely, Richard Rice, a left-handed man, and John Johnson, the hangman from Sydney, who was right-handed. They stood on each side of Fitzgerald; and I never saw two threshers in a barn move their flails with more regularity than these two man-killers did, unmoved by pity, and rather enjoying their horrid employment than otherwise. The very first blows made the blood spout out from Fitzgerald's shoulders; and I felt so disgusted and horrified, that I turned my face away from the cruel sight.

'I have witnessed many horrible scenes; but this was the most appalling sight I had ever seen. The day was windy, and I protest that although I was at least 15 yards to leeward from the sufferers, the blood, skin, and flesh blew in my face as the executioners shook it off from their cats. Fitzgerald received his whole three hundred lashes, during which Doctor [Martin] Mason used to go up to him occasionally to feel his pulse, it being contrary to law to flog a man beyond 50 lashes without having a doctor present.

'I never shall forget this humane doctor, as he smiled and said, "Go on; this man will tire you both before he fails!" During the time Fitzgerald was receiving the punishment he never uttered a groan; the only words he said were, "Flog me fair; do not strike me on the neck!" When it was over, two constables took him by the arms to help him into the cart. He said to them, "Let my arms go," and struck each of them in the pit of the stomach with his elbows, and knocked them both down; he then stepped into the cart unassisted as if he had not received a blow. The doctor remarked, "That man has strength enough to bear two hundred more."

'The next prisoner who was tied up was Paddy Galvin, a young lad about 20 years of age; he was also sentenced to receive three hundred lashes. The first hundred were given on his shoulders, and he was cut to the bone between the shoulder-blades, which were both bare. The doctor then directed the next hundred to be inflicted lower down, which reduced his flesh to such a jelly that the doctor ordered him to have the remaining hundred on the calves of his legs. During the whole time Galvin never even whimpered or flinched, if, indeed, it had been possible for him to have done so . . . He was put in the cart and sent to the hospital.'[1]

Since neither the Irish nor the Aborigines were interested in his saving their souls, Marsden set forth to New Zealand where there had been increasing contact between Europeans and Maoris, especially in the Bay of Islands. There the whalers and sealers called frequently to replenish supplies at a settlement of flax traders and timber merchants. There too some escaped convicts found work and mixed with the native population. Marsden was concerned that they were corrupting the Maori way of life, a task that clearly demanded his more righteous ministrations. So on 14 March 1814 he set out for the Bay of

Islands in his schooner, the *Active*, accompanied by three lay missionaries: John King, William Hall and Thomas Kendall.

There he conducted the first ever Christian service on New Zealand soil and began negotiations with the young chieftain Hongi Hika to establish a mission. Hongi Hika returned to Sydney with him where they concluded the deal. The young chief had bargained well. The following year he accompanied King, Hall and Kendall back to New Zealand with a boatload of firearms and enough ammunition to conduct a small war on his enemies: guns for souls – it was a price Marsden was happy to pay.

The mission was an unmitigated disaster. It made virtually no converts. Thomas Kendall abandoned his wife for the daughter of a Maori shaman and became more Maori than Christian. Indeed, he seems to have become slightly unhinged and came to believe the Maoris were descended from the Egyptians. He and Hall also ran guns for Hongi Hika's Ngapuhi tribe, who would use them to massively expand their territory in the so-called Musket Wars.

This caused some unease in the London Missionary Society, and in 1820 Kendall sailed for England with Hongi Hika and his friend Waikato to defend himself. While there, he was ordained an Anglican priest, and arranged for Hongi Hika – as 'King of New Zealand' – to meet King George. The British monarch showered the Maori with gifts, including a suit of armour, which on his return to Sydney he promptly swapped for more guns. Kendall returned to New Zealand in 1821 but relations with Marsden had fractured. The 'flogging parson' made another voyage there in 1823 to sack him personally. Then out of sheer spite he did a round of Sydney's printers, warning them against publishing Kendall's Maori grammar book.

Kendall reluctantly parted with his Maori mistress, returned to his wife and packed to leave New Zealand. However, when his ship, the *Brampton*, ran aground while leaving the harbour, Kendall attributed it to divine intervention and decided to stay. Three years later he accepted a position as clergyman to the British Consulate in Valparaiso, but it was not a success and he returned with his family to Ulladulla in New South Wales. The one saving grace in the whole episode is that his grandson Henry Kendall grew up there and would write some of Australia's most entrancing lyrical poetry about the flora and fauna of his native land.

Altogether Marsden made seven visits to New Zealand and while he did not venture north to Norfolk, his efforts ensured that New Zealand would become the headquarters for an Anglican missionary offensive in the South Pacific. They would be led in their quest by a successor to Marsden, Bishop George Augustus Selwyn. However, when Marsden died in May 1838, Selwyn was still a curate, albeit a man marked for higher things.

Educated at Eton and St John's College, Cambridge, he had rowed in the first boat race against Oxford in 1829 and returned to Eton as a tutor before being ordained as a priest. He would marry Sarah, the only daughter of a judge, Sir John Richardson, in 1839. Two years later he would begin the great adventure in the South Seas that would write its own remarkable chapter in the history of the benighted Norfolk Island.

Meanwhile the subtropical seasons passed over the island; the rich, deep foliage reclaimed the land and covered the scars slashed and burned into its open face by the imperial intruders. In far-off London, the new master of the colonial empire, the foxy-faced secretary of state for war and the colonies, Lord Bathurst, had Norfolk in his sights. Reports from New South Wales were troubling: Governor Lachlan Macquarie's 'ill considered compassion' for convicts could well be undermining the capacity of transportation to deter crime. A firmer hand was required.

The son of a Lord Chancellor, Henry Bathurst was a member of the House of Commons until he succeeded to the Earldom in 1794. He had been an influential member of the government under four prime ministers, beginning with William Pitt in 1783. He was regarded as a 'sound fellow' as an administrator but had the habit of breaking into jocular giggles at the most inappropriate occasions. However, Macquarie's compassion was no laughing matter, and in 1819 he appointed John Thomas Bigge, an Oxford graduate and former chief justice of the slave colony of Trinidad, to undertake an investigation of the New South Wales convict system. As well, Bathurst gave him three letters of 'additional instructions' suggesting the criteria he should take into account. Transportation, he said, should be made 'an object of real terror' and should he detect examples of Macquarie's humanitarian impulses, they should be reported immediately. Any leniency should be rooted out and he was free to recommend 'harsher penal settlements'.

Macquarie had transformed the colony from the rebellious shambles he had discovered on his arrival in 1810. He had established a sound administration, a solid system of emancipation on merit and a building program that laid the foundations for real progress. But the effort had taken a toll on his health, and he applied to be relieved of his post and to resume his military career. Bathurst was not opposed to the request but his response went astray en route, and when the bumptious Bigge arrived Macquarie took this as not just a refusal but a demand that he stay and face the opprobrium of his superiors in the Colonial Office.

Bigge's attitude did nothing to allay Macquarie's fears. He carried orders that the governor must comply with his directions and accord him an official respect and precedence almost equal to his own. Bigge insisted they be followed to the letter. Macquarie complied, but he didn't realise that one of the secret instructions from Bathurst was to take private, unsworn testimony from 'leading citizens' without any opportunity for Macquarie to respond. In his report, Bigge criticised Macquarie's 'mismanagement' of convicts and his 'prejudice in favour of emancipists'. He also recommended the development of a harsher regime for the penal settlement in Van Diemen's Land, and for this Bathurst was well pleased. But it didn't go far enough. Bathurst took further advice from Joseph Foveaux, and in 1821 he appointed the Scottish-born Major-General Thomas Brisbane as Macquarie's successor, a man much more attuned to the jocular colonial secretary's penal code.

Brisbane is best remembered for his interest in astronomy. He had studied the subject at Edinburgh University and during his time in Australia he catalogued some 7,385 stars of the Southern Hemisphere. However, nothing should disguise the part he played in establishing one of the more horrific crimes perpetrated by the British Empire upon its own people. And he knew exactly what he was doing.

On 22 July 1824, Bathurst sent him this dispatch:

'I have to desire that you will immediately carry into effect the occupation of Norfolk Island upon the principle of a great Hulk or Penitentiary according to the enclosed plan . . . To this island the worst description of Convicts in New South Wales and Van Diemen's Land must progressively be sent . . . at once establishing a secondary punishment *which will not admit of mitigation* . . .'[2]

Brisbane had already suggested that Norfolk become 'the *ne plus ultra* of Convict degradation' and now added his own twist of the knife in his response: 'I have . . . thought it advisable to reserve that place as one for Capital Respites and other higher class of offences. I could wish it to be understood that the felon who is sent there is forever excluded from all hope of return.'[3]

Bathurst concurred. Brisbane jumped to and in May 1825 he chartered the private trading brig *Brutus* to carry convicts and stores to Norfolk accompanied by the colonial cutter *Mermaid* with a detachment of troops under Captain Richard Turton of the 40th Regiment. The convoy arrived on 6 June and disembarked 57 convicts, 34 soldiers and 12 of the military men's wives and children. They were the advance party whose task it was to clear the regrowth and prepare buildings, so most of the convicts were tradesmen who would leave when the job was done. They were joined in December by 31 additional convicts – including several women – who would also return to the mainland.

They first built a timber convict stockade and huts for the military. Turton kept up a spanking pace. They worked 12-hour days stone cutting and lime burning, then using the materials they had fashioned for a small gaol and a much larger storehouse. Two convicts remained in the stockade each day stoking the fires beneath two big boilers filled with hot water. In the evenings the prisoners cooked their own meals of salt beef or pork with maize meal turned into a rough damper in the coals and ashes. The same system applied when the first permanent residents arrived and the advance team departed.

Meantime, on the mainland Governor Brisbane was replaced in December 1825 by an even more enthusiastic disciplinarian, Lieutenant-General Ralph Darling, who had been acting governor of Mauritius.

The Mauritians were pleased to see him go, not least because of his decision to permit a British frigate to breach quarantine there, causing a deadly outbreak of cholera. Among his first acts on arrival was to order the withdrawal of all women from Norfolk Island. As he explained to the Colonial Office in March 1826, 'My object was to hold out that settlement as a place of the extremist punishment short of death. Norfolk Island will soon have within it . . . the most depraved and dissolute characters. At present there are 115 and there are several others at this moment to be forwarded by the first opportunity.'

Darling's orders were carried by the new commandant, Irish-born Captain Vance Donaldson, and when he proclaimed them one woman ran away into the forest with her three children. They returned, starving, in less than a week but despite her pleas she was shipped out with the rest in the first available vessel. The convict men who remained were all in their thirties or younger and while most had been sentenced to hang, their crimes were often no more than burglaries or rebellion against British oppression in their native Ireland. Their sentences were commuted to life imprisonment or decades in chains.

For more serious crimes the authorities vigorously enforced the death penalty. This began with Thomas Barrett – for the theft of stores – less than a month after the arrival of the First Fleet in 1788. In the following year, Ann Davis was the first woman executed for stealing clothes and other goods from another convict. In the decade from 1826, more than 350 met the same fate. So Darling's description of the 'capital respites' as depraved and dissolute is at best an exaggeration and at worst an expression of unrestrained cruelty. Indeed, Brisbane's injunction that Norfolk was the place from which prisoners were excluded from all hope of return and Darling's determination to make it a place of 'extremist punishment short of death', ensured that its inmates would be driven to acts of desperation. The island itself was too small to provide a long-term hiding place or means of survival. The surrounding sea was a vast and unbridgeable moat. So mutiny was inevitable, and it occurred within six months of Captain Donaldson's arrival.

It had been in the planning for three months as the commandant cut rations and practised a fierce discipline. On 25 September 1826 'Black' John Goff, a notorious figure who had been in most of the penal colonies from Van Diemen's Land to Port Macquarie, put into action the plan he had devised with a score of confederates. Goff told them he *knew* there was an island where they could find sanctuary within 100 miles of Norfolk, and he may well have believed it. The geographical knowledge of the convicts was rudimentary at best, many believing that China was just over the horizon.

Goff was a black man, having been born on the Isle of Wight from a West Indian father and a white mother. He was part of a substantial population of black Britons, particularly in the seafaring trade, and they were ultra conscious – and resentful – of their status as descendants of slaves. This rebellious streak was anathema to the authorities, and Goff had paid for it with more than 2,000 lashes on his bare back and a guard's bullet that had knocked out all his front teeth.

At his signal just before morning muster, two decoys, Patrick Clynch and Robert Storey, made a dash for the forest, and Donaldson sent 30 soldiers after them. As soon as they were out of sight, Goff and the others turned on their overseers and locked them in the gaol. Then they robbed the stores and loaded their booty into three of the colony's four boats before smashing holes in the hull of the remaining craft. When the guards came running, led by Corporal Robert Wilson, one of the escapees, Edward Watson, shot him and another, William Moore, bayoneted him to death where he fell, shouting, 'I have done for one bugger' and 'You, you bugger, ought to have been the first.'[4]

Watson then shot at another soldier, Sergeant Boyle, but missed and Goff shot and wounded Private Euston then bashed him to the ground with the butt of his pistol. The fourth guard ran back to the garrison where he gave the alarm and Donaldson ordered the bugler to call the search party back. He then led the troops at the mass of about 50 escapees who had boarded two whaleboats and a launch and put out for Phillip Island 6 kilometres away to the south.

They made the journey without mishap and on arrival began cutting timber for masts for the next stage of their escape. However, Donaldson had the other boat repaired overnight and set out for the island with 25 heavily armed soldiers aboard. When Goff and his men saw them coming they tried to launch their boats but were forced back by the heavy surf. When the men of the 57th regiment found their range they drove the convicts back from the beach and landed. The fighting continued on land, but the convicts were outgunned and their ammunition soon ran out. The soldiers captured 14 of them and headed back to Norfolk. Goff and the others spread inland.

They lived in the caves and hunted goats, caught fish and dug native yams for two weeks before the soldiers returned and this time captured Goff and most of the others. However, a few held out for six months before they surrendered. One of them, John Wavers, died of exhaustion and exposure in the hospital only an hour after he returned.

Goff, Watson and Moore were taken to Sydney for trial and all three were hanged. However, in handing down his sentence to Goff, the chief justice Francis Forbes scoffed at the prisoner's plea for mitigation because of the starvation rations and fearful lashings that were the convict's lot. In doing so, he gave an extraordinary judicial blessing to a shameless regime.

'With respect to the harsh general treatment of which you complain on Norfolk Island,' he said, 'what are men sent there for? It is within the knowledge of the Court that they are never sent there except for crimes of the deepest dye; and is it then supposed that they are sent there to be indulged, to be fed with the fruits of the earth, and that they are not to work in chains?

'No, the object in sending men there is not only as a punishment for their past crimes, but to serve as a terror to others; and so far from it being a reproach, as you have stated, it is a wise project of the government in instituting that settlement for the punishment of the twice and thrice convicted felon, as a place of terror to evil doers, and in order to repress the mass of crimes in which the Colony unhappily abounds.' There could be no court of appeal from a reign of terror so heartily endorsed.

Donaldson returned to his regiment in August 1827 and was succeeded by Captain Thomas Wright of the 39th Regiment, which had been raised in 1701 and served in Ireland, the West Indies, Malta and Spain. Wright was a strong-headed individual who had smuggled his mistress aboard the convict ship HMS *Boyne* heading for New South Wales. Although she would eventually bear him three children, he was unable to take her with him to Norfolk. Indeed, his act of defiance may well have been the reason behind his appointment.

He showed a spark of humanity to his 220 prisoners when on arrival he ordered their heavy chains replaced with light ones. However, it fizzled out before the first month was up. By then he had measured out 300 acres (120 hectares) to be hoed to a depth of 18 inches (46 centimetres) and set 200 of his charges to work in gangs. It was back-breaking work and the convicts resisted. Wright responded with 50 to 100 lashes each time they failed to reach the required depth.

By October most of the mutineers had served their gaol sentences on the island and were planning a second uprising. Once again, Patrick Clynch, the freckle-faced 30-year-old from Ireland's County Longford, who had briefly been a bushranger on the mainland, took the lead. As Captain Wright walked home from a farm in the interior, Clynch leapt from his hiding place in the high grass beside the road and attacked the commandant with a club. Wright was able to ward off his attacker and staggered back to the settlement. He called out the guard, but once again Clynch eluded his pursuers.

Had he succeeded in killing Wright, the rest of the mutineers were poised to strike. However, they bided their time and three days later Clynch struck again, this time attempting to skewer the overseer with a spear fashioned from a pole with a knife bound to one end. Again Wright turned out the guard and rounded on the prisoners' camp, where they spotted Clynch heading for a swamp. Wright sent Sergeant Dennis Tunny and two privates after him with instructions, 'You know your duty, so do it!' Amid a wild hullabaloo from the prisoners, the soldiers intercepted Clynch and brought him to earth. Then, according to the convicts, they not only shot him dead but dragged his body to the gaol, placed it on the scourger's stage and forced the prisoners to file past as a warning.

A year later, Wright would be charged with his murder but acquitted when the case, prosecuted by D'Arcy Wentworth's son William Charles, collapsed under the weight of perjury from one witness and wildly contradictory testimony from Wright's second in command Lieutenant Cox. However, Wright was recalled to Sydney and replaced briefly by Captain Hunt before he too was replaced by Captain Joseph Wakefield as acting commandant.

Wakefield distinguished himself with a plan for the development of the garrison farm, but it was ignored by his successors. He would serve only 12 months before another of the sadistic monsters who populate the Norfolk saga would thrust himself upon the darkening scene. Indeed, he had been angling for the appointment since 1825 when he approached Lord Bathurst personally to plead his case. His name is best known today as a hospital for the criminally insane. It could hardly be a more fitting memorial to the life and works of James Thomas Morriset.

CHAPTER TEN

'Keep those scoundrels in order'

Until he was in his early thirties, Morisset led an unexceptionable life as a professional soldier. Born in 1780, his father – also James Thomas – was a goldsmith of Huguenot descent with a reputation for crafting commemorative swords and snuff boxes for the British aristocracy. He married Janetta Tadwell and they lived in fashionable Paddington where young James was the first born. The boy had a decent education and joined the 80th Regiment, the Staffordshire Volunteers, as an ensign in February 1798. As an 18-year-old he had his portrait painted and it reveals a beardless, pouty face below a crop of carefully coiffed black hair.

He sailed to India where his regiment was stationed and performed his duties well enough to earn promotion to lieutenant in 1800. By now the Napoleonic wars were in full swing and he was sent with the regiment to Egypt, arriving just in time for the victory celebrations following the battle of Alexandria. Five years later he had failed to gain further promotion, so while on sick leave in England he purchased a captain's commission for £1,500 in the 48th Regiment, which was soon to be engaged in the Peninsular Wars against Napoleon's forces in Spain. Captain Morisset served with no particular distinction, but on 16 May 1811, when he was 31, came the moment that would change his life. In the Battle of Albuera he was hit by part of a French artillery shell and suffered a ghastly wound to the face. It would leave him monstrously disfigured.

A fellow officer, Captain Foster Fyans, later described his face, which had 'one side considerably longer than the other, with a stationary eye as if sealed on his forehead: his mouth was large, running diagonal to his eye, filled with a mass of useless bones'.[1] While his descendants would later claim that the wound had come from a sabre cut, Morisset himself told Fyans it was 'the fruits of the Peninsular war: a 32 inch shell struck me, smashed me into atoms . . . all my bones broken, dead for a week'.

The damage went to the heart and soul of the man. While he was able to resume his duties with the regiment, as people turned away in horror and embarrassment, the terrible wound loosed a rage within. Morisset would become ever more deeply resentful. Soon he would be obsessed with the need to find an outlet among the well-made men who would come within his power to torture and mutilate. When the 48th was posted to New South Wales in 1817, he would revel in his vicious punishment of the convicts in his charge.

In December 1818, he was appointed commandant at Newcastle, and on a visit Governor Macquarie noted his 'efficiency' in dealing with convict labour. Even more telling, the flint-eyed Commissioner Bigge found him a man after his own disciplinarian's heart and praised the way he adapted special punishments to each individual prisoner. Promoted to major, he was appointed in November 1823 to Bathurst, where he relieved Captain William Lawson, who with W. C. Wentworth and the wealthy settler Gregory Blaxland had found a way across the Blue Mountains to the bounteous plains of the Wiradjuri people.

When the Aboriginals resisted the imperial incursions, Governor Brisbane declared martial law in the area and Morisset led the reprisals designed to crush the uprising. Brisbane was delighted with the result. As he reported to the jocular Lord Bathurst, 'I felt it necessary to augment the detachment at Bathurst to 75 men who were divided into various small parties, each headed by a magistrate who proceeded in different directions in towards the interior of the country . . . This system of keeping these unfortunate people in a constant state of alarm soon brought them to a sense of their duty, and . . . "Saturday", their great and most warlike chieftain has been with me *to receive his pardon* and he, with most of his tribe, attended the annual conference held here on the 28th November . . .'

However, while hunting down blacks afforded a certain satisfaction, Morisset's real goal was to be given charge of Brisbane's *ne plus ultra* of punishment, Norfolk Island. He took leave to England in 1824 to petition Bathurst personally for, in his own words, 'I [was] the man to keep these scoundrels in order . . . If the Duke of Wellington searched throughout the army of Great Britain he could not equal me. I understand all their priggings.'[2]

To underscore his commitment, Morisset made a great show of informing himself of the minutiae of prisoner control. 'Prior to leaving England I attended Bow Street daily and visited every police office in London. I was ashamed almost of being a soldier, ha, ha, and receiving pay in idleness.'[3] Bathurst was impressed by Morisset's submission of an 'excellent system' of strict convict subjugation, and eagerly recommended his appointment to the new governor, Ralph Darling. Assured of his position at a munificent £600 a year, the disfigured 46-year-old was now able to secure a wife in 23-year-old Louisa Emily Vaux, from an Isle of Wight family. When they left England the following year she had produced a baby girl, Janetta Louisa.

Morisset had already fathered a child in New South Wales. Ambrose Australia Gripers Morisset was born on 22 January 1825 to Johanna Deasey and baptised at St John's Parramatta on 6 February 1825. They had met in Bathurst, and he may well have married her in 1824 before setting out for England. However, he would never acknowledge the woman thereafter; nor his paternity of the child.

When Morisset arrived back in Sydney en route to his Norfolk Island post, Governor Darling raised objections to the appointment. While he was of one mind in the treatment of convicts, the presence of Morisset's wife and child presented a problem. Under Darling's decree they would have to remain on the mainland, but Morisset was adamant that they accompany him. Darling was also concerned that other commandants in Port Macquarie, Moreton Bay and elsewhere were receiving a mere £182/10/- and Morisset's £600 'would be a cause of dissatisfaction', particularly since Morisset was also on an additional lieutenant-colonel's pay.[4]

Until he received orders to the contrary, Darling appointed Morisset to the vacant post of superintendent of police, which he reluctantly accepted. For two years viperous exchanges passed between Sydney and Whitehall. Finally, Morisset broke the stalemate by relinquishing his army pay, and in February 1829 he received his orders to proceed to Norfolk as lieutenant-governor. However, he was further delayed by a request of his own. During his time in Newcastle he was impressed by the agony that could be inflicted on the convicts by chaining them to a treadmill, where they could endure days and weeks of grinding labour before they collapsed. He wanted one for his new post. Alas, the Colonial Office jibbed at the cost, some £2,250, and suggested substituting 'some other description of punishment for that which the Treadmill was intended to afford'.[5]

Morisset would accept the challenge.

He finally arrived on 26 May 1829. By then a second daughter, Edith Julia Eliza, had been born and they were also accompanied by his wife's brother Henry Vaux, whom he made deputy commissary general. Mrs Morisset brought her own female servant.

The commandant's powers of punishment were limited – at least in theory – to 300 lashes of the cat. But there was no limit to the number of times the sentence could be carried out. As well, he could confine a prisoner to his cell and place him on bread and water; and he could add three years to his sentence without reference to any other authority. But in truth he had the power of life and death over the 500 and more prisoners in his grip. And he could devise punishments of his own (in place of the treadmill) that were not mentioned in the official code. For example, he could have his scourger devise a heavier cat that cracked the prisoners' ribs. He could apply a crude wooden gag to the mouth to increase their agony. He could work them in heavy chains and send them to cut stone and coral up to their waists in the sea. And he could confine them in the 'dumb cell' pioneered by Foveaux, holding them in total darkness in water that stank with their own and others' excreta. All of these he applied within months of his arrival. And since no clergyman could be induced to tend such an odious flock, Morisset himself would bless his own rule each Sunday when all were obliged to assemble to hear the lesson from that hideously twisted mouth.

Inevitably, the prisoners revolted. As a chain gang returned from their work in the quarry, they turned on their overseer, smashed him to the ground with a pick handle, attacked him with their hammers and left him for dead. They then knocked off their irons, took his keys and released other prisoners and prepared to rush the garrison. However, the overseer regained consciousness, staggered there before them and raised the alarm. First on the scene was Captain Charles Sturt.

Best known as the explorer who pioneered great tracts of the Murray–Darling basin and became obsessed with the discovery of an inland sea, Sturt had returned ill and exhausted from his latest expedition down the length of the Murrumbidgee. The posting to head the garrison on Norfolk would help him recuperate before returning to the field. He acted quickly, calling out the guard and locking all exits from the gaol.

Inside, the prisoners spent the night planning their tactics, but in the morning they found themselves outmanoeuvred at every turn. Finally they surrendered. All were placed in heavy irons and locked in tiny cells. However, one bright spark called through his high window that he was prepared to name the ringleaders if Sturt would attend him. The explorer hurried to the wall beneath the cell and waited for the message. Instead he received the contents of a wooden half barrel filled with urine and slops.

The practical joker had misjudged his man. The usually equable soldier, educated at Harrow and friend to other notables like Alan Cunningham, John Oxley and Hamilton Hume, lost his temper. Encouraged by Morisset, he had all 70 within the walls placed in turn on the triangle and flogged.

Sturt's time on the island turned into a nightmare and, despite plans to send him to New Zealand as resident or a new expedition to the Darling, he was forced to take leave in England. On the journey his eyesight, which had been failing, broke down completely, leaving him totally blind. Although medical treatment would be moderately successful, he would never truly recover his health.

Two convicts, Laurence Frayne and Aaron Price, left records of their experience under Morisset. They were very different characters and their responses provide a two-dimensional perspective to the regime of terror. Price was an Englishman who, like Patrick Clynch, was assigned to Vicars Jacob, a Sydney merchant with properties in the lower Hunter Valley around Maitland. And like Clynch he absconded to join a bushranging gang led by Patrick Riley. However, when they arrived on Norfolk the Irishman Clynch continued to rebel against his treatment while Price buckled under, and over the next 30 years on the island would progress from convict to police runner, constable, overseer and finally principal overseer.

Frayne, like many of his fellows, was a young, dark-haired and blue-eyed Irishman, convicted of theft in Dublin and sent to New South Wales in 1826. Over the next four years he repeatedly absconded until the authorities lost patience and condemned him to Norfolk. Lashed to the bone on board the *Lucy Ann*, which carried him there, he was in a desperate state when he arrived. Maggots were eating his flesh. 'My shoulders,' he wrote later, 'were actually in a state of decomposition the stench of which I could not bear myself . . . In this state immediately after my landing I was sent to carry salt beef on my back with the salt brine as well as pressure stinging my mutilated and mortified flesh up to Longridge. I really longed for instant death.'[6]

He held such men as Price in vile contempt. 'Indulgence,' he wrote, 'was only got by traffic in human blood.' They were the informers in Foveaux's system, expanded by Morisset and his successors to destroy any sense of solidarity between the prisoners. Frayne knew them to be the enemy who were 'capable of any act of perfidy or blood no matter how black or horrifying such a deed might be'.[7]

He was soon brought before Morisset for breaking a flagstone in the quarry. The commandant waved away his defence and sentenced him to 100 lashes. But instead of accepting his punishment he shouted back at the colonel calling him a tyrant. And when Morisset replied that no man had ever dared say that about him, 'I said that they knew the consequences too well to tell him so. "But I tell you in stark naked blunt English that you are as great a tyrant as Nero ever was."'[8]

There might well be a dash of retrospective bravado in Frayne's account, but there can be little doubt that Morisset then took a close personal interest in breaking the young Irishman's spirit. He ordered another hundred strokes and stood by to assure himself it was given 'as severe as the scourgers could possibly inflict it'. And when he came before him two months later charged with assaulting another informer, Morisset was waiting. 'I will give you 300 at three different whippings,' he gloated.

After the first 100 Frayne was returned to his gaol cell for a week until his back scabbed. Then Morisset sent the tame assistant surgeon Alexander Gamack to see if he could take the second hundred without dying in the triangle. Frayne demanded they get it over with, and after the flogging with the heavy cat he was thrown back into his cell. In an attempt to ease the pain, Frayne poured his water ration into a slight depression in the stone floor, urinated in it to add depth, then laid his burning back into the sharply painful then soothing mix. 'I was literally alive with maggots and vermin,' he says. 'I even hated the look and appearance of myself.'[9]

However, relief arrived with the government vessel *Governor Phillip* from Sydney carrying orders that limited all floggings for a single offence to 100 lashes, and Laurence Frayne was released back into the convict community. And soon afterwards, an even more welcome relief came his way when he discovered two of the convict girls who worked at Government House had been gaoled overnight for having offended vice-regal propriety. One of them was from Frayne's home town and he found a way to sneak into their cell that night. 'They knew too well the Colonel's feelings towards me,' he says. 'They were equally anxious as myself to annoy the Colonel.' Indeed, it added spice to a night of joyous (if careful) sexual pleasuring. The memory would remain undimmed till his dying day.

Frayne's reprieve was due to the orders of the new Dublin-born governor Richard Bourke whose first acts on arrival in 1831 were to substitute civil juries for military boards in criminal cases and limit the sentences imposed on convicts to 100 lashes. Bourke represented a more liberal approach to the colony in general, and although he showed scant interest in Norfolk, Morisset would have been aware that his sadistic excesses would not find the same degree of acquiescence that he had received from Darling. Moreover, vigorous little newspapers had arisen in the colony and one in particular, the *Sydney Monitor*, edited by Edward Smith Hall, took a special interest in the island. Hall was instrumental in establishing the Bank of New South Wales, and with some justice took the credit for having Governor Darling recalled.

Hall wrote directly to Lord Bathurst's successor as colonial secretary, Lord Goderich, claiming that the Norfolk convicts were 'made the prey of hunger and nakedness at the caprice of monsters in human form. If the wretches at Norfolk Island were fiends instead of men they could not have been worse treated. There is no parallel to the cruelties practised on them.' He recalled Commissioner Bigge's report that noted the backs of Morisset's prisoners at Newcastle were 'furrowed and knotted' as a result of constant flogging. 'That scourging was inflicted by Colonel Morisset [who] of all officers who was ever employed to take charge of a settlement is one of the most improper that could have been selected by H.M. Government.'[10]

For the other officers on the island, life was one of intense boredom punctuated by periods of high tension when prisoners mutinied or murdered their overseers or each other. Captain Foster Fyans, for example, waxed lyrical as he approached the island. 'A more interesting and lovely scene of beauty cannot be described,' he wrote.[11] 'All days [are] alike in this heavenly climate. The island is small but luxuriantly rich, abundance of lemons, guavas, pomegranates, custard apple and other fruits indigenous to the soil . . . The trees throughout the year bear fruit and in many parts the ground is covered with most magnificent lemons every day in the year. To me the island appeared a fairyland and so beautiful in comparison with New South Wales.

'The valleys are provided with numerous exotics in plants, and streams of the finest water. A week or ten days might with great pleasure be expended in visiting the island. The cliffs are abrupt, the sea rolling under awfully sublime, at a distance of many hundred feet.' However, it was only a few months before Fyans was bemoaning his fate. 'I was soon acquainted with every part of the island. I was fond of shooting and exercise but soon loathed repetition of the visits. Many a day I bent my steps to Mount Pitt . . . if possible to enjoy a sight of a ship. Many and many an hour I have passed unhappily enough in this mood.'

There were diversions. Fyans was particularly taken with the regular visits of whales, particularly when they were attacked by thresher sharks. The thresher, he wrote, 'strikes on the whale, rises perpendicularly, lashing the whale to his full length. I have counted five large thrashers [sic] on one whale for upwards of an hour, the whale diving and rising constantly with his tormentors. The whale often dies from the wounds received . . .'

One weekend in 1831, Mrs Morisset's brother Henry Vaux took his dogs – two red setters and two big Newfoundlands – to a favourite fishing spot off the rocks. He was accompanied by his convict servant and his friend, Ensign Fortescue, with his military batman Milligan and another convict. Vaux was intent on his line when, according to Fyans, 'the sea suddenly receded from the rock to a considerable distance of some hundreds of yards'. It then returned and, 'Milligan rushed on Fortescue, pulling him down, with his legs wedged into a hole in the rock; held him manfully when the sea passed over, washing all away before it.'[12]

Fortunately, Fortescue and Milligan escaped unhurt. Not so Vaux, the two convicts and the four dogs. 'All were seen nearly a quarter of a mile [420 metres] out. Vaux was a fine swimmer, surrounded by his dogs; [there were] hopes that he might have escaped for he was nearer the land than the others. But it was impossible; all were devoured by sharks.' This came as a terrible blow to Mrs Morisset, who took to her sick bed for several weeks.

Government House was in mourning; and just at that time the government summarily rejected Morisset's request for a land grant of 2,560 acres (1,036 hectares). The mutual hatred between the commandant and his prisoners festered. He began to suffer headaches and periods of black despond when not even the prospect of a particularly vicious flogging could rouse him from his doleful mood. But when he applied to be relieved, Lord Goderich replied, somewhat waspishly via the governor: 'Col. Morisset should be reminded that it was at his own solicitations that he was appointed to his present command, and convicts of the descriptions of those placed at Norfolk Island was the chief ground for accepting his services as Commandant.'

This only fuelled his resentment, and from 1832 onwards he appears to have fluctuated between an ungovernable rage – for which the prisoners suffered – and periods of lassitude and total lack of interest in running the settlement. According to Margaret Hazzard, 'Violence was always in the air at this time. An atmosphere of insuppressible [*sic*] violence pervaded the gaol and violence was met with violence – the floggings increased to match the crimes and as the lashings increased so did the crimes.'[13]

The island itself seemed to shake with rage. On 29 May 1832 Price wrote in his diary, 'About 5 p.m. a violent shock resembling an earthquake was felt. Several prisoners thrown down. Many officers said the hills shook so violently they expected them to be thrown down too. Bells at Government House rang for several minutes and inmates ran for safety. Mrs Morisset fainted at the door. Everyone on the island became uneasy for their safety.'

During the periods of Morisset's prostration, Captain Fyans took charge and followed his lead in ruling by the lash, quickly gaining the soubriquet 'Flogger Fyans'. By now there were more than 750 prisoners on the island, and they slept cheek by jowl in hammocks only 20 inches (50 centimetres) apart with up to 120 in each upper-storey dormitory.

Their propinquity permitted plans to be laid for revolt. And in a world without women it gave easy access to homosexual release. Indeed, Norfolk Island would soon become a byword for 'unnatural' sex.

Meantime, Fyans worried that, with Morisset's withdrawal to his darkened room punishments were not being carried out. 'On making inquiry, an old and trusty constable flatly informed me that not a solitary case of punishment had been inflicted since the commandant's non-attendance at office,' he wrote.[14] 'On the following morning I attended the police office when to my horror the list [for punishment] amounted to 50 names from the different gangs on work . . . the convict population on the island were in one mass nearly one thousand doubly-convicted felons concocting plans of infamy.'

He hurried to Government House. 'I begged [Morisset] to look over the list and direct me how to act. "Settle them in any way you deem fit," was the reply.' The two men argued about who should take the decision to order the floggings until finally Fyans – in his telling of the confrontation – demanded the commandant act or he would walk away from the task. Morisset replied, 'You are under my orders. I shall ship you off the island by [sic] the first opportunity and report you for mutiny.' Fyans turned on his heel and went to his quarters. 'Shortly after this,' he says, 'not exceeding an hour, I had an official letter authorising me to inflict such punishments as awarded in the police office, where I lost no time in bending my steps.' Once there, he sentenced 22 convicts to a minimum 50 lashes each. 'This prompt and timely dealing soon brought matters to a more healthy state,' he says.

But all was not as it appeared. 'From information daily given to me by [Aaron] Price the constable, who had his information from the convicts, a mutiny was to take place.' Fyans found this difficult to credit, since among the convicts 'the greatest regularity prevailed'. But the next night a prisoner was found murdered in his hammock and soon afterwards Price, 'came as he always did to visit me after dark' and again raised the alarm. 'After bell toll,' he said, 'every man on the island will be on to you.' A grateful Fyans offered him a glass of brandy. Price declined. 'Drinking led me to evil,' he said, 'and made me a convict.'

In fact, the convicts, led by John Knatchbull, the 42-year-old son of an English baronet who had fallen from naval commander to convicted forger and pickpocket, planned to take over the island and reserve for Morisset and Fyans a particularly cruel and lingering fate. They would hang them, but take them down before death claimed them and divide them in quarters, each fourth to decorate a compass point on the island. Price and another informer, James Ledgwick, would be burned alive.

The next morning, the bell tolled and nothing happened; the same the following day. But then on the third there was a shot from the gaol and the convicts rushed the guard there. 'The guard behaved bravely: two men were killed, the others all seriously injured in defending themselves,' Fyans says. Then 300 from the work gangs joined in from behind armed only with gardening and quarrying tools. The soldiers ran from the garrison buckling their gear on.

'We formed on a rise about eighty yards from the melee,' says Fyans. 'I could barely speak from the effects of the run. When I gave the word, "Fire away independently," my hearty fellows did so . . . We almost immediately advanced, driving some five hundred of these cowardly fellows before us towards their barracks; but any fellow proceeding in the direction of Long Ridge was fired on, and a good few were wounded.'

From the ridge came another gang of convicts carrying wooden lances crudely tempered in fire. 'We gave them a few shot,' says Fyans. 'We followed, driving them into the barracks.' There he reported to Morisset who, in Fyans' telling, was befuddled and distrait, that there were still at least a hundred convicts at large. 'Never fear, Colonel,' said the Captain, 'as soon as our men refresh themselves, a party shall go out, scour the Island, and shoot as many of the lawless scoundrels as we can for you.'

In the end, nine men were killed and scores wounded. The uprising petered out, and by the end of January 1834 the authorities were back in control and eager for retribution. It took Fyans and his officers five months to interrogate all the witnesses for the trial to come. Meantime, the floggers worked overtime lashing the convicts *en masse* by flaming torches. They no longer cried for mercy. Instead, they pleaded for death to end their suffering.

Morisset had applied for 12 months leave of absence due to ill health a year before, and now it was finally granted. In fact, he had no intention of returning, and in February he left the island forever. Mrs Morisset completed the packing and departed with her children and six convict servants – three male and three female – on the *Governor Phillip* on 10 March 1834. Once on the mainland, the 54-year-old Morisset sold his army commission and sought a civil post in the administration. None was forthcoming. He returned to Bathurst, where he bought a property, and was appointed a magistrate in 1838. However, three years later he lost everything when the Bank of Australia crashed. He was forced to sell the farm and reserve part of his meagre salary to pay his debts. His hold on the magistracy was tenuous but he warded off all attempts to dismiss him and died in harness on 17 August 1852, aged 72. Mrs Morisset, now destitute, appealed to the government for a pension.

CHAPTER ELEVEN

Trouble on Pitcairn

While Norfolk was enduring its convulsion of violence, across the ocean on Pitcairn the inhabitants were also being swept into a maelstrom of conflict, one that would see them uprooted and transplanted, returned and overwhelmed by a commandant at least as unhinged as Morisset at his most manic.

It began gradually, a few puffs of wind ahead of the wild tumult to come. In the five years from 1819 when Captains Staines and Pipon visited, some 13 vessels called into the island, mostly whalers seeking fresh water and vegetables, which the Pitcairners were happy to supply. An East Indiaman, the *Hercules* under Captain James Henderson donated some much needed carpenter's tools and big iron boilers, which the islanders could use to obtain salt from the seawater. They would later be employed as stills in making a new version of the ti-tree liquor that had wrought such havoc among the original mutineers. On his return to India, Henderson placed an advertisement in the *Calcutta Journal* seeking donations, and on his next voyage to South America was able to deliver ploughs, cooking utensils and even a 7 metre cutter to allow the Pitcairners to fish further out to sea than was possible in their primitive canoes.

In October 1823, the English whaler *Cyrus* anchored offshore and the captain John Hall spent much of the evening in conversation with John Adams. By now there were 45 in the community and Adams was in his 56th year. He was concerned that the young people needed a more vigorous educator than his barely literate self. According to Rosalind Young, a descendant of Edward Young, writing towards the end of the 19th century, 'The captain promised to do what he could . . . and asked if any of [the crew] would be willing to accede to the request. After a few minutes hesitation, John Buffett, a young man twenty-six years of age stepped forward.'[1]

Buffett had been a cabinetmaker's apprentice in his native Bristol and had run away to join the Royal Navy. He was shipwrecked in the Gulf of St Lawrence and later cast away on the coast of California. From there he made his way to Honolulu, where he joined the *Cyrus*. Rosalind Young writes, 'Among his shipmates on board was a youth about 19 years of age named John Evans, a native of London. For love of Buffett he determined to remain on the island, and for this purpose he ran away from the ship.

'Being of very small build, he contrived to hide himself in the hollow stump of a tree until the vessel had sailed and it was safe for him to make his appearance. As there was no help for it, Evans also was allowed to become a member of the community.'[2]

Buffet quickly settled in and within a few months had married Dorothy, a daughter of Ned Young in a ceremony conducted by Adams. Some time afterwards, the diminutive Evans sought the hand of Adams's daughter Rachel, his senior by almost 10 years. According to Rosalind, 'The old man did not approve . . . however, the matter was referred to the daughter for decision. Her answer came quick, short and decided: "Try it, daddy."' Evans gave her a ring 'formed of the outer circle of a limpet shell'. They produced no children.

Adams was kept busy in this period solemnising unions in idiosyncratic Pitcairn fashion as the mutineers' descendants began the process of interbreeding in what would become a bewildering genetic web. Unimpressed with the mutineers' progeny, he groomed Buffett for leadership. However, it was an ambition that would not be realised.

In 1825, the Royal Navy ship HMS *Blossom* under Captain Frederick Beechy called into the island and Beechy remained on shore for 16 days. He recorded 36 men and 35 women in the community, of whom only five were the original Tahitian emigrants. The village consisted of five houses on a cleared area sloping towards the sea, with others located more distant from the small settlement.

The visitors ate at a different house each night, the food being cooked in earthen ovens Tahitian style but served at table with a variety of Western cutlery and crockery, particularly at the house of Fletcher Christian's son Thursday October. Beechy informed them that their home-grown calendar had been at fault for many years. Their host changed his name overnight to become Friday October Christian.

The men ate first and the women served before taking their own meals separately.

According to Beechy's report, 'Yams constituted the principal food, either baked, boiled or mixed with cocoanut, made into cakes, and eaten with molasses extracted from the ti-root. Pork was seldom indulged in; the people lived on fruit and vegetables; and with such a simple diet, early rising and much exercise, they were subject to few diseases.'

By now Buffett had taken over the teaching duties, although his only books were the Bible and the Book of Common Prayer. These did additional service on Sunday when Adams conducted no fewer than five separate services. The surviving mutineer had now become a fully fledged patriarch, the final arbiter of all customs and disputes. And during several sessions he provided Beechy with yet another version of his life, the uprising on the *Bounty* (in which he was by now little more than a startled observer) and the early, murderous days on the island (same again).

Beechy was no fool and he weighed Adams's account against Edward Young's journal, which he partially copied. On his departure, the journal remained with Adams and was 'lost' soon after. Nevertheless, the naval officer saw no reason to recommend the British Government intervene in the island's affairs. Indeed, he praised Buffett's school teaching and religious instruction. 'He is also a clever and useful mechanic, as a shipwright and joiner, and is much beloved by the community.'[3] And for the next three years life continued as before but for one significant change: John Buffett reactivated the still and began producing ti-tree liquor. Soon he was extending his instruction of the older girls into the pleasures – for him at least – of sex. He would eventually father at least two illegitimate children.[4]

In 1828, two men suddenly arrived in an 18 ton sealing sloop with the express intention of remaining on the island. They were an exceedingly odd couple – an American, Noah Bunker, and an Irish-born deserter who from youth had taken the name George Hunn Nobbs. While Nobbs was a fantasist who invented various tales about his family background, Bunker told John Buffett that their ship was fitted out from Callao in Peru for a sealing expedition. They had travelled 200 kilometres south, where the rest of the crew was landed to kill and skin seals while he and Nobbs explored further south.

Then, as related by Nobbs's great-great grandson Raymond, 'On their return they found the ship's crew and boat missing and Bunker, in debt for the fitting out of the sloop, and fearful that if they returned without any skins his creditors would seize the vessel, suggested their both going to Pitcairn's [*sic*] Island. Nobbs replied that he had wished to go there for some time . . . and so agreed to sail to the island.'⁵

In fact, the greater likelihood is that the two men abandoned their crewmates and stole the ship. And the islanders led by Adams – a practised liar himself – held grave suspicions about them. After the 5,600 kilometre journey across the Pacific, Bunker was in poor condition and after eight days deliberation Adams finally gave them permission to remain. Bunker was also deeply distressed from some actions in his recent past, which he refused to discuss, and when Fletcher Christian's granddaughter Peggy rejected his advances his threw himself off a cliff. According to Rosalind Young, 'By some means his fall was broken and his suicidal intentions were frustrated.'⁶ However, shortly afterwards he poisoned himself with an overdose of laudanum.

Edward Quintal had taken the American into his care and claimed that he had bequeathed him the boat. But Nobbs refused to listen and demolished it to provide planks for his house. Quintal would never forgive him.

By now Adams, at 59, was in decline, and Nobbs set out to assert himself ahead of Buffett and any other claimants to the patriarchal succession. To bolster his case he claimed his father was a member of the British aristocracy, one Francis Rawdon-Hastings, the Earl of Moira and his mother Jemima French, the daughter of an Irish baronet. Both were untrue. He was in fact the illegitimate son of a serving maid with no aristocratic connections – legitimate or otherwise – who abandoned him to a childless couple who lived near Yarmouth in the English county that shared the name of his eventual home: Norfolk.

To Adams and the simple Pitcairners who held imperial Britain in awe and trepidation, such credentials commanded respect and even reverence. Yet there was something about the man that didn't ring true. It was the same for stories of his wild adventures, beginning with his running away to sea at 12 and fighting fearsome battles against the elements of nature – and Spanish pirates – in most of the seven seas.

The truth remains cloudy. It is highly likely that he did enlist in the navy as a 12-year-old and served on various naval and merchant vessels; and that he spent time in India during part of the administration of Francis Rawdon-Hastings as governor-general, which might explain his choice of the earl as his 'father'. However, it is clear that from at least 1824 he had made up his mind to visit Pitcairn, which in the penny papers and among church missions had become something of a fabled isle.

Three months into his residence, a Belgian trader, Jules-Antoine Moerenhout, called into the island seeking volunteers to join him on a pearl diving operation in the islands to the west. He was thoroughly unimpressed with Nobbs. While Adams was failing he had divided the community so that as Buffett preached and said prayers in one house, Nobbs was carrying out a similar service in another. 'I took him aside,' Moerenhout wrote, 'and told him frankly what I thought . . . it was ridiculous and absurd for him to act as a pastor to people who were kind and simple enough to receive him without knowing him.'[7] This view was reinforced a year later by a visiting ship's surgeon, Robert Guthrie who, according to Raymond Nobbs, 'questioned [his] motives and regarded him as not merely cunning but also "too proud to labour the ground" and "a selfish, canting hypocrite".'

Buffett had fallen foul of Adams over (of all things) theology. In his lessons and sermons, the old patriarch relied exclusively on the Old Testament. And when Buffett began to introduce the Christian concept of forgiveness and redemption through the intercession of Jesus Christ, the old man accused him of undermining his strict regime. Nobbs saw his opportunity to widen the breach by siding with Adams. He also gained the hand of Fletcher Christian's young granddaughter Sarah to bolster his claims. When Adams died in March 1929, the succession had not been decided.

The power struggle became ever more overt as Nobbs established his own school, and soon Buffett had only eight pupils to Nobbs's 15. He had persuaded the community to pay him in kind from the common store of meat and vegetables so that he need not 'labour the ground'. Buffett saw the writing on the wall and surrendered the field, but not without a powerful, lingering resentment. The two men would never truly reconcile, but Edward Young, named for his father, acted as a go-between and became the community's chief mediator in internecine family disputes until Nobbs himself assumed untrammelled leadership.

However, before that could occur the entire community would be swept into a vortex of chaos and confusion. It had begun in 1825 when Adams told Captain Beechy he was concerned that the population would soon outgrow the island's resources. Beechy agreed and passed his misgivings on to the government, where it engaged the active interest of Sir John Barrow, a key figure in the founding of the Royal Geographical Society. Adams had suggested removal to New South Wales or Tasmania, but the church missionary societies and their representatives in Tahiti pressed the case for a return to their 'homeland'. One of the Pitcairn women, Jenny Young, had left the island in 1817 on an American whaler and was now in Tahiti.[8] Jenny told the missionaries (or so they said) that the others would be more than willing to follow her lead.

The missionaries had reached Tahiti as far back as 1797 in the *Duff*, but most of the men had been seduced by the uninhibitied sensuality of the Tahitian women and left the church. Others had fled to New South Wales. However, in the early 19th century the Reverend Henry Nott from the London Missionary Society was able to gain the support of the Tahitian King Pomare II who in 1815 finally agreed to be baptised into the church. So the missionaries had achieved a position of considerable influence in the archipelago.

By 1831 the population on Pitcairn had risen to 135 but it was poised to explode as there were 87 females, mostly of child-bearing age. And by now the men were spoiled for choice.

In far-off London, they decided, 'something must be done' and fell to a discussion of the various alternatives. Barrow, a writer as well as an administrator, had just published his *Eventful History of the Mutiny and Piratical Seizure of* HMS *Bounty* and his strong preference for Tahiti carried the day. Orders went out from the naval officer-in-chief in India and the NSW governor, Ralph Darling to send Captain Alexander Sandilands on HMS *Comet* accompanied by the barque *Lucy Anne* to carry out the transfer.

They arrived on 28 February 1831 and Sandilands 'made known to the inhabitants the object of the mission'.[9] The next day he called a meeting of the heads of all the families. 'Having fully explained to them that they were perfectly at liberty either to remove to Otaheite or remain where they were, I directed Mr Henry, who was employed by the Government of New South Wales to accompany the expedition, to give them every information in his power, which – from his being thoroughly acquainted with the manners and laws of Otaheite, as well as having been present at the meeting held by the late King Pomare and the chiefs with the promise of land, protection and assistance – he was well calculated to afford.' Half the Pitcairners agreed immediately to make the move and the following day 'the remainder came to the same resolution'.

In fact, their motives were mixed. As the descendants of mutineers they were inherently nervous about their status in British law. They were in awe of the majesty of the Royal Navy and did not want to offend those who had gone to so much trouble and expense on their behalf. And there was a natural desire to see the land their Tahitian mothers and grandmothers had spoken about so affectionately. In any case, according to Sandilands, 'They all immediately commenced preparations for embarking by carrying down to the landing place yams, potatoes and household goods which were continued to be embarked in the ships until the 7th of March; on the morning of which the entire inhabitants were on board the *Lucy Anne*.' The voyage was uneventful and they arrived at Papiete Harbour 16 days later where they found the island 'under the government of Queen Pomare, daughter of the late King, but I regret to say, upon the very eve of a civil war'.[10]

According to an anonymous correspondent (later revealed as Jules-Antoine Moerenhout) in the *United Services Journal* of 15 May 1831, a number of the chiefs under the influence of the missionaries were in rebellion against the queen. At issue was a clash of cultures – the queen seeking to regain the guilt-free sexual nature of her society, and the missionaries demanding a puritanical adherence to the middle class mores of 19th century Britain.

Open warfare was avoided but the Pitcairners were caught in the middle. According to Moerenhout, 'Nothing could be worse than to bring these good and virtuous people into this gulf of corruption. The first moral lesson they received on their arrival was to see about 50 women of Tahiti swim off to the ships in which they were, and commit in their presence, with the sailors, such acts of debauchery that they instantly desired to return to their own island.'

Moerenhout was overstating the case. The Pitcairners might have been proselytised by Adams, Buffett and Nobbs in the ways of outward modesty, but there is every reason to believe that they had a healthy appetite for sex, unencumbered by the puritanical taboos. A much more serious concern was their exposure to the diseases that had become endemic in Tahiti. Six weeks after they took up residence on the fertile land granted them, six had succumbed to fevers, including two men with families of six children each. Another 11 would die – including community stalwarts Friday October Christian and Edward Young – before their passage home could be secured four months later.

Nobbs was opposed to their returning. He had established a relationship with Queen Pomare, who adopted his infant son Reuben and wanted to bring him up with her own children. Buffett led those who wanted to leave, and Moerenhout arranged for an advance party led by Buffett and his family to return to Pitcairn on one of his pearling schooners to tend the livestock and crops they had left behind. It was a difficult voyage and for a time they were stranded on Lord Howe Island where another of the Christian family died.

Back on Tahiti, the Pitcairners sold what few possessions they had, and with the assistance of the European community there finally raised the funds to charter an American brig, the *Charles Dagget*, to sail them back to their island, arriving on 2 September 1831. It was an ambivalent homecoming. Not only had they lost 17 members of their small community, but their exposure to the underbelly of Tahitian society, where visiting seamen plied the natives with rum and exploited the women's carefree attitude to sex, had lit a spark among them. Once back in Pitcairn, they fired up the liquor stills and in no time 'drunkenness and licentiousness returned to the island'.[11]

Some of the islanders, notably the Quintal family, petitioned the London Missionary Society to send a pastor to replace both Buffett and Nobbs who had also taken to drink. But before they could respond, into this volatile mix came a catalyst that could only have been designed by a vengeful fate. It took the form of a fantasist and conman who would make Nobbs's imaginings about his aristocratic parentage appear almost benign daydreams by comparison. Calling himself Lord Joshua Hill, the tall, white-haired mythomaniac arrived from Tahiti in the barque *Maria* in October 1832, claiming to have been sent there by the British Government to take charge of the island's affairs.

He arrived to find Nobbs drunk and the community totally fragmented.[12] The situation might have been made for him. At first he lived with Nobbs, but within two months he had not only dismissed him from his teaching role but expelled him from his own house. It now became Government House, with Lord Hill the incumbent for an indefinite term. At least half the islanders – led by the Quintal family – supported him. Nobbs, Buffett and Evans were forced into an uneasy coalition fronted by Charles Christian as Hill made his grab for power.

On 30 May 1833, HMS *Challenger* arrived at the island. Captain Charles Fremantle came ashore and later reported that at first he had doubts about Hill's bona fides. 'It appeared so extraordinary [that] a gentleman of Mr Hill's age [60] and apparent respectability, coming from England for the express purpose of residing on Pitcairn's Island, that I at first thought he must be some adventurer, more likely to do harm than good. [But] as he had broken up all their stills and formed them into a Temperance Society, I gave him all the assistance in my power to support him in that situation.'

Alas, Captain Freemantle should have trusted his first impression. Hill was born in 1773, possibly in America, but his early life remains clouded. We know that he left England in 1830 for Hawaii where the governor refused him a grant of land. He fetched up in Tahiti in October 1831, a few weeks after the

Pitcairners had departed. Jules-Antoine Moerenhout was quickly on his case. 'The missionaries believed him to be a person of importance,' he says, 'and they presented him to the Queen.' However, the Belgian found him a person of 'childlike vanity, boundless pride, dangerous fanaticism and implacable hatred for anyone who opposes him'. Indeed, even the missionaries were pleased to see the back of him when he persuaded the English captain of the *Maria* to take him to Pitcairn.

Following Freemantle's visit, Hill confronted his perceived enemies, denouncing Nobbs, Buffett and Evans as 'lousy foreigners' and accusing them of stealing the islanders' birthright of land by marriage. Buffett wrote later, 'We and our families received letters from him to be ready to leave forthwith.' Then, as judge and jury, he humiliated all three by ordering them to be flogged for some trivial offence. Buffett and Evans took their stripes from one of the burly Quintal boys. Nobbs escaped the lash only through being bedridden at the time.

When the whaler *Tuscan* touched by on 8 March 1834, Hill ordered them to leave. According to Raymond Nobbs, 'Captain Stavars, the surgeon Frederick Bennett and two missionaries from the London Missionary Society bound for Tahiti were sympathetic to the Englishmen's plight and an offer was made for them and their families of transport to Tahiti.' It is a measure of Hill's bravado that the men left but the families stayed behind. Moreover, the missionaries made no protest to their superiors about Hill's administration or the banishment of the three exiles. Once delivered to Tahiti, Buffett became a mate on a trading vessel while Nobbs took Evans with him as a missionary to the Gambier Islands. However, all three sent letters and petitions to the British authorities in Valparaiso seeking redress.

Back on Pitcairn, Hill appointed a cadre of elders, sub-elders and cadets to enforce his rule. They built a gaol to house the victims of his draconian regime and Hill ensured it was well occupied. However, Lord Acton's homily of the corrupting tendencies of power took their inevitable toll on the dictator's grandiose self-esteem. When Arthur Quintal's 11-year-old daughter was brought before him for stealing yams, he decided she should be executed. He called Quintal to his presence and informed him of the sentence. And when the father rebelled, Hill grabbed his sword and the two men fought an unequal battle until another young islander passing by saw the fight, ran to get his musket and threatened to blow Hill's head off. By then Quintal had been scarred for life. But Hill's reign of terror was effectively over. According to Rosalind Young, 'He was then allowed to rise and retire peaceably to his room. Nothing further was done to him, but he did not receive his sword back again until the day when, friendless and unloved, he left the island forever.'

That would not occur until 1837, and by then Nobbs, Buffet and Evans had returned. And while the good graces between the Nobbs-Christian and Buffett families would never be fully restored, George Hunn Nobbs had learned some valuable lessons. While he resumed the role of schoolteacher and pastor, he ensured that John Buffett was fully employed instructing the young men in woodwork and his newly acquired skills of navigation in a workshop class he called the Mutual Improvement Society.

CHAPTER TWELVE

'The most heart-rending scene'

By the time Judge William Burton arrived on Norfolk at the end of June 1834, a formal charge of mutiny had been brought against 137 prisoners who had rebelled against Morisset, although only 55 would stand trial. The crown solicitor, David Chambers, who accompanied the judge decided that the evidence against the others – invariably from convict informers – would make a mockery of proceedings. But since they included the brains behind the uprising, John Knatchbull, the entire judicial process had already become a sanctimonious sham.

Judge Burton was a former naval officer, a fiercely anti-Catholic Anglican who couldn't understand why the convicts appeared 'to gather no heartening effect from the beauties of creation around them, but to make a Hell of that which else might be Heaven'. He was even more shocked when the prisoners, the oldest of whom was only 35, appeared before him 'grey, wizened, their eyes dull and unseeing, the skin stretched taut on the cheeks . . . awful to behold'.[1]

The trial was conducted in a purpose-built room adjoining the convict barracks. They were represented in court by John Plaistowe, a lawyer whose drinking habits on the island became notorious. He was forced to apologise publicly to one Captain Church for throwing insults 'while being under the influence of wine'.[2] His appeals to the four-man military jury were largely ignored and they found 35 of the accused guilty. Burton sentenced 29 of them to hang. He was about to leave when one of the other convicted prisoners burst out, 'Your Honour, sentence has been passed on us before, and we thought we should have been executed, and prepared to die, and wish we had been executed then. It was no mercy to send us to this place. I do not ask for life. I do not want to be spared on condition of living here; life is not worth having on such terms.' Burton was deeply affected. 'To appeals like these,' he wrote later, 'the human heart could not be insensible.' He decided to take the matter up with the new commandant, Major Joseph Anderson.

Born in Scotland in July 1790, Anderson had been a professional soldier since joining the 50th Regiment at 15 and had fought in numerous battles against the French. He was promoted steadily and secured his majority in 1826. The 50th was posted to New South Wales in 1834 and almost immediately Governor Bourke singled out the fierce looking Scot with his bristling beard to command the penal colony. He arrived in March with his wife Mary, the daughter of a general, whom he had married in England eight years previously, together with their family of one son and four daughters.

When Burton approached him, he found Anderson thoroughly familiar with the 1,400 or more convicts in his charge through the same kind of informer system developed by his predecessors. He grudgingly agreed to Burton's request that the hangings be delayed until he returned to the mainland for consultations with the governor. Back in Sydney, the judge addressed Bourke and his Executive Council with such passion that – somewhat ironically – they commuted the sentences of 16 of the condemned men to hard labour for life. However, he also gained Bourke's agreement to send two clergymen to hear the final confessions of those destined for the hangman's noose. The governor enlisted the Reverend H. T. Stiles, Anglican rector of Windsor Parish and the Catholic vicar-general of Australia, Father William Ullathorne. Both men travelled on the *Isabella* and arrived in September, a week before the executions were to take place.

When they disembarked both clergymen went immediately to visit their coreligionists. Both were shocked to the marrow by the encounter. In his memoirs, the then Bishop Ullathorne wrote, 'A soldier was appointed to guide me to the prison . . . and now I have to record the most heart-rending scene that I ever witnessed.

'The prison was in the form of a square, on one side of which stood a row of low cells, covered with a roof of shingles. The turnkey unlocked the first door and said, "Stand aside, Sir." Then came forth a yellow exhalation, the produce of the bodies of the men confined therein.

'The exhalation cleared off, and I entered and found five men chained to a traversing bar. I spoke to them from my heart and after preparing them and obtaining their names I announced to

them who were reprieved from death and which of them were
to die after five days were passed. I thus went from cell to cell
until I had seen them all.

'It is a literal fact that each man who heard his reprieve wept
bitterly, and that each man who heard of his condemnation to
death went down on his knees with dry eyes and thanked God.'

Both clergymen were shaken, the more so when immediately
afterwards they went on to a reception at Government House
where Reverend Stiles reported, 'I found a brilliant assembly
there, in strange contrast to the human miseries in which my
soul had just been steeped.'

The 'brilliance' of the occasion with the smartly uniformed
officers and their fashionably clad wives was enhanced by what
Anderson described as 'bounteous living', with imported wines
and where the military had fresh meat daily from the flocks
of 'thousands of sheep and hundreds of cattle'. Moreover, 'the
officers were allowed to buy as much more as they wished, and
flour also at a nominal price of twopence a pound . . . My garden
at Orange Vale was a splendid one abounding with everything
one could desire. We made about 400 lb of the best coffee
annually . . . my pigs and poultry were kept near Government
House, together with dozens of turkeys, geese, guinea-fowls and
ducks . . . we made the best bacon that was ever known . . . the
public dairy was near my house and every officer, soldier and
free person on the Island got a daily allowance of milk and
butter. With all these advantages we lived most comfortably
and almost for nothing.'[3]

Anderson had ordered the construction of a gallows by the
great gate of the gaol as well as a stockade in front of it big
enough to encircle half the prisoners who would be ordered

there to watch the execution. The other half would be penned inside with a view from behind. On 22 September 1834, the convicts were assembled fore and aft, and Anderson stood before them to order each among them to take a lesson from their fellow inmates' fate. He ended, 'If any of you attempt to move or show any sign of resistance, the officer in the stockade has my positive order to open fire at once.'

The first seven men were led from their cells dressed in thin cream calico, the oldest 29 and the youngest, William McCulloch, only 21. McCulloch begged Reverend Stiles to write to his mother in England and tell her that he begged forgiveness. All were hooded then 'dropped' simultaneously as the prisoners watched in silence. And the following day the 'lesson' was repeated. Then the clergymen sailed away.

Anderson, the parsimonious Scot, decided the temporary courtroom might be put to use as a church for the officers and their families, and petitioned the governor to send a minister for the purpose. He was joined in this by Stiles and Ullathorne, but no one could be found to venture across the sea to what was becoming known as 'Sodom Isle'. In the all-male confines of the gaol, 'unnatural crime' was the order of the night in dormitories, where anal rape became almost a rite of passage for new arrivals. Indeed, when two English Quaker missionaries, James Backhouse and George Washington Walker visited the settlement at the behest of Governor Bourke in 1835, they quickly became aware of the 'crime most revolting to nature' and suggested solitary sleeping cells. They spent a month there and undertook some pastoral work but no permanent minister would arrive until 1837.

In the meantime, Anderson discovered two convicts – one Anglican and one Catholic – who had studied some theology before falling from grace, and they conducted services in exchange for a commutation of their sentences and a shilling a week. Backhouse also suggested the courtroom might be used for reading and writing classes after the convicts finished their daily labours. Anderson agreed, but the idea withered on the vine as the prisoners returned from the fields utterly exhausted and frequently bleeding from the lash. And in any case they were doomed never to put their learning to use, since any pleas for mercy or redemption would never leave the island.

However, Anderson did not need Backhouse's urging to begin alterations to the ramshackle timber gaol. Almost from the day he arrived, he embarked on a building program that would eventually result in a massive rectangular wall containing an octagonal stone structure so brutal, cramped and claustrophobic that it might have been designed to torture its inmates to madness, murder and suicide. And, spurred by the lash, they would build it themselves.

Anderson's reign has overtones of a Cecil B. DeMille production, with his slaves divided between hoeing the unforgiving farmland and dragging the great stones from the quarries to the building sites on the flat between the roiling sea and the hills behind. But at Norfolk the blood was real. And it gouted from the backs of prisoners like William Riley, who in the two years following the mutiny received a total of 1,000 strokes of the cat; or Michael Burns who in less than three years – and in heavy chains – endured no fewer than 2,000 lashes. Not surprisingly, both were Irishmen, and their crimes on the island included 'singing a song', no doubt an Irish ballad of rebellion against the empire.[4]

The English officers, by contrast, passed their days in pleasantries. The young ensign Abel D. W. Best of the 80th Regiment, assigned there for a year from 1838, kept a diary that barely mentions the convicts but rejoices in the social life of the ruling coterie. September 1838, for example, 'was a great day of employment to us bachelors of Norfolk Island. We purposed giving a ball in the mess room the following day & determined to do it in a style hitherto unknown. A great quantity of evergreens were brought in and disposed around the room so as to make it resemble a shady bower. Over the Orchestra was a transparency expressing our welcome to our guests. The supper room was disposed as an armoury & and a transparency over the door inscribed with the words "Eat drink & be merry".'

Then on the 26 September, 'Arose early, bathed and rendered what assistance I could to the committee of management; as soon as my services were dispensed with I went out shooting returning at 7 p.m. My sport was a wild cat. At nine the company began to assemble and as ushered into the ball room expressed great satisfaction with the grace & beauty of its appearance . . . Dancing was kept up till midnight when supper was announced. The supper room afforded quite as much gratification to our guests as the Ballroom . . . A table in the form of a T occupied the centre & one end of the room bearing on it all the luxuries of Norfolk Island. When eating had ceased several toasts were proposed and songs sung. Dancing was then resumed until past five when the party broke up . . .'

In October, they organised a cricket match between teams from the 50th and 80th Regiments. He requisitioned a team of convicts to prepare the ground, 'which was in a wretched state, cut up by carts and overgrown with weeds'. On the day of the match, 'There was great excitement; in the barracks, men rushing violently about and betting figs of tobacco on the result of the game, on the cricket ground a pitching of wickets and tents. At half past twelve the playing commenced and lasted till five when the 50th were declared victorious. This was a result I had expected, few of our men having taken a bat in hand since leaving England . . . A pig with a soaped tail was then turned loose and afforded great amusement after which the men ran races in sacks. All these diversions having ceased we returned the men with the pig to their barracks and me to my room where dinner was ready; when this was disposed of we adjourned to the mess room and danced all night . . .'

When visitors arrived from passing ships they were entertained enthusiastically. On 6 February 1839, for example, 'While sitting at luncheon Mr Hayne, commander of the *Alice* joined our party. He is quiet and gentlemanly and one of the handsomest men I ever saw. We soon dispersed in search of various amusements and assembled again at seven to dinner. We sat late and heard some good singing from Mr Turner. He has a good voice and some taste but wants scientific teaching. Towards four in the morning some of the party waxed boisterous and chairs flew like flies about the room to the infinite danger of the spectators of the fray. As soon as the storm had passed and the principles [*sic*] carried off to bed the rest of the party dispersed . . .'

When dealing with the convicts Anderson's by-the-book methods contained the seeds of their own undoing. For example, he refused to consider Backhouse's suggestion that he employ bullocks to plough the land and simultaneously fertilise it with their droppings, as had been the practice for centuries the world over. Instead, convicts wielded their hoes in lines across a field, with the strongest placed as pacesetters at each end; those towards the centre would be lashed if they fell behind, so they cut shallow with a resulting loss of productivity.

This in turn raised the cost of feeding the population, and when Anderson sought to substitute potatoes for the daily ration of maize meal the convicts revolted. Anderson simply starved them into submission, and was known thereafter as 'Potato Joe'.

The building program was equally flawed by relying on the go-slow tactics of slave labour. The resident surgeon, Dr Alexander Gamack, compounded Anderson's problems by 'laying off' convicts he considered too ill or injured to work. The commandant raged against him and his malingerers and by the end of 1836 succeeded in having him replaced by the less experienced Dr Patrick Harnett, an Irish Catholic aged only 26, who had arrived in NSW from County Limerick in 1832 as an assistant surgeon. Harnett bowed to Anderson's demands and cut the daily 'sick list' in half. Those sent back to work included a new arrival, young William Castleton, who had been convicted of a minor offence in York and transported for seven years, arriving in Sydney on the HMS *Admiral* in 1830.

On Norfolk he complained of 'bowel trouble' and was sent back to work. The next day and the one after, he pleaded his case. Harnett called him 'work shy' and threatened to send him to the commandant. The following day he returned with a cell mate who swore he'd seen 'blood run down his legs'. Harnett carried out his threat and Castleton was brought to court on 9 December and sentenced to 50 lashes. The flogger strapped him to the triangle and delivered 37 before the prisoner collapsed.

Harnett ordered him taken down and he was transferred to the island's version of a convict hospital – a dank, airless, stone structure, where he died in agony six days later.

Unfortunately for Harnett and Anderson, the incident – which would otherwise be lost to history – coincided with the brief residence on the island of a freelance minister, Thomas Atkins, who had been recommended by the London Missionary Society, and whom the turnkey Aaron Price would call 'the prisoners' friend'. Atkins, who was just 29, possessed a somewhat erratic and restless personality. He protested volubly at Anderson's 'petty tyranny' and engaged in a war of words with the commandant, with each seeking Governor Bourke's backing.

Bourke sided with Anderson, and Atkins left the island in blazing anger on the colonial brig *Governor Phillip* and reached Sydney via Moreton Bay in April 1837, where he began a virulent campaign against Anderson's rule. An anonymous correspondent for the *Perth Gazette and Western Australian Journal* reported an interview with him, describing Norfolk and its 1,500 convicts as 'an emporium of crime and pollution'. It detailed the death of William Castleton and the raging argument between Atkins and Anderson. 'At this,' says the correspondent, 'we are by no means surprised, knowing as we do from experience, the disposition and demeanor of this petty tyrant [Anderson], this would-be important personage, to those about and under him who are sycophantic enough not to possess a mind of their own.'

The answer, he says, was 'to recall Major Anderson who has rendered the abode of the civil officers at that penal settlement a perfect Pandemonium . . . to be reproved if not cashiered'. Both Anderson and Harnett would continue in office until mid-1839, when the major would resume his military career, and with his brother John, a general, would eventually take up a massive 85,000 acres (34,400 hectares) of land in the rich Goulburn Valley, become colonel of his regiment and on retirement settle in Melbourne. He would be a nominated member of the Legislative Council of Victoria from 1852 to 1856, where he would campaign against Chinese and other riff-raff despoiling the southern province.

Harnett would be appointed colonial surgeon and open a private practice in Macquarie Street while he and his extended family took up choice holdings on the slopes of the Monaro. He would not live to enjoy the squatter's life in retirement. He died five years after his return from Norfolk, aged only 34.

Anderson's enduring legacy on the island was the three-storey commissariat store, which bears his name chiselled in stone and would be converted to a church by the Pitcairners. He was also responsible for the officers' houses on Military Row (renamed Quality Row without a hint of irony) as well as the foundations of the partially completed octangular prison. He also left behind a grotesque chronicle of human suffering. William Castleton was only one of the numberless victims who fell beneath his imperial lash.

On his departure, the whip hand passed to Major Thomas Bunbury of the 80th Regiment, who had arrived in January 1839 but would not assume command until Anderson's departure. Like Anderson, he was a veteran of the Peninsular Wars with a good record in combat. However, he had been born in Gibraltar, the illegitimate son to an unknown mother by Major Benjamin Bunbury, and this remained an indelible stain on his career prospects. By the time he reached Norfolk his father had died in gruesome circumstances. In 1827, he and his only legitimate son, 18-year-old Henry Mill Bunbury, were taking the air in a pony chaise some 3 miles from the Bunbury manor when something spooked their horse and the vehicle overturned. The two Bunburys were trapped beneath the chaise and subjected to three hours of kicking by the horse before a passer-by came to their rescue. The major lingered speechless for several days before he died. Thomas made no mention of his death in his two-volume memoir *Recollections of a Veteran*.

He had arrived in Sydney in 1838, and before taking up his appointment met with the new governor, Sir George Gipps. It was not a success. According to Bunbury, he was received 'with a great deal of haughtiness and petulance' and they parted 'with the mutual dislike greatly increased'. Nevertheless, he was determined to shine in the new posting, and before leaving Sydney had studied all aspects of the island's resources and devised a plan to make it self-sufficient, most notably by countermanding Anderson's absurd regulations preventing use of the plough. When he finally took control in April, he also attacked the sick list with a new rule: 'If a man is too sick to work he is too sick to eat.'

In his memoir he congratulated himself on its effect. 'The line of would-be patients at the hospital diminished by 50 per cent,'[5] he wrote. As it turned out, the new rule was too clever by half. But there was little else to boast of. In his brief reign, Bunbury was bedevilled by an attempted escape by convicts and – more seriously – a mutiny of the soldiers under his command.

The escape attempt occurred when a party of officers who had spent the morning fishing were excitedly hauling the net to the beach. A nearby a prison gang saw their opportunity and rushed through the surf to the boat, threw out the crew of 'trusties' on board, and made for the open sea. According to Ensign Best, 'The alarm was instantly given and two of the fastest boats started in pursuit, four soldiers in each. As soon as they were within range [they] opened fire; the runaways finding no chance for escape threw down their oars. They were brought back, tried, found guilty, and in a very few minutes each had received 300 lashes.'

Anderson's men of the 50th left behind the genesis of the mutiny that would bring Bunbury down. The departing soldiers had sold to Bunbury's men of the 80th the gardens they had been allowed to cultivate, together with the huts in which they stored the vegetables and other crops they had grown. They were located behind the old barracks in what was known as 'Irish Town', and Bunbury quickly realised that his troops resented being called from their gardening to their military duties, particularly when they were able to trade their produce to convicts 'too sick to eat' for goods they had stolen or scavenged from the officers. The huts, he believed (with some justice) were the trading posts and the repository of convict loot.

On 1 July, without notice to the troops, he ordered an overseer and his convict gang to pull down a garden hut. Word flashed around the garrison, and when the demolition party arrived in Irish Town the soldiers 'assembled in a very riotous manner'[6] and drove them away. When Bunbury heard of the outrage, he issued a garrison order upbraiding his men, and declared that the huts would now be demolished under his personal supervision.

He assembled a demolition team and advanced on Irish Town. He saw 'a party of about 30 to 40 men [who] had forced their way out of the new barracks and were rushing with loaded muskets towards the place where I stood.' Bunbury held his ground, declaring that he would cut down the first man that advanced a single step farther. 'You will have to trample over my dead body before you pass,' he said. This was tantamount to rebellion, a capital offence. However, before shots were fired a tropical storm unleashed itself and the men retired to the veranda of the barracks where they formed 'armed and accoutred' and ready for action.

Bunbury drew back from the confrontation, and when the rain slackened addressed the mutineers. 'Eventually,' he says, 'they quietly returned to their duties, but not before demanding the full mainland ration of spirits in their daily issue.' Bunbury dismissed this out of hand and told them that they should not have paid for their gardens which he now proposed to withdraw from single soldiers, who instead would be supplied with vegetables from the government gardens. One penny per man per day would be debited from their pay and an extra halfpenny when melons were supplied. The soldiers were not pleased, which was hardly surprising since deductions for rations and necessities already reduced their pay to less than sixpence a day. Archdeacon John McEnroe, who had arrived on the island on 4 November 1838 to minister to the Catholic convicts, witnessed the mutiny and blamed it on a 'blundering' Bunbury.

On 23 July, Bunbury finally penned his report to Governor Gibbs. In addition to a detailed account of the mutiny, he levelled direct and implied criticism of his predecessor's administration of the settlement, not only in relation to the soldiers' gardens, but claiming that there were no daily parades of troops on duty, failure of troops to appear on parades, and generally 'a relaxed state of discipline'. However, Anderson was still in Sydney and he responded with Scottish outrage. Gibbs clearly felt his initial poor impressions of Bunbury were warranted and ordered his recall. He would languish in Sydney for nine months before being posted to the Bay of Islands in New Zealand, where he would eventually carve out a successful career and, after a round of negotiations with Maori chiefs, declare British sovereignty over the South Island.

Meantime, Irish-born Major Thomas Ryan took over temporary administration of the island, but events in the British Parliament and at Whitehall would soon bring a radical change to New South Wales as a penal colony; and a revolutionary transformation of its most violent and notorious manifestation in the South Pacific.

Captain Cook's landing place, Norfolk Island

Captain John Hunter

A miniature portrait of William Bligh
(c 1814)

Early years – Norfolk Island pre-1800

The *Maeander* in great peril in Sydney Bay, Norfolk Island, c 1856

The loss of HMS *Sirius* in 1790

A whipping post

George Adams, his wife, and Quintal on Norfolk Island, c 1860

The remnants of the Gallows Gate

The Bloody Bridge, Norfolk Island, 1946

Cutting up a whale

Captain Charles Robert Pinney, Administrator of Norfolk
Island in the 1930s

A picnic in honour of the royal visit of 1946 – given by descendants of the *Bounty* mutineers

St Barnabas (formerly Melanesian Mission) in the 1940s

Looking south from Mount Pitt, the highest point on Norfolk Island

The Georgian courthouse at Kingston, today

(Roger Maynard)

Glenn McNeil on his way to court

(Roger Maynard)

CHAPTER THIRTEEN

Winds of change

On Pitcairn, too, change was afoot. In 1838, a 16-gun British Navy sloop, HMS *Fly*, under the command of a minor aristocrat, Captain Russell Elliot, called in to the island to discover the residents anxious to formalise their place within the empire. They were recovering from a frightening visit by an American whaling crew who prowled the island for two weeks demanding sex with the women while the men defended the community with their firearms.

Also, there was continuing tension between the Pitcairn-born Edward Quintal and the three Englishmen: Nobbs, Buffett and Evans. While Nobbs had consolidated his position as spiritual leader, the Mutual Improvement Society led by Buffett had collapsed through lack of interest and he now fashioned furniture from the native mero tree. Their wives attended to cultivation. The ineffectual Evans spent his days in his garden.

When Captain Elliot stepped ashore on 30 November, he found himself accosted on all sides to produce a 'constitution' that would provide imperial recognition and a code of laws. Accordingly, the Honourable Russell Elliot – without any official backing – presented a Union Jack to the community with due ceremony together with a few high-sounding principles on ship's paper. Although the British Parliament declined to include Pitcairn in the empire until 1887, the islanders regarded Elliott's document as their imperial imprimatur. It did at least establish the position of magistrate to be elected annually 'by the free vote of all the inhabitants in the island – male and female – who had reached the age of 18'. The captain also included a provision for compulsory education from the ages of five to 15. The islanders themselves added a code of 10 laws governing the control of dogs; punishment for killing cats; compensation for the damage done by stray pigs; cultivation of land; prohibition of alcohol; and banning women from boarding visiting vessels without the permission of the magistrate.

They then elected the burly Quintal to the bench.

In the small community of just 104 – evenly divided by gender – it was not easy for the magistrate to maintain the judicial aloofness of more metropolitan societies. This was particularly so in Quintal's case since, according to Rosalind Young, 'When aroused by anger [he] was capable of committing deeds of cruelty.'[1] On one occasion, she says, when he was engaged in a dispute with John Evans, 'both men lost control over themselves. The quarrel increased and Quintal, being a powerful man, brought it to a termination by lifting Evans, who was small, as easily as he would a child, and throwing him violently into a pigsty, thereby causing him serious injury.'

Quintal was re-elected.

That year – 1840 – Nobbs was particularly gratified by the arrival of the London Missionary Society ship *Camden*, with Captain Robert Clark Morgan in command. The Reverend Mr Heath and the captain went ashore with presents from the governor of New South Wales, Sir George Gipps, and enough Bibles to distribute one to each family. Nobbs hosted them and after three services during the day and evening the *Camden* spread her sails, beat to windward, and disappeared over the horizon. However, by the time she reached the New Hebrides they had taken aboard one of the more adventurous early missionaries, John Williams, who had recently returned from England with copies of the New Testament translated into Samoan. When they anchored off Tanna, Williams went ashore with Captain Morgan and the missionaries James Harris and Arthur Cunningham. According to church historian Graeme Kent, 'They handed out gifts according to custom, and Williams and Harris walked along the beach in search of a drink of water.[2]

'This changed the attitude of the islanders who had been reserved but not antagonistic. They had been preparing for a feast . . . and they were suddenly afraid that Williams and his companion would stumble across the feasting grounds and steal their food, as previous Europeans had done. Panic stricken, some of the Erromangans surrounded the two missionaries. One of the leaders, Raniani, had seen his own son killed by visiting Europeans, and it seems he struck the first blow with a club.

'The Europeans turned to run back to their boat. Cunningham and Captain Morgan, who had not ventured as far as the other two, reached it, but Harris fell while attempting to leap across a stream of water, and was killed with clubs and spears. Williams too stumbled and was felled with a club. The Erromangans stood over him thrusting with their spears until he was dead. Then the natives dragged the two dead missionaries into the undergrowth and later ate them.'

The next year, Fletcher Christian's original companion, Isabella or 'Mainmast', died. This signalled the parting of one of the final links with the first settlers. The sole survivor now was Susannah, who was only 14 when she sailed with the mutineers on the *Bounty*. She had been Edward Young's first wife, and had decapitated her countryman Titahiti while he slept. Aged 30, she married 15-year-old Thursday October Christian, the first male born on the island, so bore grandchildren to the mutineers as well as children by them. Her death would not come until 1850.

The women's traditional clothing now gave way to the European styles seen on the wives of visiting captains. At first the long-waisted, bone-ribbed dresses were kept for Sunday best, but in time they became standard wear throughout the week. This new sense of modesty won the approval of Nobbs and the visiting clergymen. However, it did nothing to dampen the ardour of the Pitcairn men, young and old, and the average age for girls tying the marital knot – often when already pregnant – fell to between 14 and 15.[3]

More and more ships called into the island – at least 350 between 1833 and 1850 – and as a regular stopover for American whalers seeking water and fresh vegetables Pitcairn's economy prospered as the sailors traded clothing and tools as well as currency. At the same time, the several branches of Christianity extended their efforts throughout the Pacific to convert the heathens to their particular readings of the testaments. According to the London Missionary Society's official records, 'Between 1835 and 1844 thirty-four Englishmen and thirty Englishwomen entered the Pacific as missionary agents.'

However, it was the established Church of England, headed by Queen Victoria as Defender of the Faith, that would make the most powerful impact on Norfolk Island. At first, the church was confined to the single diocese of Australia, which at the time included New Zealand. However, when the Archbishop of Canterbury William Howley appointed the 32-year-old curate of Windsor, Cambridge-educated George Augustus Selwyn, to the post, the letters patent contained an error that would have far-reaching consequences. Instead of defining the northern boundary of the diocese as 34 degrees 30 minutes south, the church bureaucrat wrote 'north' – thus stretching Selwyn's authority far beyond New Zealand to include the islands of Melanesia.

Selwyn, the enthusiast, made no attempt to correct the error. On the contrary, he took his cue from Howley who urged him to regard New Zealand as 'a fountain diffusing the streams of salvation over the islands and coasts of the Pacific'. Actually, Howley was quoting the unfortunate John Williams, who famously described his Tahitian mission as a 'fountain from whence the streams of salvation are to flow to the numerous islands and clusters scattered over that extensive ocean'.[4] News that he had been killed and consumed on Tanna had apparently not reached Canterbury at the time of Howley's exhortation.

Selwyn, with wife and child, left England in December 1841. On the voyage he studied navigation and was soon envisioning 'a central missionary college drawing pupils from all parts of the South Pacific'.[5] His principal competitor would be the London

Missionary Society with their non-denominational but rather more Protestant and Congregational approach to saving souls. However, while they had stolen a march on the Anglicans in Tahiti, they were having a series of unhappy setbacks elsewhere.

In the New Hebrides island of Futuna, for example, they landed two Samoan teachers, Samson and Abela, in 1841. They spent three years with their wives and children preaching and gathering converts. They were enjoying some success until 1845 when an epidemic struck. The islanders blamed the 'sacred men' and killed them all. The same year, the Reverend Arnold Murray ferried two islander teachers to New Caledonia. When he returned two years later, he discovered one of the men had died only weeks after being landed, while the other had only just survived. Nonetheless, he left two replacements, one of whom wrote, 'We have joy, for the word of God is growing in this land . . . a few days ago a heathen came to me to enquire about casting away his idols. I told him an idol is nothing at all; that Jehovah is the true God; that he made the heavens, the earth and all things; that He has pitied us in our sins and death, and had sent his son Jesus to be our saviour.'

Alas, according to historian Graeme Kent, his optimism was misplaced. 'Unfortunately, the missionaries had little success on New Caledonia,' he says, 'and the weeping teachers were taken away on the next mission boat. Soon after they left there was internecine strife on the islands . . . and most of the natives who had been converted were slaughtered.'[6]

Selwyn was at first preoccupied with his New Zealand base, and for three years travelled around the islands by sea and on foot. His pastoral peregrinations were complicated by a Maori rebellion in the far north – a sad corollary of the actions of Thomas Kendall, the missionary gun-runner – and vicious disputes with the entrenched London Missionary Society missionaries over their qualifications for ordination. Nevertheless, his enthusiasm to extend his bailiwick to incorporate the islands north to Melanesia, including Norfolk, was undimmed.

The winds of change were also blowing on the New South Wales mainland, assisted in no small part by the Quaker missionaries James Backhouse and George Washington Walker. They had made detailed submissions to an 1837 Parliamentary Select Committee of the House of Commons chaired by the urbane 26-year-old member for East Cornwall, Sir William Molesworth, to consider the whole issue of convict transportation. Molesworth, whose looks were disfigured by childhood scrofula and who had been sent down from Cambridge after fighting a duel with his tutor, began the hearings opposed in principle to the practice. He ended it appalled by 'the horrid details of the penal settlements' where 'every kind and gentle feeling of human nature is constantly outraged by the perpetual spectacle of punishment and misery – by the frequent infliction of the lash – by the gangs of slaves in irons . . . till the heart of the immigrant is gradually deadened to the suffering of others and he becomes at last as cruel as the other gaolers in these vast prisons'.

The committee reported to the house in August the next year, and with the firm backing of the home secretary Lord John Russell and the under-secretary for the colonies Sir George Grey, transportation would be ended. The last New South Wales convict ship would arrive in Sydney in November 1840. However, Molesworth's concerns did not extend to the *ne plus ultra* of imperial sadism. Norfolk Island was specifically exempted from the new arrangements. So too was Port Arthur in Van Diemen's Land; and in Hobart, by happy coincidence, resided the only man who would emerge from the sordid history of Norfolk Island with credit: 51-year-old former naval officer Captain Alexander Maconochie.

Alexander was born in Edinburgh to a wealthy lawyer – also Alexander M'Konochie but with a more traditional spelling. His mother, Ann Margaret, was the second of his father's wives and Alexander the fourth of his six children, three of whom were born out of wedlock to other (unknown) mothers. His father died when young Alexander was only nine, and while he lived with his mother, his uncle Allan Maconochie saw to his education. Allan was also a lawyer, and in 1796 was appointed to the bench and ennobled as Lord Meadowbank. Alexander at first had ambitions to follow a legal career, but the maps of the newly explored oceans studied in his dusty schoolroom beckoned him to a wider world and at 15 he joined the Royal Navy. The following year, 1804, he became a midshipman under the watchful eye of another relative, Admiral Alexander Cochrane.

He served in the West Indies, and later, when Horatio Nelson was chasing the French fleet, Admiral Cochrane called a conference of his commanding officers on board the *Victory* in the Port of Paria, off Trinidad. Cochrane chose Maconochie to accompany him. 'I was standing on her quarter-deck,' he says, 'when Lord Nelson came out of the cabin with a large glass under his arm, and crossing to where I stood on the lee side, he said to me, "Youngster, give me a shoulder," and made a motion to employ me; but changing his mind he turned up the poop ladder. He looked heated and impatient, and finding the French fleet had sailed . . . made sail for England. I never saw him afterwards.'[7] A year later he would find enduring fame in the Battle of Trafalgar.

Maconochie would remain in West Indian waters and acquire a good working knowledge of Spanish. In 1810, he joined the 18-gun brig HMS *Grasshopper* under Captain Henry Fanshaw and the following year they were escorting a massive convoy in the Baltic when hit by a freak storm that roared in from the north. It devastated the fleet. Four warships and nearly 200 merchantmen were wrecked and sunk off the Dutch coast. The *Grasshopper* almost shared their fate.

Maconochie was on watch at 3 a.m. as the ships struggled to stay afloat. Suddenly he saw another ship heave across his weather bow. 'I called out to ease the helm up, to pass under her stern,' Maconochie says. 'And to the mistake I thus made we owed our deliverance . . . for at this moment [the other ship] struck the ground where she was ultimately lost and not a soul saved. Passing under her stern we struck the same sands end on and with a little dragging dropped into smooth water at seven fathoms and immediately cast anchor.'[8]

It was a narrow escape but when the day dawned and the wind died they found themselves surrounded by a hostile Dutch fleet. Captain Fanshaw had no choice but to surrender. He and his crew were taken prisoner and handed over to the French. Maconochie was about to endure an experience that would provide a first-hand insight into the plight of the prisoner utterly dependent on the good graces of his gaoler. Its effect would be felt most dramatically by the several thousand inmates who would eventually come under his supervision on the other side of the world.

Few details of his captivity are known. He was clearly reluctant to describe his experience in subsequent correspondence despite the fact that he would become a prolific and professional writer. However, we do know that Napoleon's soldiers hated the British with a passion and that they forced the *Grasshopper*'s officers and men to march through a bitter winter to Verdun, where British prisoners of war had been confined in the forbidding citadels of Charlemont and Valenciennes since 1803. He was held for more than two years until Napoleon's abdication in April 1814. In that time, he made the acquaintance of an unnamed English lawyer and his wife who had been interned when war broke out during their French honeymoon. Maconochie regained his interest in the law, and to fill the time the lawyer agreed to tutor him. However, once he was released he rejoined Admiral Cochrane's command.

He served in the war against America and in 1815 was promoted to commander and master of the HMS *Trave* and later the HMS *Calliope*.

When the troops were being returned from Canada to England in preparation for the battle of Waterloo, his ship was sent ahead to report the fleet's movements. He crossed the Atlantic in only 19 days. It was his last military action, and at the end of a triumphant year he, like thousands of others, was paid off. He returned to live with his mother in Edinburgh. There was, however, one more lesson to be gleaned from his war years. He wrote later, 'At Quebec the idea first occurred to me of a principle in discipline which I afterwards carried into effect to a great extent at Norfolk Island. It was that of mutual responsibility of my men.

'The desertion from our shipping of men anxious to hasten to the seat of war was almost universal. To check it, it became common in our fleet to grant no leave of absence. It occurred to me to grant it on a system requiring those who obtained it to return on board before their companions in the watch could receive the same favour; and without saying no-one ever broke this contract . . . such a breach of faith very seldom occurred.'[9] Thus the concept of group responsibility was firmly implanted.

By his own admission Maconochie was uncharacteristically idle in the six years that followed his war service. But while he sought no paid work, he did devote himself to both research and writing on the subject that engaged him so deeply as a boy – the great world beyond the confines of Europe and Britain's place within it. His first published work, which appeared in 1816, urged the government to establish a settlement on the Sandwich Islands (Hawaii) lest the Americans or the Russians jump the colonial gun. Two years later, in a more substantial booklet, he urged the establishment of a free port at the Cape of Good Hope and another somewhere on the shores of the Pacific to facilitate British international trade. His efforts were noted in high places and promoted by his patron Lord Cochrane. But it was not until his mother died in 1821 and he married the following year that he gave serious thought to building a career.

His bride, Mary Hutton Browne from a solid Northumberland family, was 27, some eight years his junior. When their first child was born in February 1823, they moved to a farm at Fife on Scotland's east coast. There the family grew until there were two girls and four boys. All required schooling that could not be found in rural Fife so he moved to London in 1828 and immediately involved himself in 'the branch of geography which may be called ethical or political geography'. He was ahead of his time. No such academic discipline existed. But there was growing interest in the subject in imperial circles and within a year he had helped to form the Geographical Society of London. It soon attracted the attention and patronage of the king – William IV – and adopted the name by which it is still known, the Royal Geographical Society. Maconochie was its founding secretary and subsequently the first professor of geography at London's University College.

His portrait, painted in 1836, reveals a high, domed forehead above dark, somewhat suspicious eyes, a long nose and a well-shaped if narrow mouth – altogether a thoughtful and concerned character splendidly uniformed as a naval captain and bearing the insignia of a knight of the Royal Hanoverian Guelphic Order over his left breast. It had been instituted by George IV when he was prince regent, and although it was a signal honour, it did not permit him the knightly appellation of 'Sir'.

Nevertheless, he had risen in remarkably quick time to a position of note. And in the formation of the Geographical Society he had been joined by a former naval colleague, Captain John Franklin, who had a very distinguished military record. He had been a midshipman under Matthew Flinders on the HMS *Investigator* in the circumnavigation of Australia. He was second in command under Captain Frederick Beechy in a search of the Northwest Passage; and he had led an overland expedition across Canada to Arctic America during 1819–22, covering more than 8,000 kilometres and enduring appalling hardships.

They became firm friends, and when the newly knighted Franklin was offered the post of lieutenant-governor of Van Diemen's Land he asked Maconochie to become his official private secretary. He made the offer on the understanding – confirmed by Lord Glenelg, the secretary of state for colonies – that it would be a precursor to Maconochie himself receiving an independent appointment once he was established in the colony. In the meantime, Maconochie had been approached by the London Society for the Improvement of Prison Discipline to make enquiries and complete a questionnaire on the efficacy of the system in Van Diemen's Land. Shortly after their arrival in Hobart in January 1837 Maconochie began his investigations. He had come to the task, he says, 'rather impressed in its favour; but being charged to study it, and having some habit of scanning, and reasoning on, social exhibitions, I could not long be deceived; nor was I, in truth, above two months before I saw the principle [*sic*] of its mistakes.'[10] The wonder is that it took as long as two months. Franklin was replacing Colonel George Arthur, whose administration was as cruel and tyrannical as any across the southern colonies.

Initially, the two naval officers worked well together. However, some of Arthur's bureaucrats remained in place, and they plotted to drive a wedge between Franklin and his dangerously liberal secretary. By playing on Franklin's high opinion of himself, they gradually weaned him away from the man who was his senior in the naval hierarchy. But the real break came through Maconochie's growing fascination with the colonial penal administration. In his correspondence with the London Prison Discipline Society, Maconochie called the system on Van Diemen's Land 'cruel, uncertain, prodigal; ineffectual either for reform or example [and] can only be maintained by extreme severity'. Moreover, 'Some of its most important enactments are systematically broken by the government itself.'[11]

He assumed his views would be treated as confidential advice. But without his knowledge, his reports were elevated to the status of an official government paper and used by the Molesworth Committee to support the case for ending transportation. When they were included in the final report, Franklin was outraged. He had no choice, he said, but to demand Maconochie's resignation. The two families had been living under the same roof at Government House, so the situation became awkward in the extreme. Mary Maconochie wrote to their family friend Sir George Back, 'It is a most cruel position to place us in – in an expensive colony, and our young family to educate, and there are no advantages for them here in any way.' Of the Franklins, she wrote, 'For Lady Franklin I shall ever feel warmly attracted [but] for Sir John I never thought much and since our sojourn here less and less.'

Fortunately Government House was capacious enough to accommodate them in separate apartments while Maconochie sought a new situation. But for almost two years none was forthcoming and he occupied himself with extending his studies of the convict system. The result was a lengthy work, *Thoughts on Convict Management and Other Subjects Connected with the Australian Penal Colonies*. It was published in 1839 in London under the more manageable title *Australiana*.

It struck a chord with the new Whig policy makers towards transportation, and towards the end of the year Franklin was able to pass on the news that Governor Gipps was authorised to offer him the position of superintendent of the penal settlement at Norfolk Island. Maconochie travelled immediately to Sydney to accept the post in a personal interview with Sir George. By then he had refined his views on penology and developed a highly detailed system of 'marks'. The underlying philosophy was that since punishment didn't work as an effective deterrent and the lash simply brutalised prisoner and gaoler alike (together with the society that condoned and encouraged it), an entirely new approach was needed. In his regime, prisoners would be treated as social human beings rather than beasts to be penned and flogged. But they would have to earn this new perception by their behaviour towards their fellow inmates and the authorities responsible for them. The length and conditions of their captivity would be determined in large degree by their response to the tasks set for them.

Each prisoner would be able to earn – by labour and good conduct – a fixed number of 'marks of commendation', perhaps 5,000 in total.[12] And once that figure was reached, he would be free to return to society. The process would begin with his entry into the system when there would be a 'short period of restraint and deprivation with the object of inducing penitence and humility'. When that was completed he would begin to earn his shelter, food and clothing by the accumulation of marks from regular allotted tasks. Disciplinary offences would result in marks being subtracted. But as he built up his tally, the prisoner would be allowed to join in small gangs where they would gain marks as a unit. In this, Maconochie would rehearse the findings from his experiment with his sailors at Quebec.

Throughout the prisoner's detention, anything that tended to degrade or deprive him of his self-perception as a 'social being' would be avoided. Brutal punishments such as the use of leg irons, neck chains, 'spreadeagling', the gag and the lash would be used only in the most extraordinary circumstances. The uniform would not be designed to humiliate; nor would the prisoner be required to display servility in his approach to prison officials. As superintendent, he would be the final arbiter of the marks to be awarded and the timing of the prisoners' parole or release.

Gipps, himself a broad-minded Whig, listened with growing fascination – tinged, no doubt, with the occasional frisson of alarm – as Maconochie outlined his scheme in minute detail. He had been aware of the broad thrust of the reformer's approach, but this was easily the most radical proposal ever put before the governor of a penal colony, albeit one that was in the process of gradual transformation. Maconochie concluded his outline, thoroughly satisfied that Gipps was 'a most excellent man, just, equitable and high-minded' and who had received him 'in a very kindly fashion'.[13] There was, however, one point on which the governor would not budge. Under no circumstances would Gipps permit him to apply the system to the repeat offenders already on the island. They were beyond the pale; it would be reserved exclusively for the new arrivals from England.

Maconochie argued that 'To coop up 1,500 men on a small island under two systems, one more advantageous than the other, would breed jealousy and quarrelling between them and infallibly injure both.'

Gipps stood his ground.

'I offered even to give up Norfolk Island,' Maconochie says, 'and try my experiment on a much smaller scale in some retired nook in New South Wales . . . though already seeing the rock on which I should ultimately split with Sir George, I was forced to acquiesce.'[14]

Gipps confided his fears about the enterprise to his diary that night: 'Captain Maconochie avows his opinion that the first object of all convict discipline should be the reformation of the criminal,' he wrote. 'This opinion, however agreeable it may be to the dictates of humanity, is not, I believe, the received one of legislators who rather require as the first object of convict discipline that it should be a terror to evildoers.'

By then Maconochie was returning *poste haste* to Hobart to wind up his affairs and prepare the family for their transportation to a new home, the cruellest and most notorious prison in the empire. He could barely contain his excitement.

CHAPTER FOURTEEN

A living hell

The Maconochie family – all eight of them – stepped ashore from the *Nautilus* onto Norfolk's rich and fecund soil on 6 March 1840. Mary Ann, whom everyone called Minnie, was the eldest of the brood, and at 17 her father's favourite. She was followed by Catherine, 15, Alexander, 13, and the three younger boys, James, George and Francis. It had been a pleasant, uneventful passage from Sydney despite the fact that their fellow passengers included 300 convicts transported in the same ship from Dublin.

Maconochie had negotiated an agreeable salary of £800 a year plus a fine residence and rations. At the time, the New South Wales solicitor-general received the same amount but was responsible for his own food and accommodation. He had also persuaded Gipps to allow him the choice of his own administrative team in John Simm as overseer of works, James Reid as assistant surgeon, a chief of police and two sergeants. And perhaps most consequential, he brought an assistant superintendent,

Charles Ormsby, who would deal with the doubly convicted 'old hands' and as magistrate would assist Maconochie with summary justice.

Clearly, this was to be a complete changing of the guard, and the prison population was already aware that something radical was afoot. The inmates' rumour machine had been working overtime ever since his appointment. The shipload of 'new hands' would serve their time with a similar number of first offenders soon to arrive on the island, as well as the 'double-dyed felons' – somewhere between 1,200 and 1,400 – already enduring the torments of retribution as prescribed by imperial edict.

Maconochie's immediate predecessor, the 49-year-old Irishman Major Thomas Ryan, had already shipped out suffering from an undefined illness, and Maconochie, together with his military commander Colonel Hulme, was greeted by the ranking military officer, who passed on Ryan's apologies and good wishes. Coincidentally, Ryan had been on hand in Hobart four years previously to swear in Sir John Franklin as lieutenant-governor of Van Diemen's Land. At the time he was somewhat bedraggled after a beating administered by a fellow officer who had caught him *in flagrante* with his wife. At Norfolk he had taken over from the stop-gap commandant, Captain Charles Best, a very fat character with a bawdy laugh who suffered a fate shared by many who ventured into the roiling waters of Sydney Bay.

On 14 February, Best was out in his cutter on a journey to Phillip Island to retrieve some prisoners who had been banished there. The day was fine and the boat well managed, but according to a convict eyewitness, Thomas Cook, 'By the time the coxswain had brought her convenient to the bar the seas rose and with a fury seldom witnessed the boat was caught and thrown up perpendicular. She was again struck and thrown completely over.' Rescuers put out immediately but while they were able to retrieve eight convicts and the coxswain, 'lamentable to relate the honourable Charles Best, Mr McLean the superintendent of agriculture and a soldier were drowned'.[1]

Colonel Hulme's troops of the 96th Regiment of Foot together with members of the 80th already on the island, escorted the prisoners off the ship and up the hill on the 2.5 kilometre journey to the agricultural station at Longridge. There, separated from contamination by the old hands, they would be housed in timber barracks and put to work in the fields.

Maconochie had made it his business during the two-week voyage to get to know as many of the convicts as possible. Once he had settled his family he travelled to Longridge to explain his marks system in detail. Those who earned 6,000 marks, he told them, would discharge a seven-year sentence; for 10 years the figure would be 7,000 and for life, 8,000. They could either spend a portion of their marks on 'luxuries' – extra food, clothing and tobacco, for example – or devote all their energies to the accumulation of the total. If they chose the latter they could obtain a ticket-of-leave (in essence a parole) in one year, two years, and two-and-a-half respectively.

He then turned his attention to the old hands and found, 'A more demoniacal looking assemblage could not be imagined. The most formidable sight I ever beheld was the sea of faces upturned to me when I first addressed them.'[2] Their quarters were filthy and overcrowded. Anderson's octagonal gaol was not much advanced from the time he left, although the stone walls surrounding it were now completed. The prisoners were forced to bow their heads in servile respect, and not just to officers, soldiers and guards, but to empty sentry boxes as they passed. Their food, taken outdoors in the lumber yard, was little more than slops eaten without utensils; and in an act of particular viciousness, Anderson had ordered the orange trees that had spread across the island cut down to prevent the convicts picking the fruit for themselves. The result, Maconochie wrote, was hardly surprising since, 'in every way their feelings were habitually outraged and their self-respect destroyed'.

He was deeply affected, and that day he decided to defy Governor Gipps and extend his marks system to the old hands. It was a fateful decision. It would transform conditions on Norfolk and the lives of the great majority of prisoners; but ultimately it would lead to Maconochie's dismissal and a return to brutal barbarism on an island already seeped in convict blood. It might have escaped the attention of outside authorities, at least until its long-term benefits could be demonstrated, but for the enthusiastic new commandant's next decision. The young Queen Victoria had come to the throne in 1837, and three years later on 24 May she would celebrate her 21st birthday. There would be rejoicing throughout the empire and Maconochie decided it was the perfect occasion to put his belief in mutual responsibility to the test. If successful it would show the most obdurate of his critics that his system was based on sound principles. And if it failed . . . well, he would have to make adjustments. But it couldn't fail, and that was an end to it.

Nevertheless, when he declared on 20 May that 'On Monday, 25 May, Her Gracious Majesty Queen Victoria's birthday will be celebrated by a Public Holiday', he must have experienced a frisson of nervous tension. In the morning, he said, the soldiers would fire a 21-gun salute and the gaol gates would be opened.

The prisoners would be allowed to wander the island everywhere but in the forests. They would all receive a ration of fresh pork and it would be eaten at an open-air midday 'dinner', which he would attend. Officers would also be invited, and after the meal they would all drink Her Majesty's health in rum punch 'with suitable honours'. In the afternoon, prisoners would stage a play and a variety performance at the gaol and it would be repeated later at Longridge. Then in the evening for an hour from 7 p.m. there would be a fireworks display until the bugle sounded to return the convicts to their beds. The news was received with a mixture of wonderment bordering on disbelief.

Coincidentally, that day a ship arrived from Sydney bearing a letter from Governor Gipps in response to Maconochie's report that he had included the old hands in the marks system. Gipps was furious and delivered what he described as 'a sharp rebuke'. It must have given Maconochie pause. However, he proceeded with the celebrations and paid for the rum himself. 'It was mixed with lemons,' he wrote, 'and scarcely smelt of spirits; it went, as was intended, to the hearts and not the heads of those who drank it.' The entire day turned out to be a great success, and the following day he issued a note congratulating the prisoners: 'Not a single irregularity, or even anything approaching an irregularity, took place. At the appointed hour, every man returned quietly to his ward; some even anticipated the hour.'[3]

However, it was inevitable that word of such a remarkable turn of events would quickly spread from the confines of the island. Ships were arriving frequently and leaving with messages from soldiers, administrators and convicts to ever expanding circles. Within a month it was the talk of Sydney. Newspaper cartoons lampooned Maconochie; outraged citizens protested at the very thought of convicts drinking rum on 'the Island of the damned'.[4] And the further it spread the wilder the story became. The Launceston missionary John West – later editor of the *Sydney Morning Herald* – wrote, 'The very notion of Maconochie seemed to be illustrated by the experiment. The contrast with the past system created the greatest amazement, and the description of this extraordinary scene excited universal laughter.'[5]

Not quite universal. Gipps was appalled. Lord John Russell, the home secretary in London, whose Whig government was facing an election, was apoplectic. Gipps tried to escape censure himself by reporting that, 'Though my disapproval of Captain Maconochie's proceedings was . . . received by him on the 20th May, no attention whatever was paid by him to my communications.' Lord Russell suggested that he be recalled from Norfolk and a severe disciplinarian be installed in his stead. However, the message would take time to reach the Antipodes, and in 1841 his government fell to the Tories of Sir Robert Peel. That would probably have sealed Maconochie's fate in any case, but from a Westminster perspective Norfolk Island was not even a third-order issue, and interest soon faded.

Meantime, Gipps lectured the superintendent sternly but reasonably. 'Deeply impressed with the truth of your own principles,' he said, 'you appear to His Excellency [Russell] to have set to work with the idea that everything was to give way before you. Deep-rooted feelings or convictions, especially those of the inhabitants of this colony, were to be set aside as idle prejudices, and even the safety of New South Wales endangered.'

Unheeding, Maconochie pressed ahead with his system, and on the ground at least it was soon making great strides. He had brought £50 worth of books from Sydney and almost £150 worth of musical instruments and song sheets. He established a library with an educated Irish prisoner in charge, and soon he required two assistants; while in the evenings various musical groups were conscientiously rehearsing their repertoire. The gaol was more peaceable, and at Longridge the first offenders were generally concerned with raising the tally of their marks.

Some of his staff members were unimpressed, particularly when drought struck the island in 1841. The grain crop failed and Gipps was reluctant to part with scarce supplies on the mainland. Maconochie transferred a troublesome Ormsby from his charge over the old hands to become superintendent of agriculture. But the man remained recalcitrant, and in late 1841 Maconochie charged him with a plot to steal and kill sheep and put the blame on a Jewish convict, Joseph Cohen, whom Maconochie had appointed to care for the island's flock. But when he established a board of inquiry into the charge, they perversely found in Ormsby's favour. Maconochie sent him back to Sydney anyway.

His commissariat officer, J. W. Smith, opposed his decision to issue breeding sows to newly minted ticket-of-leave holders on the island to establish their households. But his opposition went deeper. He reported secretly to his superior on the mainland, Deputy Commissary General David Miller, 'A most radical change is wanted here immediately. The place bears no more resemblance to what a penal establishment should be than a playhouse does to a church.'[6]

Maconochie was more concerned with two intractable problems among his prison population – homosexuality and the Ring. 'Crimes against nature' had long been a notorious feature of prison life and Maconochie knew the only sure way to reduce its practice was by the introduction of a female alternative. But all his attempts to persuade Gipps to include women convicts in subsequent transports were rebuffed. 'Women have never yet been sent to Norfolk Island,' the governor wrote, 'and the universal impression is that it would be highly dangerous to have them there (not less on account of the male convicts than of the troops who guard them).'[7]

Maconochie responded by having lights set in the formerly darkened dormitories to discourage liaisons, but if anything the 'crime' increased. Indeed, it was far more common among the new hands than the old. And it was one area where his usually liberal nature deserted him. 'When I heard of it,' he wrote, 'I followed it right to a conclusion either of guilt or false accusation. When a man was found guilty he was punished with the lash.'

The Ring – a group of ruthless, incorrigible old hands – dominated the lumber yard where the prisoners 'broke in' new arrivals with anal rape if they resisted their advances. They had ruled in the prison's shadows ever since Foveaux. According to Robert Pringle Stuart, a magistrate from Van Diemen's Land who investigated conditions on the island in 1846, 'They exerted absolute power in the most tyrannical manner'. Their values were a complete inversion of Maconochie's. 'There are no means of protecting a man,' Stuart wrote, 'who may have brought on himself odium on account of good conduct . . . or having given evidence against the so-called "ring".' Stuart was writing about a later period but while Maconochie was able to loosen their grip he was never able to break it.

Governor Gipps made an unannounced visit to the colony in 1843 and stayed for six days. 'I visited every part of it, minutely inspected every establishment and separately questioned or examined every person holding some position of authority,' he wrote.[8] His conclusions were surprising, even to Maconochie. He was generally very pleased, but he was especially impressed with the condition of the old hands. 'They seem far superior mentally and morally to the New Hands and strikingly superior to them in cleanliness,' he wrote. He even approved of the application of the marks system to them, and admitted that his earlier judgements had been 'over hasty'.

Nevertheless, following his departure Maconochie struggled with continual reports reaching the island that he was about to be removed despite the fact that his system was producing good results. And while he constantly sought to discharge men to the mainland on tickets-of-leave once they had reached the necessary totals, Gipps felt he was being too lenient and declined to act on many of his recommendations.

Unbeknown to either man, the Colonial Office under Lord Stanley had already decided to recall Maconochie. The news was on its way to New South Wales as Gipps was writing notes on the island for his favourable report. And when Stanley received it he responded, 'It does not alter but rather confirms my opinion of the necessity for the measures which Her Majesty's Government have adopted with reference to the treatment of convicts at that settlement.' In short, Norfolk would return to a regime of official torment, a place of terror and human degradation.

It was a bitter blow for Maconochie, the more so because his family life had suffered along with his professional career. The boys were happy enough and well tutored by their mother;

their second daughter Catherine had married a Lieutenant Hill of the 96th Regiment at only 16 and departed immediately for their new posting in Delhi. But it was his beloved Minnie who was causing the greatest heartache.

Early in the piece she had begun to take music lessons from a convict, usually unnamed but said to be one David Ankers,[9] a new hand who had taught piano in London before his transportation for forgery. Maconochie appointed him the official bandmaster and welcomed him into the residence. But as he gave Minnie violin lessons, love blossomed between them. When Mrs Maconochie discovered the affair, the superintendent was shocked, then torn with indecision. Should he follow the dictates of his philosophy and accept that Ankers might be on the road to redemption? Or should he bow to the values of a society that would snigger behind its hand and banish his daughter to the outer darkness? In the end, they decided there was really no choice, and in 1842 they sent her away to London to live with her aunt. When Maconochie returned to England, Minnie would become her father's confidential secretary, and in 1849 follow him to his posting as governor of Birmingham's new prison, designed with his theories in mind. There she would die, unmarried, at only 32.

As his ship departed the island in March 1844, the reformer could at least take consolation from the fact that 920 doubly convicted men had been discharged over the four-year term of his administration. And three years later, less than 5 per cent would have reoffended. More than 600 new hands had earned their ticket-of-leave through his marks system, and they too had departed the island for Van Diemen's Land. They would never know how lucky they were. For under Maconochie's replacement, Major Joseph Childs, the island and its inhabitants would become a living hell.

Childs, in the view of the *Edinburgh Review*, brought to Norfolk in February 1844 his 'utter imbecility', and his administration soon bordered on anarchy. Hand-picked by Lord Stanley, the 56-year-old marine officer had fought in the Napoleonic wars and established a reputation as a strict disciplinarian. But that was within the chain of military command. A penal colony with its devolution of power among petty civilian bureaucrats, cunning convict overseers and sadistic floggers was beyond his simple ken. And with Stanley's riding instructions for 'constant vigilance and inflexible rigour' there was nothing to restrain him or the sadists under his command. In a single year, they would inflict no fewer than 20,000 lashes upon the bleeding backs of the men in their charge.

According to the Reverend Thomas Rogers, an Anglican minister posted there, on some mornings, 'The ground on which the men stood at the triangles was saturated with human gore as if a bucket of blood had been spilled on it, covering a space three feet in diameter and running out in various directions in little streams two or three feet long. I have seen this.'[10]

Stanley was particularly concerned – even obsessed – with homosexuality among the prisoners, and believed it could be beaten out of them with 'appropriate punishments . . . sufficient to restrain the immoralities'. Clearly, it was a view shared by Childs's civilian magistrate, the 30-year-old London lawyer Samuel Barrow, who had arrived two years earlier in Van Diemen's Land. Barrow quickly developed a taste for inflicting pain on the prisoners, whether for their 'immoralities' or the most trivial of infractions. And when Childs complained that chains and the lash were insufficient to deal with the 'double-dyed felons', Barrow declared himself willing to concoct variations on the most vicious instruments of torture in the sadist's armoury.

Childs's complaint was directed to the new lieutenant-governor of Van Diemen's Land, the oddly named Sir John Eardley Eardley-Wilmot, who had been at Oxford with Stanley. The colonial secretary regarded his university classmate as 'a muddle-brained blockhead', but he could at least be relied upon to carry out orders without question. And since transportation was no longer permitted to New South Wales, Stanley transferred overall responsibility for Norfolk Island to the Warwickshire baronet, thus combining the two locations still receiving Britain's discards.

Eardley-Wilmot never set foot on Norfolk, so was unaware that among Barrow's innovations were the tube gag, a timber cylinder thrust into the mouth, held in position by straps and cutting off most of the prisoner's air supply. Invariably the prisoner bled from the mouth and soon ulcers formed on the lips and gums. According to medical historian Professor Bryan Gandevia, 'The bridle [also a Barrow favourite] was a similar instrument, a metal head frame supporting the gag; Norfolk Island had its own variant, which covered the mouth with leather, leaving only a small breathing orifice.[11]

'Hanging the subject up by the thumbs for some hours was also employed at Norfolk Island, probably with a wooden peg below one foot to take part of the weight.

'The spread-eagle is a self-explanatory term; the arms "were painfully stretched out to ringbolts". A new instrument of torture, named "the stretcher", was an iron frame like a bedstead with transverse bars about a foot apart. The convict was lashed to this on his back and left with his head hanging unsupported over the end.

'The straightjacket was also employed; in one notorious case a man suspected of tampering with his eyes [to be placed on the sick list] was put on an iron bed in a jacket and left for about a fortnight; when he attempted to complain of the pressure sores on his back, he received a flogging for insolence. Convicts were easily punished more than once for the same offence, without "legal" processes; often secondary punishments led to some extension of total sentence . . . there was little concern for justice, or equitable punishment, real or even apparent.'

Unsurprisingly, the Ring flourished as a shadow power in this world of unsurpassed malevolence. And it was into this community that there arrived in 1845 a young man who personified the horrors that underlay the British Empire of the day: William Westwood, who at 16 had been taken for robbery in his native Essex and transported for 14 years. He was described by the co-author of his autobiography Thomas Rogers as having 'fair features' with 'small white teeth, so small and so white as to give a somewhat feminine appearance, made more feminine by thin red lips, small mouth, well-shaped chin and a gentle nature'. He quickly acquired the nickname Jacky Jacky.

On arrival in New South Wales, he says, he was sent to slave on the property of a Captain King near Goulburn. 'The treatment I received there,' he writes, 'was such that I would rather have met death in any shape.' After several months he absconded and fell in with a bushranger, Paddy Curran, and together they were 'a terror to the settlers'.

However, when Curran attempted to rape the wife of a grazier, Westwood intervened, threatened to shoot Curran, and in the aftermath went his own way. He soon gained a reputation for daring and for selecting the most tyrannical of the landholders to rob and humiliate, notably 'Black Francis' McArthur of the Bungendore district. In fact, it was in the town of Bungendore where he was first captured and taken to Berrima gaol, from which he removed the roof shingles and slipped away in the night.

There followed seven months of such hi-jinx on the Sydney to Goulburn road that he became the most famous highwayman in the colony, with an ever-growing price on his head. However, the reward tempted the daughter of a grog shanty, who seduced him in the parlour, and when he was undone cried out to her father, who with a passing carpenter held him down and belaboured him until he surrendered.

For the next five years he endured the horrors of Port Arthur and other prisons, punctuated by a series of extraordinary escapes, most notably in Van Diemen's Land, where he took to the bush and found himself on a promontory. 'When we made the place we started for,' he writes, 'I could see the mainland [of Tasmania] two miles distant.

'It was a long swim for a beginner [but] my comrades plunged into the sea and I followed, resolved to reach the mainland or perish in the attempt. After swimming about a mile my comrades were seized by sharks or other monsters of the deep. I struggled on and at length reached the mainland but was ignorant of the bush and naked as I was born. This did not weigh with me for a moment when I thought of the fate of my comrades, taken in the moment when they thought their release was sure.'

He staggered through the trackless bush until he was totally exhausted and the troopers tracked him down. They returned him to Hobart Town Gaol, where he was sentenced to be transported to Norfolk Island. By now the cheery young 'Jacky Jacky' was no more. And the inhuman treatment meted out with such disregard for justice or even reason produced a being at the edge of insanity, one whom even the most hardened members of the Ring treated with caution. In the first half of 1846, Barrow's sadism was at its zenith.

'The crisis was approaching,' Westwood writes.

CHAPTER FIFTEEN

'Less than human'

Major Childs's imbecility had not gone unnoticed, either at the Colonial Office in Whitehall or at Government House, Hobart Town. By 1845 Sir Eardley-Wilmot and his Controller-General of Convicts, Colonel William Champ were receiving disturbing news of a descent into disorder verging on anarchy. They commissioned the Hobart Town magistrate Robert Pringle Stuart to investigate, and in May 1846 he submitted a devastating report.

There were almost 2,000 convicts on the island at the time – more than 1,000 at the Sydney Bay settlement now known as Kingston, about 600 on the plateau at Longridge and 328 at Cascades on the north of the island. He provided a rare description of the convict buildings at Kingston, which included 'the prisoners' barracks in which they sleep – three storeys high consisting of a centre and two wings, substantially built of sandstone and contains 22 wards calculated to accommodate

790 men . . . the largest contains 100; the smallest 15 with the exception of one fitted with 7 separate divisions under lock, in which are placed certain men addicted to unnatural offences.'

As well, there were the lumber yard in which they messed, the hospitals and the gaols, old and new. 'Near the cookhouse,' Stuart wrote, 'is a large privy; an uncovered soil-pit is at the rear outside, and an open drain, communicating with the settlement creek, not far below the waterhole whence the water supply of officers is drawn. Much disgusting annoyance is, of course, felt from the exhalation of this nuisance, and I can easily imagine, when the creek is flooded, that the contents of the waterhole are rendered impure and offensive . . .

'At the gaol entrance stands the gallows; so placed that you cannot pass the doorway without coming almost in contact with this engine of death. It is never removed. The gaol is generally crowded, is badly ventilated, low, and damp; the prisoners have each a straw mat, and a blanket, which forms a bed on the stone floor.' This was bad enough, but he was shocked to the marrow by the homosexuality rife within the gaol. 'I visited the wards unexpectedly at night, at 8 o'clock, and found them oppressively hot . . . on the doors being opened men were scrambling into their own beds from others, in a hurried manner, concealment evidently being their object.

'It is my painful duty to state that atrocities of the most shocking, odious character are there perpetrated, and that unnatural crime is indulged in to excess; that the young have no chance of escaping from abuse and even forcible violation is resorted to. A terrorism is sternly and resolutely maintained, to revenge not merely exposure but even complaint; and threats of murder, too likely to be carried into effect from the violent, desperate characters here associated are made more alarming by the general practice of carrying knives.

'I am told, and I can believe, that upwards of 100 – I have heard that as many as 150 – couples can be pointed out, who habitually associate for this most detestable practice, and moral perception is so completely absorbed that they are said to be "married", "man and wife" . . . There are [also] known to be, and called, common prostitutes, who for a trifling consideration surrender themselves for this odious purpose.'

But moral outrage aside, it was the pervading power of the Ring that constituted the most damning aspect of the report. Childs had in effect surrendered the running of the gaol to the most vicious of its inmates. Stuart saw an example of the Ring's defiance when Lieutenant George Bott ordered Private Richard Pilkington to take a banned tobacco pipe from a man smoking in the cookhouse. He was received, says Stuart, 'with a look of the most ineffable disdain'. The prisoner walked away, hands in pockets, to join the Ring. Bott then ordered Chief Constable Alfred Baldock to take the man into custody. 'The whole yard was now like a beehive,' says Stuart, 'and Mr Bott expressed his conviction that there would be a riot.' The convict then became truculent to Bott, 'struck him two very violent blows in the face' and returned to his mates. No attempt was made to follow him. Bott said, 'We had better retire, Mr Stuart, I see them getting out their knives.'

Immediately after Eardley-Wilmot received the report he ordered Childs's recall. However, before that could occur his imbecility would trigger an outbreak of violence unequalled since the Morisset mutiny 12 years earlier. The spark was his decision that the prisoners no longer be permitted to cook their own maize meal; from now on they would get the bread baked in the communal kitchen.

When the loaves were issued the prisoners threw them away. According to Chief Constable Baldock, 'These innovations gave very great dissatisfaction to the prisoners and much grumbling ensued.' It was exacerbated by members of the Ring who were conspiring with the cook for the best rations 'pilfered from their half-starved fellow prisoners'. Soon, he said, 'reports were again rife of an intention to break out in acts of insubordination, and 50 men were stated to be about to take to the bush.'[1]

Childs withdrew the order. But then on the night of 30 June, the convict Charles West, who slept in the same ward as Jacky Jacky, heard the clatter of carts sounding suspiciously like the authorities were removing the prisoners' utensils. 'On the bullock drivers coming in, they told us that the pots and kettles had been taken away,' West reported.[2]

Westwood was at the school, where he was among the few seeking to keep their minds alive under the tuition of Reverend Rogers. When he returned and heard the news, West said, he became angry. 'He said the wretches wanted a damned good thrashing.' He brooded through the night. According to Martin Cash, the Tasmanian bushranger also there at the time, Westwood was in a sorry state. 'He had been flogged, goaded and tantalised till he was reduced to a lunatic and a savage.'[3]

West recalled that the next morning 'The prisoners were very disorderly at chapel. After chapel was over I saw them consulting together in the lumber yard.' Westwood then assumed leadership: 'Jacky Jacky went into the shed and said, "What do you say. Shall we one and all go into the store for our pots and kettles?" In a loud tone they answered "Yes" and immediately rushed out of the lumber yard in a body.'

Martin Cash watched as Jacky Jacky headed the mob of some 20 prisoners, all of whom were armed with staves and bludgeons. 'Having entered the cookhouse,' he writes, 'Jacky killed a free overseer named Smith with a single blow of the cudgel, on which the gang again returned to the lumber yard, making their egress through a covered archway leading out to the mechanics' shops where there was a watchman stationed on duty. Westwood on passing him spattered his brains against the brickwork near which he had been sitting, crouched and paralysed with fear. The next movement was in the direction of the lime kiln huts where some constables were stationed.[4]

'Westwood, having by this time exchanged his brain-spattered bludgeon for an axe, entered the hut and clove the skull of one of the constables, upon which another constable who happened to be in bed and witnessed the occurrence exclaimed, "Mind, I saw who did that."

'He had scarcely uttered the sentence, however, when Westwood struck him down to the earth and afterwards literally cut him to pieces.' They then headed for the residence of the hated Samuel Barrow, whom they had christened 'The Christ Killer', but the sight of uniforms there effectively ended the mutiny. Lieutenant Bott and a troop of soldiers imposed order.

At the lime kiln hut, one constable was dead and another mortally wounded, soon to die; in the sub-overseers' mess room three men were severely wounded and others 'much cut and bruised'. In the lumber yard, free overseer Stephen Smith and John Morris the gatekeeper were dead. Three of them — and perhaps all four — had been killed by Westwood himself.

Samuel Barrow acted immediately, ordering that 'all prisoners should be mustered and those upon whom any marks of blood or other suspicious circumstances appeared, should be apprehended and confined.' In a letter to Colonel Champ, he said, 'About twenty-five to thirty I have tried summarily for the tumult and riot, and inflicted in most instances the punishment of twelve months imprisonment with hard labour in chains.' He scoffed at the prisoners' complaints about their cooking arrangements. 'To attribute the recent painful exhibitions of a thirst for blood to the mere depriving the prisoners of an unsanctioned indulgence is, in my opinion, a perfect fallacy.' He did not admit the obvious: that his own vicious cruelty allied to Childs's capricious and erratic administration lay at the base of the eruption.

His solution was more of the same, since, 'a latent thirst for blood is [not] quenched . . . there is still a smouldering flame that will again burst out with a yet more frightful and devastating fury *unless strong remedial measures are speedily adopted.*' In the result, 26 men were committed for trial – nine for the assault of the overseer and 17 for wilful murder of Constable John Morris. As it happened, seven men on the island were already facing capital charges and Childs had requested the presence of a criminal court justice several weeks before the mutiny. On 26 July, Judge Francis Burgess arrived on the *Lady Franklin*, completely unaware of what awaited him – literally dozens of defendants whose lives were now in his hands.

It was too much. Within a few days he had become ill and hastened home on the *Lady Franklin*'s return voyage. However, the ship had also brought to the island a character of much sterner stuff – Childs's replacement, the civil commandant John Giles Price. Childs welcomed him briefly and departed for England, where he remained with the marines until his retirement as major-general in 1857. He spent his later years in Cornwall where he finally expired in 1870, aged 83.

Meantime, Price saw the prosecution of the mutineers as a heaven-sent opportunity to break the power of the Ring and impose his own personal tyranny. He conducted many of the depositions himself, and was well prepared when the replacement judge, Justice Fielding Browne, arrived on 3 September. Robert Pringle Stuart also returned as prosecutor, but despite the prisoners' pleas no counsel was provided for their defence.

While awaiting trial, Jacky Jacky had again attempted to escape, and Price blamed Reverend Rogers when a steel spring saw was discovered in his cell. He was removed to another, ringbolted to the wall by his hands and fastened to the floor by leg irons. He was, however, permitted to attend the court – held in the school room – when his trial began on 23 September. It was a farce. The accused now numbered 14, and all pleaded not guilty and stood at the bar jeering as Pringle Stuart questioned the witnesses.

In his statements Westwood acknowledged his guilt but sought to establish the innocence of several others. The evidence was quite clear that he alone had killed Morris, but 12 were convicted on the same charge. The other two – John Morton and William Lloyd – escaped the noose but were condemned to endure the malevolent rule of Commandant Price, who looked on throughout the nine-day trial.

Rogers and the Roman Catholic priest, Father Bond, met with the condemned men in their cells each day until 13 October, a clear spring morning, when the first six men, Jacky Jacky among them, were led from their cells to the base of the new multiple gallows built within the gaol yard. The military were armed and ready to respond to the first sign of restlessness among the prisoners assembled to watch the execution.

The condemned men's arms were heavily pinioned but their irons were struck off so they could mount the gallows' steps. Aaron Price, the turnkey, noted the scene in his diary. 'Ropes adjusted by the two executioners, White and Hammond . . . Mr Rogers in attendance on them, having been up the whole night preceding. Burial service was read by Mr Rogers . . . after which they had close communication with each of a very affecting character applicable to the awful situation to which they had brought themselves. All united in singing a hymn, and after it Kenyan [about to be hanged] sang one alone. Last moment at a quarter past eight . . . drop was 6 ft. One or two severely convulsed for a few minutes but all appeared to die almost at once.'

The bodies were cut down and the next six brought forward, taken up and hanged. Then they too were cut down, the 12 bodies thrown into the rough wooden coffins and hauled away on three bullock carts to a disused sawpit just beyond the consecrated cemetery ground, where they were hastily buried. The mass grave of the 12 mutineers has never been marked, and is known as Murderers' Mound. Its exact location is still said to be a mystery; however, some bones have been uncovered by a rising tide, and a visit by the author in 2012 established its probable position some distance from the tourist marker.

In his autobiography Westwood writes, 'You, gentle reader, will shudder at my cruelty. But I only took life. If [the gaolers] did not in a moment send a man to his last account, they inflicted on him many a lingering death. For years they tortured men's minds as well as their bodies, and after years of mental and bodily torture, sent them to a premature grave. This is what I call refined cruelty, and it is carried out, I blush to own, by Englishmen, under the enlightened British Government. Will this be believed hereafter, that this happened in the nineteenth century?'

. On the night before his execution, Westwood had written to one of the few who had treated him with kindness, the former chaplain of Port Arthur. '. . . I started life with a good feeling for my fellowman,' he says. 'Before I well knew the responsibility of my station in life, I had forfeited my birthright. I became a slave, and was sent far from my dear native country, my parents, my brother and sisters – torn from all that was dear to me, and that for a trifling offence.

'Since then I have been treated more like a beast than a man, until nature could bear no more. I was like many others, driven to despair by the oppressive and tyrannical conduct of those whose duty it was to prevent us from being treated in this way. Yet these men are courted by society; and the British Government, deceived by the interested representations of these men, continues to carry on a system that has and still continues to ruin the prospects of the souls and bodies of thousands of British subjects . . .

'Sir, the strong ties of earth will soon be wrenched, and the burning fever of this life will soon be quenched, and my grave will be a haven – a resting place for me, William Westwood. Sir, out of the bitter cup of misery I have drunk from my sixteenth year – ten long years – and the sweet draught is that which takes away the misery of living death; it is the fiend that deceives no man; all will then be quiet – no tyrant there will disturb my repose, I hope.'

He was one month beyond his 26th birthday.

The judge then dealt with the men accused prior to the mutiny, five of whom were also hanged. He and the other court officials departed on 12 December; and that day the old gallows was dismantled on the order of Commandant Price. The new ones remained.

Price was unquestionably the most malicious and vindictive of the entire procession of malignant misfits and mindless brutes who administered the imperial orders on Norfolk. And he was indisputably a child of the establishment, the fourth son of Sir Rose Price, whose family fortune came from great sugar estates in Jamaica worked by his 247 slaves. John Giles Price was educated at Charterhouse followed by Oxford's Brasenose College. However, there are no records of his graduating from the university, and the years between 1827 and 1836, when he left England for the Antipodes, are mysteriously blank. There have been strong suggestions – based on his familiarity with convict argot and underworld manners and customs – that he spent some time 'inside'. Certainly by this time his father had wasted most of the family inheritance on an outlandish estate in Cornwall with its own brewery, pack of hounds and a mansion known locally as Price's Folly. It may well be that the young gambler saw the inside of a debtor's prison. But whatever the experience, it left him with an obsessive interest in criminal behaviour and a pathological need to dominate and demean malefactors.

He was a big man, well over six feet with a wide, loose mouth. He wore a monocle in his left eye and fixed his hearers with a knowing, unblinking stare. On arrival in Tasmania he took up land at Risdon and was welcomed into the polite society of Hobart Town. In 1838, aged 29, he married 24-year-old Mary Franklin, a niece of the lieutenant-governor, Sir John Franklin. He was no friend of the Maconochies, much less the 'wrong-headed and dangerous' system of marks advanced by Alexander. In 1839, Price left his farm under the care of an overseer to put his own stamp on the criminal administration, taking up the joint positions of muster-master in the Convict Department and assistant police magistrate. This gave him entrée to a world where men could be cowed into submission and reduced to pitiable mendicants. He examined all convicts on their arrival in Van Diemen's Land, recorded their histories and dispatched details on request to other departments with his own perceptions included. The convict milieu exerted such an overwhelming fascination for him that he would not only revel in its brutishness; it would drive him to his own violent death at convict hands.

According to his biographer, Justice Sir John Barry, 'He was attracted to the evil in them even as he was repelled by it. He regarded them as less than human, with no claim to justice in a civilised sense, but his vanity nevertheless demanded they should move in submissive terror of him.'[5] So when Eardley-Wilmot required a replacement for Commandant Childs he needed look no further than Price, who had established a formidable reputation as an 'iron-fisted' dispenser of colonial justice. But while Price was eager, despite some unnamed health issues, there were countervailing forces, notably his wife Mary who by now was the mother of five children under seven. As well, the ascendancy of Hobart Town did not want to lose their chief protector.

Price was deaf to all but the call of his demons, and set out for Norfolk Island with Eardley-Wilmot's 'perfect confidence in his prudence, zeal, and knowledge of the duties and trust reposed in him [so that] days after his arrival everything will be restored to order and regularity . . . and above all that separation [of the convicts] at night and continued surveillance without which nameless horrors are perpetrated.'[6]

Having dealt with the mutineers, Price turned his attention to the other sources of influence and authority on the island. In short order, he withdrew the Reverend Rogers's commission as a justice of the peace and as an acting magistrate. Samuel Barrow was sent packing, although he remained in the penal system and would bring his questionable talents to bear as the first governor of Melbourne's Pentridge Prison. Price then suspended Gilbert Robertson, the superintendent of agriculture, who had previously received high praise for his job. He had achieved good results without constant recourse to the lash, and this alone marked him down in Price's book. But worse, he was not prepared to kowtow to the commandant.

Robertson protested the suspension, and there followed a series of increasingly acerbic letters between them, ending with Robertson's appeal that his wife and sick daughter were becoming desperately distressed; he pleaded for some generosity of spirit. Price's sneering reply crushed all hope, and Robertson and his children were driven from the island. The daughter Elizabeth was too ill to travel, and although his wife remained to oversee her care, she died in January 1847 within weeks of her father's departure. She was buried on the island.

Others who showed the slightest independence of mind soon followed and were replaced by toadies from the island or men Price had known in Hobart Town. Reverend Rogers hung on for as long as he could endure it and sent a steady stream of complaints to his superiors detailing Price's 'barbarous inhumanity' to the prisoners. All to no avail; he departed the island in February 1847 and took up a parish near Launceston. There for the next several years he campaigned against Price and his sadism.

Among his examples were a convict cart driver being flogged with 36 lashes for finding a young bird and taming it; and a convict cleaner charged with having government papers improperly in his possession when he was cleaning them from the police office floor. When he tried to defend himself Price shouted, 'Give him the gag!' Under his regime, men were thrown into solitary for 14 days for such trivialities as 'not walking fast enough when going out to work'; 'not being in rank when the bell rang'; 'being in at the privy when the bell rang'; 'having fat in his possession'; 'walking in the prison yard'.

With a workforce of 2,000 prisoners, Price recommenced the building of the octagonal (now redesigned pentagonal) gaol within the stone walls. This provided ample tiny cells for prisoners to serve their 'solitary' sentences fed only bread and water in darkness for up to three months at a time. And when they emerged to the glaring light they were flogged before being returned to the chain gangs.

Most devastating to prison morale was his obsessive revival of the informer system. He played favourites ruthlessly, but even the most compliant found themselves spurned for the slightest infraction and then betrayed by their patron with a quiet word to their rival or victim of their tales. Among his leading 'stoolies' was Martin Cash, although this apparently slipped his memory when writing his autobiography. Price's presence among the prisoners, either personally or through spies, was ubiquitous. The only area where he had no control was the military garrison, which was under the command of Major William Harold of the 11th Regiment and later Major George de Winton of the 99th. But even there he had the right – frequently exercised – to call for assistance from the guard.

In Hobart Town, Eardley-Wilmot read Price's reports with unabashed satisfaction. Order had been restored, just as he expected. Thus encouraged, he decided that the 'new hands' should be shipped back to Van Diemen's Land and in their place he would send all the doubly convicted men who were causing trouble at Port Arthur across the sea to Price's colony. The idea also appealed to his successor, Lieutenant-Governor Sir William Denison, and from 1847 it was an accepted part of the system.

The roll call of men broken beyond redemption echoed across the years to 1853. Typical was Mark Jeffrey who engaged Price's special attention as a brash country boy and suffered at his hands 'humiliation, indignities and persecution until my heart sickened and my senses revolted'.[7] In the quarry gang, Jeffrey worked with 16 kilograms of iron chains held between his ankles as he smashed the rock face with splintery pickhandles. And when he answered back to his overseer he was lashed until the blood ran. Price came to see him and stared through his monocle, saying, 'How do you like it by this time, Big Mark?'[8]

Jeffrey survived to join the chorus of hatred for the man who took such ferocious pleasure in torment. As the years passed, Price became ever more 'iron-fisted' in his treatment of the men beneath him. Finally, the authorities in Hobart Town began to take note of the ever rising tally of whippings in the reports arriving from Norfolk. By 1852 when Anglican Bishop Charles Wilton visited the settlement he discovered, 'gloom, sullen despondency, despair of leaving the island. About a fortnight before, for some cause they were ignorant of, the commandant ordered every man wearing chains to have both legs secured – "chains crossed" – which adds, I am told, greatly to the punishment especially to those in heavy irons. On Sunday 14 March, out of 270 who attended the church only 52 were without them.

'Complaints regarding the frequency of the lash were great indeed . . . the state of the yard, from the blood running down men's backs, mingled with the water used in washing them when taken down from the triangle – the degrading scene of a large number of men standing in the outer yard waiting their turn to be tortured, and the more humiliating spectacle presented by those who had undergone the scourging, were painful to listen to and now raises a blush . . .'[9]

Called upon to explain the soaring number of lashes, Price responded with a long, rambling letter of extraordinary self-justification. He claimed that the convicts were simply unwilling to exert self-control and follow his regulations which he said were 'no more stringent than those imposed on soldiers, or indeed on boys at public schools in England'. He claimed that flogging was not even his preferred method of punishment. 'Were I asked what punishment I consider most effective,' he said, 'I would reply that of isolated cells. Were there a sufficiency of these, the most refractory might be tamed and corporal punishment abolished by law.'

Denison, not unnaturally, was unconvinced. The authorities now began to consider seriously the abandonment of the settlement, which was costing far more than keeping the prisoners at Port Arthur. Price himself was concerned that his children were unable to be educated on the island, and his health was again in doubt from 'some unspecified and mysterious malady'.[10] It is tempting to identify it as syphilis, which would go some way to explain his increasingly unhinged behaviour, but there is no independent evidence to support this.

Denison removed Price and his family from the island on 17 January 1853 on health grounds, although he retained the position and salary for a further 12 months. He sought posts outside Australia but in vain. Then, apparently recovered, he was appointed inspector-general of penal establishments for Victoria and moved the family to a residence within the Pentridge stockade, replacing Samuel Barrow. There he remained for four years, instituting a regime so harsh and unforgiving that there arose a citizen's committee, backed by the Melbourne *Age*, demanding his dismissal. Price fought back, supported by the rival *Argus*, but the Victorian Legislative Assembly was also having doubts about the wisdom of retaining him. Then, on the afternoon on 26 March 1857 at the port of Williamstown across the bay from Melbourne, he was finally cornered by kismet.

He had housed several hundred convicts in the stinking hulks *Lysander* and *Success* and put them to work on the Williamstown wharf. Conditions aboard were appalling and the warders regularly underfed the men and enriched themselves. At about 4 p.m. he joined the other officials in a tour of inspection on the wharf. A group of convicts gathered about protesting their treatment.

And when he scorned their claims the convicts snatched up pieces of quarried rock and hurled them at the party.

According to eyewitnesses, Price raised a hand to protect his head and instinctively turned away. The spell of his personality was broken. A group surged forward. Several convicts seized him. He broke loose and began to run. A heavy stone struck him in the back and he fell. He got up and attempted to make his escape but stumbled in a gutter and fell again. Dazed, he was getting to his feet when a convict struck him with a shovel. A mob of howling men surged about him, dragging him along as they struck him with stones and fists until he was unconscious. Then they dropped him and made a run for freedom.

Armed guards soon rounded them up, and one convict, Simon Russell, went to his aid, raised his face from the wet earth and helped him to breathe. Two others came to assist. They lifted him into a barrow and wheeled him to the nearby lighthouse, where he was attended by Dr John Wilkins. There was nothing he could do. Price's skull had been crushed. Apart from a momentary lapse into consciousness, he was beyond recall and died at 4 p.m. the following day.

The *Age* editorialised, 'There can be no doubt whatever that Mr. Price was guilty of the cruelty attributed to him, and that his untimely and unfortunate end is the melancholy result of that vindictive feeling which his own conduct has fostered in the minds of the convicts under his charge . . . He was a cruel man, and his cruelty came back to him.'

CHAPTER SIXTEEN

Perpetrating a sham

Price's departure from Norfolk Island marked the beginning of the end. He was replaced by the senior military officer on the island, Captain Rupert Deering, who almost immediately sent in his resignation; but not before a party of nine convicts shanghaied a government boat and made their escape from Sydney Bay to the open sea. Deering and his posse gave chase but the convicts out-rowed them; a cyclone struck; the seas rose and Deering was forced back to the shelter of the island without two of his crewmen, Private Boardmore and the coxswain James Forsythe, who were knocked overboard and drowned. Most of the convicts survived the tempest and when the boat came ashore on the coast of New South Wales several were recaptured and sent to Port Arthur.

They were forerunners of their fellows on Norfolk who were now being shipped out in groups of 68 on the *Lady Franklin* to serve the remainder of their sentences there. It was a long and untidy process supervised by Deering's replacement, Captain Harold Day of the 99th Regiment. There was some resistance to the abandonment of Norfolk Island from London, and occasionally shiploads would arrive expecting to serve their time on the 'Isle of Sodom', only to be rerouted after a few days in the increasingly commodious barracks. Ironically, the vile pentagonal gaol was just now perfectly complete, and Captain Day, who had arrived on 18 September 1853 with his wife and family, had no desire to emulate his brutish predecessors, so kept it virtually empty.

He appears to have been a thoroughly decent man. The turnkey Aaron Price, who was about to end his own 25 years on the island, noted in his diary that since Christmas that year fell on a Sunday, the commandant 'was so kind as to allow the prisoners the indulgence of half a day on Monday to keep Xmas – and also allowed the officers to invite the men to their quarters, which they did in a most liberal manner'. Day himself entertained those who failed to score an invitation from his colleagues and, according to Price, 'making glad with his kindness, and sending all to bed in good humour and with full bellies'.

In July 1854, the *Lady Franklin* brought orders that the island was to be completely vacated by January 1855. However, the authorities underestimated the enormous task of repatriating both the convict and civil population with the stores and implements of a generation, so the final transfer was not completed until exactly one year later. Even then, five trusted convicts were left behind to maintain essential services under the commissariat storekeeper, Thomas Stewart. While the authorities were finally closing the book on the most reprehensible of its imperial crimes, they were about to open another, whose secrets are even now shadowed and disguised by myth and make believe.

The Pitcairners were packing their chattels under imperial orders for the journey from their own murderous islet to one which – unbeknown to them – had witnessed the depths of human depravity.

Most were thrilled at the prospect. And all were deceived by the colonial authorities that they were being granted a new homeland as their permanent independent birthright under the British crown. It is possible that there was a measure of wishful thinking in their perceptions, but certainly the officials who persuaded them to leave Pitcairn did nothing to disabuse them.

The two guiding lights of the move were George Hunn Nobbs, still seeking to cloak his illegitimate brand in the garb of religious respectability; and the somewhat unlikely figure of Sir Fairfax Moresby, commander-in-chief of Britain's Pacific station. Moresby had been born into a military family in India in 1786, and had distinguished himself when stationed in Mauritius in the 1820s in actions against the slave trade. He was promoted to rear admiral in 1849 and commanded the Pacific station from Valparaiso. He, like many Britons of the day, was intrigued by the romantic reports of this curious Pitcairn community in the vastness of the great ocean, so apparently welcoming to callers, so modest and devout in their Christian observances.

The Pitcairners actively promoted the romantic image as the barefoot young blades rowed out to meet the ships and when they landed seeking water and fresh vegetables the women made a tidy living from their handicrafts. George Nobbs dressed in a long black coat (and shoes) as befitted his clerical pretensions, and conducted Anglican-style services at the drop of a coin into the communal plate. He still acted as schoolmaster, making a modest charge to the pupils' families – except for those children to whom he was godfather. (Soon, unsurprisingly, the latter outnumbered the paying students.) By the 1840s he was writing to officials in England as the *pater familias* of 'my people'. It is highly unlikely that he shared the correspondence with Quintal and other prominent Pitcairners.

Usually visitors stayed only long enough to record their first impressions and broadcast them, suitably embroidered, to an eager audience huddled beneath Britain's gloomy skies. But occasionally they found themselves marooned there for longer periods, such as the quintet that included the Baron de Thierry, and the Eton- and Cambridge-educated Hugh Carleton, who would later make his mark in New Zealand politics. The baron, whose aristocratic heritage was doubtful at best, had styled himself the sovereign chief of New Zealand while passing through Sydney, on grounds that the missionary-cum-gun-runner Thomas Kendall, whom he'd met in London, had purchased him a domain there for 12 rusty axes. He also had clerical pretensions, but was regularly denied ordination by the more conventional authorities. He and Hugh Carleton were both trained musicians, and they spent much of their 18 days on Pitcairn introducing the islanders to the delights of choral harmony.

By June 1846 Nobbs had overseen the building of a new church and schoolhouse that could seat 200, further evidence to ships' captains and their missionary passengers that an active Christian outpost had been established in an otherwise hostile Pacific. Indeed, the London Missionary Society's *Camden* delivered many more Bibles and prayer books, and in 1849 and

1852 visiting naval captains Wood and Wellesley respectively outdid themselves in reports presenting Pitcairn as an island of the blessed.

However, Nobbs yearned for a formal recognition of his religious authority and sent a blizzard of letters lobbying the ecclesiastical establishment for a suitable licence. He even engaged the community in the campaign, although according to Raymond Nobbs, 'The letter has the distinct flavour of the pastor's own hand and in later years some claimed that many of the petitioners had not signed their names to it at all.'[1]

But while the church authorities were unmoved, in 1851 a similar letter addressed to Sir Fairfax Moresby in Valparaiso and signed, according to Rosalind Young, 'by several of the island matrons and maidens'[2] finally brought results. In August 1852, Sir Fairfax himself arrived at the island in his flagship HMS *Portland*.

'His coming,' Young says, 'was greeted by the people with every demonstration of joy which reached its height when, gathered beneath a grove of orange trees, they listened to the band that the admiral had kindly ordered ashore, and enjoyed such delicious strains of music as they never had dreamed of.'[3] Nobbs was in seventh heaven. He and Sir Fairfax struck up an instant rapport, and according to Sir Fairfax's son and secretary, Fortescue Moresby, 'Never were so many happy smiling faces, all eager to look at the first admiral that ever came to their happy home . . . if we said a kind word to any of them, they looked so happy and pleased.

'It was now prayer time and away we all went to Church. Mr Nobbs officiated and read the prayers impressively and earnestly; the most solemn attention was paid by all present. The islanders sang two hymns in most magnificent style; I have never heard any Church singing that could equal theirs, except at Cathedrals; and the credit is largely due to Mr Carleton who was left behind by accident from a whaler in 1850.'[4]

Although he only stayed four days on the island, so impressed was the admiral that he readily acceded to Nobbs's plea to assist him in his quest for formal clerical qualifications. He not only gave him passage on his ship to Valparaiso, but also took Nobbs's daughter Jane there to further her education. He outfitted the penitent pastor and paid his passage to London for instruction, gave his family £100 to defray expenses in his absence, provided a substitute pastor from his own ship in the Reverend William Holman for the duration of his absence and a personal letter to the Bishop of London recommending his candidacy for ordination. All Nobbs's fervent prayers were answered.

The 53-year-old former sealer and soldier of fortune reached British soil on 16 October, 41 years after he first put to sea from Portsmouth. He wasted no time in presenting himself at the bishopric, where he was admitted to deacon's orders at St Mary's church, Islington and a mere five weeks later was ordained an Anglican priest by the Bishop of London, Charles Blomfield. He was taken up by the prominent politician and philanthropist Sir Thomas Dyke Ackland, and feted wherever he went.

He addressed a celebrity-studded Pitcairn Fund Committee headed by the Archbishop of Canterbury and including no fewer than three admirals of the fleet. A bank account was established to equip the islanders with everything from whale boats, tools, medicines, clocks, clothing, church bells and other impedimenta, not least a clerical wardrobe for Nobbs himself and a stipend of £50 a year. The highlight was his meeting with Queen Victoria and Albert the Prince Consort at Osborne House on the Isle of Wight, an event that Nobbs happily retold to the end of his days, usually illustrated by his most precious memento, an autographed lithograph of the Royal Family.

However, as he nodded approvingly in the gilded halls at the romantic blather about Pitcairn as some pious arcadia, Nobbs was acutely aware that he was perpetrating a sham. The community was riven with jealousy; conflict between families continually bubbled just beneath the surface. As he would later write, there was 'so much hatred and variance existing among many of the communicants' that he was reluctant to administer holy communion to them.[5] Nevertheless, he held his peace, filled his purse, and after only two months departed on the *Portland* with his naval patron, reaching Valparaiso on 12 February 1853. There he collected his daughter Jane, and his son Reuben, who had contracted tuberculosis on Pitcairn but was now ready to return.

They arrived on the admiral's flagship to a joyous welcome, not least, according to Rosalind Young, because 'the people were suffering from the effects of a severe drought and were obliged to subsist on whatever they could get, unripe pumpkins forming their principal diet.' Stores were immediately forthcoming, and she noted that Nobbs 'seemed to have acquired a somewhat more dignified bearing' following his ordination.[6]

When Admiral Moresby came ashore he convened a meeting with Magistrate Arthur Quintal, and his two councillors, Thomas Buffett and Edward Quintal, to consider moving the community holus bolus to Norfolk Island. Nobbs was ready for the larger stage and argued forcefully that they had outgrown

Pitcairn. There was a sullen resistance from some of the islanders – particularly the Adams family.

No sooner had the *Portland* sailed away than almost everyone contracted a particularly virulent strain of influenza. This, allied with the continuing drought, gradually wore down the opposition, and by 1855 a poll of the population found 153 out of 187 in favour of the move. The remainder – notably George Adams, Charles Christian, Jacob Christian, Simon Young and John Quintal – were reluctant to acquiesce. Nonetheless, early in February 1856 – after prolonged negotiations conducted by Nobbs and Moresby – the New South Wales Governor Sir William Denison chartered the 830 ton emigrant ship *Morayshire* to carry out the transfer.

She reached Pitcairn on 22 April and immediately began loading the entire population with all their goods and chattels into her capacious hold. By now the population had reached 194 despite several recent tragedies. Three of the men – William Evans, Driver Christian and Matthew McCoy – had decided to fire the old *Bounty* gun and it exploded prematurely, injuring two of them severely and mortally wounding McCoy. Reuben Nobbs surrendered to consumption and was buried on the island. Another youngster accidentally stabbed himself with a spear and died of tetanus; and Daniel McCoy fell from a cliff while walking with his young wife, broke his back and died within the hour.

According to Rosalind Young, 'By the second day of May 1856 everything was ready, and the time had come to say goodbye to the dear old spot where all their lives had been spent. Some, with buoyant hopes and bright expectations, stepped on board the ship that was to carry them away, while others – and these the far greater number – with sad hearts and tear-dimmed eyes left their island home. Utterly lonely and desolate, the little rock stood in the vast ocean as it slowly receded from view.' It had been 67 years since their mutinous ancestors had found their isolated hideaway, and despite the Pollyanna prose of Ms Young – written many years hence – the sense of foreboding was almost universal.

The journey took 36 horrendous days of seasickness, but on 8 June they negotiated the choppy waters of Slaughter Bay in whaleboats and landed at what was finally and officially known as Kingston. As the heavens opened in a typical island storm at 11 a.m., they climbed from their lighters onto the rough convict-built rock and concrete Kingston Pier. Denison had arranged for the HMS *Herald* under Captain Henry Denham to arrive several days before, and Captain Denham joined Mr Stewart on the pier to welcome each lighter ashore as the rain pelted down. Only Nobbs, Buffett and Evans had ever seen a land bigger than Pitcairn, and as the newcomers looked about they must surely have wondered at the wildly alien topography and the forbidding architecture that confronted them.

To their left was George's Hill, stripped bare of trees from the time of the first settlement, and behind it Arthur's Vale, the first flat area cleared for cultivation and still producing crops of grain. Directly ahead on a rise was the surgeon's cottage, rebuilt on the site of the first Government House. Flanking the pathway to the cottage was a series of stone buildings – the police office and the guardhouse on one side, the pier store and the abandoned crankmill on the other. A rough track led from the pier about 200 metres to a line of buildings, the most commanding being the three-storeyed soldiers' barracks, and to its right a parade ground, officers quarters and well-made colonial homes for the officers and their families. Most were in reasonable order and they were pleased to discover the street was named Quality Row. The second and permanent Government House, completed in Morisset's term, occupied the lower side of the street and overlooked the sea.

To the newcomers' right was the dominant feature – the great high stone walls enclosing the pentagonal prison and beyond that the infamous prisoners' yard and barracks that had so recently witnessed a generation of horror. The compound was only 50 metres back from the sea shore where the waters lapped gently, their surging power broken and dispersed by the line of rocks and coral that had taken so many lives. Far to the right was Emily Bay, sheltered behind a rocky point, as calm and inviting as the blue Pacific lagoon of sailors' tales. In the rise up from the bay were dotted the gravestones that told the tale of Norfolk's wicked and perilous past.

Most were totally ignorant of the malevolent policies that had created their surroundings. Sarah Nobbs wrote a few months later, 'Everything was so strange: the immense houses, the herds of cattle grazing and in the distance the gigantic Norfolk pines, filled us for the moment with amazement.'[7]

They were met at the pier by commissariat storekeeper Stewart, who had assumed the trappings of office and lived with his wife in Government House; two odd couples named Rogers and Waterson; and half a dozen convicts who had tried in vain to keep the place up to scratch. The buildings were dilapidated, the roads potholed and the farmlands in disarray. Mrs Waterson considered herself a psychic and searched among the Pitcairners for a face she had seen in a dream . . . also in vain. However, the New South Wales Government had provided a bountiful store of goods and livestock to get them started: 1,300 sheep, 250 cattle, eight horses, an unknown number of wild pigs roaming the bush together with feral goats, swarms of rabbits, and enough flour and other provender – including 45,500 pounds of biscuits – to feed them for a year. When all were safely disembarked they walked through the slush to Government House for a cup of tea.

Nobbs was initially dismayed; and he was not alone. 'Every face,' he wrote, 'wore an expression of disappointment.' He was particularly displeased to discover 'a succession of hillocks and shallow ravines covered with short, brown grass, but scarcely a tree to be seen'.[8]

He consoled himself by conducting his first church service on the island, choosing the upper floor of Major Anderson's crowning triumph, the military barracks on Quality Row. Shortly afterwards, he claimed No. 9 Quality Row as his residence after a lottery among the various heads of households. In time, he would take a more elevated position on Longridge, from whence he shone his guiding light. In fact, the plateau of Longridge would become one of the more productive areas of Norfolk until it was taken over by the United States military during World War II and transformed into the airfield that still serves the island today.

The *Herald* brought to the island a team of surveyors who would divide an area of it into 50 acre blocks, one for each of the Pitcairn families to farm. They were already well advanced in their work, and within two weeks had allocated the blocks on the southern half of the island, from Arthur's Vale on the east, Longridge in the centre, to Cascade in the north-west. Again the families drew lots for their new possessions, and at the end of the month the *Morayshire* withdrew, taking Stewart and the other caretakers back to New South Wales. The Pitcairners now had it totally to themselves.

The land transactions had been concluded amicably, partly because the Pitcairners were somewhat overwhelmed by the size of their farms, but also because they were unsure what to do with them. They had grown up with vegetable patches around their cottages and a range of fruits to be picked from the trees; they had virtually no experience of cropping or grazing larger areas and, as it turned out, very little interest in acquiring such knowledge and skills. They were not so much lazy as totally lacking the essential work ethic of the farmer. The results were predictable. The sheep contracted various diseases and many died. The cattle, other than the milkers, were neglected and soon ran wild. And the crops, mostly of Indian corn, failed three times out of five. Some of the younger adults accepted the new order but within a year others were agitating for a return to Pitcairn.

When Governor Denison arrived on the island in September 1857, he discovered that they had consumed all of the biscuits and were in desperate need of flour and other staples. He sailed directly to New Zealand, where he bought the food and arranged trading contacts that would take their wool, tallow and hides. He returned the following month, called them together and warned them that 'regular and energetic labour' was needed to make a tolerable living from the island's resources.

The Pitcairners nodded their agreement, and as soon as he departed resumed their preferred existence, spending much of their time out fishing. Others rebelled and continued their agitation for a return to Pitcairn. Nobbs damned them as 'simpletons', and of the 60 who were preparing to leave he was able to pressure 44 into giving Norfolk a second chance. But no amount of persuasion and angry vilification could prevent 16 members of two families departing in November 1858.

Alarmed at the continuing lack of direction in the community, Denison engaged a headmaster of a Hertfordshire Industrial School, Thomas Rossiter, to head a party of practical English tradesmen to provide the sinews of an infant economy. Using the Pitcairn Fund, Denison was able to bring Rossiter, James Dawe, a miller, wheelwright and blacksmith, together with their wives and families as well as Henry Blinman, a stonemason and plasterer, all the way to Sydney and then on to the island, arriving in June 1859. Rossiter was only 34 but had the authority of Denison's imprimatur and took over from the 60-year-old Nobbs and his deputy Simon Young the duties of schoolmaster as well as the island's storekeeper and chief farming instructor. It required all his tact and diplomacy to interact with the Pitcairners and, although he installed himself – at Denison's suggestion – in Government House, relations with the islanders were never easy. Dawe and Blinman soon lost patience with the Pitcairners and left within two years, never to return.

By then Denison's successor, Sir John Young, was similarly concerned that Rossiter must be encouraged to remain among 'these interesting colonists' to prevent them 'from relapsing into the listlessness which the climate and the abundance with which they are surrounded are so apt to superinduce; without [him] there might ensue a complete forgetfulness of the habits and pursuits of civilised life.'[9] Rossiter remained and developed his own farm on Longridge as the island's showplace. However, division among the former Pitcairn community continued to rumble beneath the surface, and in 1863 it erupted with a score of recalcitrants demanding to be returned to their distant home.

Rosalind Young remembered the event well. 'Four families decided to go,' she says.[10] 'These were, first, Thursday O. Christian, his wife and nine children. Mrs Christian's aged mother also accompanied them for the purpose of seeing again her son Mayhew Young who was with the first party . . .' The other families were Robert Buffett and his wife; Simon Young, who had been superseded as assistant schoolmaster by Rossiter, with Simon's mother, Hannah Adams, his wife and eight children; and Samuel Warren and his wife Agnes, the daughter of T. O. Christian. Warren was an American whaler from Rhode Island who landed on Norfolk in the early 1860s and married Agnes the night before they departed. He was 33 at the time, and according to the *Pitcairn News* 'Most Pitcairners [now] have Warren blood in them and many bear the name Warren proudly.' Their child was born shortly after their arrival on Pitcairn.[11]

This loss of a further 27 settlers had little effect on the population, which continued to increase. However, in 1863 a new threat to their autonomy entered the equation. It arrived in a form that raised an exquisite dilemma for Chaplain George Hunn Nobbs, for it was clad in the garb of ecclesiastical authority and from the very font of his own pastoral prerogative: the Church of England. And they wanted to appropriate for themselves a great chunk of *his* island.

CHAPTER SEVENTEEN

Coveting Norfolk

Bishop George Augustus Selwyn had coveted Norfolk as a base for his Melanesian Mission for at least a decade. He first visited the island with the New Zealand Governor – a fellow High Church Etonian and Cambridge graduate – Sir George Grey in 1853. By then he'd realised that Auckland was a less than ideal site for his 'college' to produce native missionaries from those he had tempted by trade goods to leave their island homes to learn the wonders of Anglican theology.

In the 11 years from 1849, at least four of the 152 Melanesians he had brought to his St John's mission school had died from the change in climate, and all were lost to the cause on their return, 'swept away by the torrent of heathenism in their own homes'.[1] Moreover, despite a rigorous teaching regime, their grasp of Christian doctrine fell somewhat short of Selwyn's Oxbridge standards. His instructors were delighted, for example, when at the end of his course one Sapandulu from Erromango in the

New Hebrides (now Vanuatu) explained his newly acquired faith: 'Me say One God; God very good; all good; God made you, made me, made everything. You good, God love you.'[2]

According to church historian David Hilliard, 'Any expectation that young Melanesians after only a few months of instruction, could as individuals successfully challenge the existing system of beliefs and behaviour, was doomed to disappointment.' However, Selwyn and his chaplain and successor John Coleridge Patteson were fired by a zeal that overwhelmed such sober rationality. They saw the move to Norfolk Island as the key to spreading worship of the creator at the apex of British imperialism to the cruel and misguided natives. The irony of their choice of locale simply didn't occur to them.

However, there were other, secular forces at work that frustrated them. While Selwyn called on his High Church contacts in London – notably prime minister-in-waiting William Gladstone and slave trade reformer William Wilberforce – to persuade the government to transfer the former penal colony to his stewardship, there was serious opposition on two fronts. Sir William Denison in Sydney was committed to the transfer of the pious Pitcairners and felt that the introduction of 'savages' from the islands might tempt them to abandon their virtuous ways. And from their own Christian ranks, the London Missionary Society – and particularly the Low Church Reverend Thomas Boyles Murray, author of an immensely popular book[3] extolling the saintliness of the Pitcairners – condemned Selwyn's ambitions.

The bishop recorded his frustrations about the manner in which 'well-meaning' people in England had taken up the Pitcairners' cause with an enthusiasm 'which is always lavished on the heroes of a romantic story and of blemished escutcheons, but which prosaic and honest folk have to go without'.[4] Nevertheless, he pressed ahead and in 1854 he travelled to England and from the great wealth of his establishment friends and relatives easily raised £10,000 to endow a Melanesian see.

Thus fortified, in May 1856 he sailed in his ship the *Southern Cross* – purpose built to transport his natives to and from their theological studies – first to Norfolk to reassure himself that the island would suit his needs, then to Sydney where he had arranged to meet again with Governor Denison. Since the Pitcairn migration was a fait accompli, he now proposed a triumvirate government for the island comprising one person appointed by the British Home Office, one by the Pitcairn community and the third by himself.

Denison was decidedly unimpressed, calling the proposal 'crude and undigested', and smelt the threat of 'ecclesiastical tyranny' over the Pitcairners.[5] Selwyn responded high-handedly that he would 'carry forward' his endeavour 'in communication with and with the consent of the Pitcairn Islanders whatever plans I may believe to be necessary to promote their spiritual welfare and the extension of the Kingdom of our Blessed Lord'.[6] He set forth for Norfolk, arriving with his wife in July 1856 as the newcomers were settling in.

Pastor Nobbs and his flock were thrilled. Totally unaware of the churchman's real agenda, Nobbs could not do enough to make him welcome, and insisted that he and Mrs Selwyn occupy Government House. However, while the bishop treated Nobbs with the respect due to a fellow churchman – albeit of relatively lowly station – Selwyn was aware that the pastor's hold over his flock was by no means complete. Indeed, John

Quintal, a long-time opponent of Nobbs, confided to him in a note, 'I beg you my dear father that we shall not be left under the teachings of a common sailor as we have been heretofore, but that you shall be the bishop over us, and shall be looking out for our souls while we are here in Norfolk Island.'[7]

Selwyn bided his time. Although he had no formal ecclesiastical authority over the island, which remained within the New South Wales diocese, Selwyn officiated over confirmation services without objection from Nobbs. And when he departed on another journey gathering native scholars from the cannibal tribes in the New Hebrides and the Solomon Islands, he left Mrs Selwyn behind to continue the softening-up process with the Pitcairners. In this, she was splendidly successful. According to Rosalind Young, 'She soon won the hearts of the people, and gave much assistance in teaching in the day school as well as the Sunday school.

'She tried to impress upon the minds of the young women and girls the importance of practising habits of cleanliness and industry while young, teaching them also to cook. This energetic lady was not satisfied with merely giving instruction, but would frequently visit her scholars at their homes to see whether those instructions had been followed or not. In this way, more lasting good was accomplished, and much real benefit resulted from her patient and conscientious labours.'

It says much about the general standards of the Pitcairners that they were in need of instruction to keep themselves clean and busy. And photographs taken at the time attest to her concerns. But by ingratiating herself with the community she was also able to gather valuable intelligence for her husband's campaign. She would quickly have learned of the resentment some families had towards Nobbs's assumption of leadership and the airs and graces he exhibited among outside officialdom. She may well have discovered his own continuing struggle to resist the demon drink. Certainly, Selwyn and Patteson were aware of his 'lapses from temperance' since his ordination. Indeed, Patteson declared himself willing, when next on Norfolk Island to have 'a plain talk with Mr Nobbs on my own account, that the Bishop might not be compromised, just letting him know that if I choose to make public what I know about him and the people etc'.

Whether Patteson made good his threat at this stage is unknown. But Nobbs was also torn by his silent acquiescence in the nonsensical perception by the English grandees of the saintliness of his fellow Pitcairners. 'Little do those in England who congratulated me on my admission into holy orders know the difficulties I have to contend with,' he told his diary. 'And I have in great measure brought them upon myself by permitting all the glowing accounts which have been transmitted home by transient visitors to remain uncontradicted, when it was my duty to have exposed their fallacy and deceptiveness.'[8]

When Selwyn proposed that the community should help spread the Gospel among the heathen by taking into their homes a few children from the islands, Nobbs was happy to comply. Indeed, he consented to take one child himself 'and will do all I can for its welfare, by God's help'. But when the bishop then proposed a mission school there was immediate resistance, and a vote among the heads of households was lost 16 to 12 with both Nobbs and the chief magistrate, Frederick Young, casting their ballots against.

The churchmen were undeterred. Patteson called at Norfolk in 1859 and was soon in private colloquy with Nobbs. Whatever may have passed between them, Nobbs then suddenly declared, 'I have quite altered my mind about the Melanesian school. I quite see that I was mistaken; and the people are considering how to correct themselves.'[9] He then threw his weight behind the idea and when the newly consecrated Patteson became acting bishop for the Melanesians from 1861, five families offered sons for his mission work, including Nobbs's sixth child, Edwin, and Young's lad, Fisher.

The following year, the new governor of New South Wales, Sir John Young, visited the island and heard of the mission school proposal first hand. His fellow Etonians, Selwyn and Patteson, had yet to take him into their confidence, and he reacted vigorously to the idea. 'I cannot conceive of anything more likely to demoralize the population and turn it from the higher type of race it now assumes back to that of mere South Sea savages,' he said in a letter to the Duke of Newcastle, secretary of state for the colonies. 'I cannot but think that the introduction of a number of half-savage youths at the period of life when their passions are least under control would be in the highest degree pernicious, and indeed fatal to the prospects of the community.'[10]

Young clearly envisioned a mob of untamed and lustful blacks making hay with the Pitcairn maidens, themselves only a generation or two from the wildly promiscuous Tahitians. It simply would not do. Newcastle, yet another Etonian, sympathised. 'I agree with you . . . and I have little doubt that your communicating with Bishop Patteson . . . he will readily abandon his intention.' Alas, Newcastle quite misjudged the fervour of his alumnus. Patteson and Selwyn were deaf to Young's objections and in 1863 they formally proposed that the mission be moved from Auckland to Norfolk and offered to buy a tract of land there from the £10,000 Selwyn had raised in England.

Suddenly a new complication arose when one of Patteson's supporters, Simon Young, decided he'd had enough of Norfolk and wanted to return to Pitcairn with his family. Patteson's response verged on the hysterical. 'I fear that you do not feel the real importance of this point on which I so greatly insist: i.e. *the most essential thing of all – the authorised ministration of the word and sacraments* [his italics]. You may not think that the ministrations of Bishop Selwyn or me, or Mr Nobbs are edifying – that is not the point. It is Christ himself, who by the hands of his ministers, regularly appointed, gives to His own people His own blessings.

'If you wilfully, and by your own act, deprive yourself and your family of this blessing, how shall you receive the blessing? Christ gives it in His own appointed way; what right have you or anyone to neglect His way, and yet think to receive the blessing?

'And if you are not doing right in going away from such privileges, you may be sure that you are not doing good to others. You will be encouraging them in a course that is not right. You ought to be using whatever influence you have to keep others from going from the blessings which you have at Norfolk Island and will *not* have at Pitcairn Island . . .'[11]

There was much more, but Simon Young and his family left anyway. The following year tragedy struck. In August 1864, Simon's eldest son Fisher, 18, and his friend Edwin Nobbs, 21, were travelling in the *Southern Cross* with Patteson on his latest mission to extract potential scholars from the islands when they reached Santa Cruz in the Solomons.

Patteson himself left a graphic, if curiously self-centred account, noting that, 'The people are large, tall and muscular. It is no doubt a very wild place – books of navigation will tell you it's the wildest in the Pacific.' Nonetheless he hoped to get 'two or three lads to come away with me'. So, on 4 August, he mounted an expedition in the schooner's whaleboat.

'There were six in the boat,' he says. 'Rowing and sailing along the coast I reached two large villages where I went ashore and spent some time with the people – great crowds of naked, armed men at each. About noon I reached a very large village at the northwest point of the island.'[12]

There he left the boat on a reef and waded alone the 200 metres to the village. 'In the boat they counted upwards of 400 men all armed (wild cannibal fellows they are) crowding about me,' he says. 'But you know I am used to that and it seems natural. I went into a large house and sat down. I knew only a few words of their language.'

His quest for scholars seems to have been unsuccessful, so he returned back across the reef with 'the people thronging around me'. The boat crew, including Edwin and Fisher backed the craft to meet him. However, once aboard, 'I saw men swimming about had got hold of it and it was evident from their expressions that they meant to hold it back. How we managed to detach their hands I can hardly tell you.

'They began shooting at once, being very close. Three canoes chased us as we began to get away – men standing up [in the canoes] and shooting [arrows]. Pearce was knocked over once, Fisher shot right through the left wrist, Edwin in the right cheek. No-one, I suppose, thought there was a chance of getting away.

'They all laboured nobly. Neither Edwin nor Fisher ever stopped their oars or stopped pulling. Thank God! a third Norfolk Islander, Hunt Christian and Joseph Atkin, an excellent lad of 20, from Auckland were not hit. Once dear Edwin, with the arrow fragment sticking out of his cheek and the blood streaming down (thinking more of me than of himself) called out, "Look out sir, Close to you." Indeed, but it was on all sides they were close to us.'

Finally they reached the schooner and climbed aboard. 'With difficulty I got the arrows out of Pearce's chest and Fisher's wrist,' he says. 'Edwin's was not a deep wound.' However, he knew, he says, that the Pitcairners were more susceptible than most to the dreaded tetanus, better known then as lockjaw. 'On the fourth day that dear lad Fisher said to me, "I can't think what makes my jaw so stiff." Then I knew that all hope was gone of his being spared.'

However, the bishop divined a bright side. 'God has been very merciful to me,' he writes. 'The very truthfulness and purity and gentleness and self denial and real simple devotion that they ever manifested and that made them so very dear to me are now my best and truest comforts. Their patient enduring of great sufferings – for it is an agonising death to die – their simple trust in God through Christ, their thankful, happy, holy disposition, shone out brightly through all. There was not one word of complaint it was all perfect peace.'

If so, this was indeed remarkable. Tetanus begins with mild spasms in the jaw muscles. As they increase in intensity they affect the chest, neck, back, and abdomen. Back muscle spasms cause arching, breathing problems and sudden, powerful, and painful contractions of muscle groups causing fractures and muscle tears.

Other symptoms include drooling, excessive sweating, fever, hand or foot spasms, and uncontrolled urination or defecation.

Patteson tended Fisher for several days. 'The last night when I left him at 1 a.m. only to lie in my clothes by his side he said faintly (his body then being rigid as a bar of iron), "Kiss me, Bishop." At 4 a.m. the last terrible struggle then he fell asleep.'

Four days later, Edwin exhibited the same symptoms. It took him eight days to die. But again, Patteson found consolation. 'For myself,' he says, 'it has been a season of much discipline. I hope it has done me good. It was hard to feel thankful that I was left. But God in great mercy took those who indeed were most ready to go.'

Patteson also received good tidings from a different quarter. In the two years since he had condemned the idea out of hand, Sir John Young had suffered a change of heart regarding the mission proposal. The departure of his namesake and other Pitcairners back to their distant islet alarmed him. If, as was rumoured, this turned into a mass exodus the result would be an administrative chaos that would not sit well with his masters in Whitehall. Moreover, the Pitcairners on Norfolk had welcomed a number of wayfarers and ne'er-do-wells into their society from the whaling vessels that frequented the place, thus forgoing the racial and social exceptionalism that had given the community its romantic status in the British imagination. And finally, he needed the money. Bishop Selwyn's £10,000 became very attractive to an administrator beset with demands on every side as tens of thousands of gold prospectors rushed the diggings on Lambing Flat, soon to commemorate the governor himself in the name of its principal township. Sir John conveyed his newfound enthusiasm to the churchmen.

Realising he now held the whip hand, Patteson hesitated. On his journeys he had landed at Curtis Island off the Queensland coast only 10 days sailing from the Solomons; and the colonial government was prepared to grant land there on condition that the school also took in local Aborigines. It was a tempting offer. However, in the end, according to Hilliard, 'Norfolk was chosen in preference to Queensland mainly because of the opportunity to "improve" the morals and intellects of the Pitcairners.'

Unmindful of such blessings to come, the Pitcairners on Norfolk were shocked when in a letter from Sir John to their chief magistrate, one of the Quintal clan, they learned the extent of the purchase of 'their' island – no less than 1,000 acres (400 hectares) of its most arable and desirable property. A series of rowdy public meetings followed. Outrage piled on heartbreak. Even Sir John's assurance that the money would go to the island's investments and would pay the £50 annual stipend for Reverend Nobbs did little to appease the agitators.

The pastor and spiritual spokesman for the community found himself in a perfect quandary. He had been the chief proponent among his fellows for close cooperation with the missionaries. And the presence of the bishop himself on the island for much of the year would add greatly to his clerical prestige. But Sir John's decision seemed to put paid to the firm belief shared by the Pitcairners that Norfolk was theirs by imperial gift. And there was no support coming from the Rossiters, now firmly ensconced at Government House.

Sir John turned for advice to his old patron in England, Sir Fairfax Moresby, now a Knight Grand Cross of the Bath and rusticating in Devon, but still highly influential in government circles. He in turn consulted the Earl of Harrowby, the former

Lord Privy Seal at the time of the migration of the Pitcairners to Norfolk. The news was not good, at least for those among them who entertained notions of self-determination. 'Their island,' reported Harrowby, 'was never promised them, nor a permanent exclusion of all other settlers. The measure was always as an experiment, and the work of carrying it out was clearly to be adapted from time to time according to the results. No doubt the whole process was to be made subordinate to their benefit, but was left to experience to decide.'[13]

Experience had clearly decided that the empire rules.

This was an issue that would arise many times in the next century and would remain unsettled – at least in the minds of some Pitcairn descendants – to this day. However, it at least provided Nobbs with an escape route from the horns of his dilemma. And a community born, quite literally, from original sin was unwilling to assert itself beyond much more than a symbolic protest. It continued to rankle, and more than a decade would pass before the two oddly distinctive communities achieved an amicable working relationship.

Meantime, the Pitcairners successfully avoided Rossiter's attempts to inculcate a farmer's work ethic and a sound knowledge of animal husbandry. They preferred a freewheeling life on the open ocean and, as whalers like Sam Warren regaled them with tales of their adventures, they devoted most of their energies to the hunt for the great mammals of the sea. Even Reverend Nobbs – perhaps recalling the excitement of his own seafaring days – supported their ventures. He told of one particularly frolicsome occasion to Admiral Moresby in December 1868 when a six-man boat commanded by Frederick Young speared a 'cow whale' some 5 kilometres offshore.

'The great animal,' he wrote (in part), 'very quietly turned the boat bottom up without staving a plank, and then went off some distance. The crew set about righting the boat but could not free her from water; however, they got the oars lashed athwart and though the gunwale was level with the sea, commenced paddling homewards.

'To their surprise they saw the wounded whale coming towards the boat, either supposing it to be her calf, which lay dead some two miles off, or actuated by a desire for vengeance. The crew leapt overboard; the irritated monster placed her head on the boat and there remained motionless for some time. Then she retired a short distance and the head-man swam back and got a lance ready, determined to use it if the whale came back again within reach.

'She did return and the dauntless Young, swimming up to her, thrust the lance several times into her spout hole! Feeling the smart, the whale settled down some fathoms, came up swiftly, and smashed the boat and oars into fragments.

'There was now no alternative but to strike out for land. One of the crew, an English sailor could not swim; but two of our people bid him put an arm on each of their necks . . . The last time they saw the whale she was in a very weak state from loss of blood but still remaining by the debris of the boat.

'And now for three long weary hours did the immersed whalers exert their energies to the utmost but, the current setting off, they had not gained more than a mile. The poor sailor was almost exhausted [and] a lad of 16, one of our own people was growing tired. That which seemed to alarm the lad most was the presence of immense sharks whose fins were continually coming in contact with his legs.

'At length my son Fletcher, seeing nothing of Young's boat for several hours, left off chasing whales and went in quest of it . . . After pulling nearly a mile the steersman fancied he saw three black spots in the water and said "Pull, boys! There they are!" Soon they had the three swimmers on board but they were afraid what had become of the other three, fearing they were either drowned or eaten by the sharks; but one of the rescued men said, "Pull on! The others can't be far off", and about half a mile further on they were happily met with, but in a most exhausted state. Another half-hour would have sealed their fate. No one was hurt, though the English sailor was still weak and pallid.'

CHAPTER EIGHTEEN

'Still cannibals and headhunters'

The Melanesian Mission on Norfolk, christened St Barnabas after the legendary missionary who accompanied St Paul, opened its doors for business in November 1866. Bishop Patteson had secured a very good deal in negotiations with the NSW governor – the entire 400 hectares, representing about one-fifth of the island's arable land, cost a mere £1,830/10/-.

He and his staff immediately set to transfer their scholars from Auckland to assist in building the accommodation, classrooms and chapel – as well as a road from Kingston to the mission. Patteson took the *Southern Cross* on another recruiting drive to the New Hebrides and the Solomons. More hands were needed to prepare the land for cropping and to tend the sheep and cattle that would supply meat and dairy to the inmates. And while he had been able to make only one annual trip from New Zealand to the islands – returning with about 60 scholars – now he could make several.

The mission farm soon proved a bonanza. Tropical and temperate fruits of every kind abounded — bananas, guavas, apricots, peaches, oranges and lemons were all to be had for the picking. And the full range of vegetables sprouted from the rich red soil. Which is not to say the operation ran altogether smoothly. As a New Zealand-educated housemaster, Charles Elliot Fox, was to record somewhat later, 'The people of the islands were still cannibals and headhunters,' and there was constant friction between the young men from different island groups.

'One Christmas Eve a New Hebridean stabbed a little Mala boy during a quarrel and blood flowed,' he says. 'In less than five minutes some one hundred and fifty Solomon Islanders had thrown off all their clothes and, stark naked, seized axes, knives, spears, anything that came to hand, and were in full cry after some 60 New Hebrideans, who for their part were going all out for the sea coast.[1]

'Below the school grounds were a number of small houses, one belonging to each island, where the boys used to cook the fish they had caught, and smoke, and enjoy themselves. The armed and naked Solomon Islanders rushed for those owned by the New Hebrideans to slaughter anyone they could find in them — but they were all quickly emptied except for one in which a quiet New Hebridean "head cook" sat smoking. As the Solomon Islanders rushed down to it they shouted "Anyone in there?" and the New Hebridean very wisely shouted, "No!" and the Solomon Islanders rushed on past it.

'These riots were not common but they did occur from time to time. On this occasion it was [the headmaster] who quelled it by the vigorous use of a stockwhip.'

All religious instruction was carried out in Mota, the language of one small island, chosen because it was the only Melanesian language within the ken of the first headmaster, Lonsdale Pritt. But according to Fox, 'There could not have been a better choice. It was a good foundation for learning other Melanesian languages later.' Fox himself was a gifted linguist and quickly picked it up. However, it took him some time to adjust to the islanders' temperaments.

The boys and young men slept on bare boards with a single blanket, and Bishop Patteson would go into the dormitories in the morning and pull the blankets off 'with shouts of merry laughter'. 'In the beginning,' Fox says, 'I did try something of the sort, and the sleeping dog suddenly became a raging tiger, leaping at me and wrestling me round the dormitory. These boys were the sons of cannibals and headhunters and not far below the surface in those days was a hot and fierce temper.'[2]

The daily routine followed strict timetable regulated by bells. A school day began at 6 a.m.; there were mattins at seven; breakfast in the hall at 7.30; and schoolwork for an hour and a half from eight. 'After morning school,' Fox says, 'the boys fell in and were sent out to work, each set to its particular job. Half a mile from the school were the large gardens which supplied us with food. Europeans and Melanesians worked these together daily, clearing, weeding and planting. We also kept in order five miles of island roads.'

Dinner was at 1 o'clock, and at two there were more scheduled classes followed by singing at three. 'Sometimes,' says Fox, 'we had what we called "working holidays", i.e. instead of school we worked from 8 a.m. to 5 p.m. on the gardens or roads. Some boys also learnt to milk and look after cattle, sheep and horses;

others worked in the printing and carpentry shops; others did the cooking.

'About a dozen boys cooked each week, with a white man at the head of them, who usually was someone fresh from Oxford or Cambridge who had never cooked in his life before, but he happened to be the last to join the staff.'[3]

According to David Hilliard, 'The ethos of the Norfolk Island school was less egalitarian than it was of a benevolent clerical paternalism. The model was the family with the bishop as the unquestioned head and governing mind, the clergy as older brothers and the Melanesians as children in civilization at various stages of development, to be helped, encouraged, taught, weeded out and carefully disciplined by the "unwritten law of love".'[4]

Christmas seems to have been the high point of the year, and it is clear that despite their High Church strictures, Patteson and his staff were prepared to accommodate some local customs. They encouraged the boys to present their own plays and dances. The New Hebridean dances were usually narrative dramas, while the Solomon Islanders imitated fishing, hunting or fighting. 'In the old days,' Fox says, 'dancing parties used to travel from village to village, and often it was exciting for the spectators as the dancers had weapons concealed and would suddenly fall on the spectators in the middle of the dance and slaughter them.'

On one occasion at St Barnabas, there was an echo of the 'old days' when the mission nurse, 'Sister Kate', was alone in the small hospital and was suddenly 'chased round the ward by a sick boy with a carving knife. She dashed into her room, locked the door, leaned out of the window and rang a large bell about 2 a.m. We all turned out on that dark night to search for the Solomon Islander with the carving knife. We found him in a deep ditch half a mile from the hospital, and his nocturnal wandering cured him of pneumonia.'[5]

Lonsdale Pritt's successor as headmaster, Robert Henry Codrington, a clerical fellow of Oxford's Wadham College, worked closely with Patteson and was the dominant figure during Patteson's many absences on recruiting missions. He would remain on Norfolk for 20 years studying Melanesian customs and language. He affected a patrician air, 'proud of his intellectual pre-eminence, a caustic commentator on the foibles of his colleagues'.[6]

Patteson was principally concerned with his charges' spiritual welfare. In High Church fashion, they celebrated all the major saints' days. For the daily chapel services, he arranged a connected series of psalms, Bible readings and narrative hymns in Mota, composed by himself, to commemorate the main sacred Christian events and doctrines.

On the Sunday the theme would be of Jesus's resurrection; followed in order by the 'gift of the spirit', the 'nativity', 'epiphany', 'betrayal' (although his hymn on Judas was considered to be so terrifying it was later omitted), 'ascension', 'crucifixion' and 'burial'.

Many fell by the wayside. Indeed, by 1868, 20 years after Bishop Selwyn's first voyages, apart from a few dying infants, only 26 Melanesians had been baptised, one of whom had died and two had fallen back into 'habits of indifference, if not utter neglect of their teaching'.[7] Of the remainder, only 12 had been offered for confirmation. That year, Selwyn retired from the field as Bishop of New Zealand, returning to England where he became Bishop of Lichfield in Staffordshire. The disposition of the £10,000 he had raised for the Norfolk Island purchase is unclear, although it may well have contributed to some elements of the mission. But overwhelmingly, St Barnabas was financed by Patteson's own substantial private income, royalties from a religious novel, *The Daisy Chain*, written by his relative Charlotte Yonge, and donations from churchgoers in Australia and New Zealand.

However, the mission could not have survived without the free labour provided by the scholars. This may well account for Patteson's refusal to condemn the Kanaka slave trade that was gathering pace in the South Pacific as sugar planters in Queensland and Fiji 'recruited' workers from the same islands as the bishop. He favoured a sterner regulation of the trade to protect the islanders from violence, fraud and murder. But he could divine undoubted benefits for 'pagans if they were properly treated and could see for themselves a functioning Christian society'.[8]

The islanders themselves could be forgiven for believing that they were being exploited from all sides. The European missionaries from the school, New Zealander Joseph Atkin and Irishman Charles Brooke, who returned with some of the boys and remained for a time on their home islands, reported 'difficulties' in dealing with the villagers. And when the returning scholars attempted to enlighten their fellows with their newfound Christian revelations, they were either ignored, banished or beaten up. By 1871 the situation was becoming seriously fraught as Patteson set out in April on yet another recruiting drive in the *Southern Cross*.

At almost every port of call he discovered that 'blackbirders' had preceded him. At Whitsuntide Island, many men had been carried off by a 'thief ship'; and nearby Merlev had suffered the loss of nearly every able-bodied man. In the Floridas, Patteson was told that 50 islanders had been lured aboard with trade goods and all had been carried off to Queensland. At another port Europeans on the same ship had dropped large stones from the deck onto the surrounding canoes then dragged the natives from the water and made off with them.

He spent three months at Mota where he had established a foothold 13 years before. The *Southern Cross* picked him up on 19 August and sailed to the Solomons to collect Atkin and Brooke, who were staying on San Cristobal and Nggela respectively. Brooke was full of fearful tales of confrontation by two hostile chiefs, but since he tended to dramatise his experiences 'after the fashion of the Irish' Patteson was unconcerned. They then headed eastward to the populous island of Santa Cruz and on 20 September anchored off the nearby reef-enclosed island of Nukapu. Patteson planned to use the small island as a springboard for the evangelisation of its big, populous neighbour.

According to the official version of the tragic events to come, on the morning of 21 September, Patteson conducted a Bible class for the new recruits on the ship, reading them the story of the martyrdom of Stephen. He ended the lesson with these words: 'We are all Christians here on this ship. Any one of us might be asked to give up his life for God, just as Stephen was in the Bible. This might happen to any one of us, to you or to me. It might happen today.'[9]

The reaction of the young initiates (if it really occurred) is not recorded. At 11.30 a.m. the ship's boat was lowered containing Patteson, Atkin and three native graduates from St Barnabas. The rowers pulled for the reef where six canoes awaited. When the boat reached the reef, the tide was out and it was impossible to row to the shore. So Patteson transferred to one of the canoes and was taken to the beach while the others waited for him in the boat. Three canoes approached the boat and the native paddlers asked where they came from. Atkin replied that he was from New Zealand, while his native companions were from San Cristobal (Bauro) and Mota. 'At this,' says church chronicler Graeme Kent, 'the canoes began to drift away. Suddenly the men of Nukapu discharged arrows at the men in the boat, shouting "This is for New Zealand man! This is for Bauro man! This is for Mota man!" The arrows tore into three of the four men in the boat!'

One of the natives was struck six times, another once, and Atkin was wounded in the left shoulder. The other native escaped injury by throwing himself to the bottom of the boat. They instantly retreated. 'In spite of their injuries,' says Kent, 'the four men managed to row back to the *Southern Cross* where they were helped on board by the horrified crew and schoolboys. Then they all turned their attention to the shore, wondering what had happened to the bishop.

'By then John Coleridge Patteson was dead.'[10]

The exact circumstances surrounding his death are still disputed. In the official church version, he was killed in revenge for the actions of a blackbirder who had recently visited the island. However, Hilliard says it is more likely that Patteson had unwittingly broken a local custom by giving a present to a lower-caste chief and 'either a smaller one or none at all to the Santa Cruz man who conceived himself the more important personage.'[11] All that can be said for certain is that after Patteson landed he and the village chief, one Moto, entered a palm-leaf hut and while Patteson lay down on a mat reserved for guests the chief went to get some food. When he returned he found Patteson dead, his skull smashed in by a heavy wooden mallet.

Meanwhile, Atkin was determined to return to the island with some of the schoolboys who volunteered to go with the party. The ship's mate, Mr Bongarde, armed himself with a pistol and took charge of the boat. By this time, the rising tide permitted them to pole their way over the reef, and when they arrived ashore they discovered the bishop's body already washed and prepared for burial by the village women. They returned with it to the *Southern Cross*, and the following day, far out to sea, Joseph Atkin officiated at the burial ceremony before committing it to the deep. Soon afterwards he began to suffer the fearful symptoms of tetanus, and both he and the wounded native succumbed before the *Southern Cross* reached Norfolk. The young Melanesian initiates on board believed that their new religion had died with the bishop, and it was only with difficulty that they were persuaded that 'school' would continue.

Patteson's 'martyrdom' in the Christian cause created a powerful emotional response in New Zealand and Australia, and a memorial fund was established in Sydney. Imperial Britain took more direct action. The government sent the HMS *Rosario*, an 11-gun navy sloop commanded by Lieutenant A. H. Markham, to Nukapu, arriving on 29 November. Markham shelled the island with two 40-pounders, then sent a well-armed landing party ashore to burn the village and destroy their canoes.

Markham reported the islanders' casualties as 'severe', although the number of dead and wounded was uncounted.

Patteson's memorial fund was used to build the lofty stone chapel of St Barnabas with imported Devonshire marble and stained glass windows by the British artist and designer Sir

Edward Coley Burne-Jones. The novelist Charlotte Yonge provided the magnificent pipe organ. Thomas Kendall, the missionary and gun-runner, came from New Zealand to oversee the felling and dressing of the pine logs for the outer shell. It was completed in 1880. By then Patteson had been succeeded, somewhat reluctantly, by John Selwyn, the second son of Bishop George Selwyn, and was only 29 when he was elected to the vacant see in 1874. 'I sometimes long with all my heart that they had not made me Bishop,' he confided to his mother. 'The inner spirit of it which my father and Bishop Patteson had so strongly is lacking utterly.'[12]

This meant that it fell to headmaster Codrington to provide the inspirational vigour to the mission, but the bumptious pedagogue was not temperamentally suited to the task. So for a time the enterprise languished. In this it reflected the falling fortunes of its cohabitants on Norfolk. The Pitcairners were themselves facing an impending social upheaval. By 1881 George Hunn Nobbs was preparing for his end. He wrote to his old friend and patron, Sir Fairfax Moresby, 'I am fast drifting towards death's bay . . . the fact cannot be concealed from others, as well as myself, that I am rapidly becoming a very old man. My good wife is also frequently an invalid.'

His community, which in 1869 had numbered 326, continued to grow from within. But they also accommodated visiting whalers, mainly from America, who brought with them a plentiful supply of spirituous liquors and – equally troublesome for Nobbs – the revivalist literature that was sweeping their country. The latter was made the more attractive by its being anathema to the Anglicans of the mission whose occupation of 'their' island – particularly when allied to Codrington's high-handed attitudes – many still resented. Nobbs was the only real conduit between the two communities. He called on the clerical staff to assist him in his pastoral duties. They responded willingly but they could only do so much to resist a general lowering of the moral tone. According to Raymond Nobbs, 'Throughout the seventies the references by the mission staff to the increasing "scandals of the town people" were not without foundation. The 11 cases of fornication which were actually brought before the chief magistrate's court in 1876 alone might well indicate a wider practice.'[13]

Nobbs decided to ask his youngest son Sydney, who had been ordained in 1872 in England and was now a curate in Chichester, to take his place as chaplain to the islanders. At first the Pitcairners objected strongly, but in time they had a change of heart and sent a petition offering him the role of clergyman and schoolteacher. Sydney declined. He apparently shared his father's aristocratic pretentions, for he changed his surname to Rawdon and remained in England as a clergyman for the rest of his life.

As Nobbs's health declined still further, he sought Codrington's help to secure a replacement from England, but no takers could be found. This was the situation when the New South Wales governor Lord Augustus Loftus, a minor aristocrat who had spent his life trading on his peerage, visited the island in April 1884. Accompanied by his son and aide-de-camp Lieutenant A. B. B. Loftus and a photographer to record his vice-regal progress, he stayed at the home of Francis Nobbs for the four days of his visit. According to his official report, he confronted the former Pitcairners at a meeting of the island parliament and 'deprecated the way in which the land was allowed to go to ruin'. Of the total 8,600 acres (3,480 hectares) of the entire island less than 180 acres (72 hectares) were under cultivation by the community. He strongly objected to their social exclusiveness and particularly objected to cousins being allowed to marry freely. By contrast, he argued that the presence of the Anglican mission was 'advantageous in every respect'. According to a *Sydney Morning Herald* report, the community accepted the vice-regal opprobrium 'calmly', then continued as before.

When the patriarch died on 7 November 1884 and was buried at Kingston among the departed officers and convicts of the two penal settlements, the community – now numbering 470 – was still without a spiritual guide. The vacuum was filled almost immediately by the arrival of a challenger to the Anglican dominance of both communities: the Methodist evangelists. In the New Hebrides and the Solomons, their revivalist message had struck a responsive chord, particularly after Patteson's death stripped him of the wondrous authority the natives had invested in him. And when his companion on that fateful voyage, Charles Brooke, had to be dismissed from the mission in 1874 for his scandalous homosexuality among the native boys, the standing of the Anglicans fell still further.

It was restored to some degree in the Solomons after a dispute between a Norfolk Island graduate, Charles Sapimbuana, and a local chieftain in October 1880 led to an attack on the crew of a British man-of-war schooner, HMS *Sandfly*, on a survey of the Nggela coastline. When a party led by Lieutenant Bower went ashore, three of his men were killed. Bower hid in the hollow of a banyan tree but was quickly discovered, bashed to death and partially eaten. The following month the British responded with a bombardment of the district by HMS *Emerald*, and early in 1881 the 16-gun HMS *Cormorant* arrived at the same time as the *Southern Cross* carrying Bishop Selwyn. They captured some of the murder suspects and after the pretence of a trial executed them on the spot.

Selwyn was 'uneasy' about the inherent injustice of the proceedings. But according to Hilliard, 'The Melanesian Mission had been demonstrated to be a political agent, linked on terms of friendship with the all-powerful British man-of-war. Not surprisingly, its position was thereby strengthened . . .'[14]

No such happy coincidence occurred within the Pitcairn community. On the contrary, only two months after the death of Pastor Nobbs, there arrived on Norfolk the Methodist missionary Reverend Albert H. Phelps and his equally committed wife. By 15 August they were preaching in the home of Parkin Christian to about 40 attentive Pitcairners. Two weeks later, they organised a gospel temperance meeting on the flat in front of Quality Row. However, their evangelising split the community, and on 5 October their opponents held a mass meeting in an attempt to prevent the formation of a formal Methodist Church on Norfolk. Opponents within the inextricable Pitcairn family mix came to blows and the chief magistrate, Arthur Quintal, was forced to swear in special constables in an attempt to restore order. He was only partially successful and the Methodist preachers continued to gain converts. Within two years, the former military barracks had been converted to a church and was dedicated to its Methodist doctrines in August 1886.

It was not the only division within the former Pitcairn community. Reverend Alfred Penny at St Barnabas at the time wrote, 'The Norfolkers of today, whatever else may be said of them at Pitcairn Island, may be divided into two classes: those who work and those who don't.[15]

'The industrious ones keep the lazy ones. There are many who are living in comfort, in well-built, pretty homes, their allotments stocked with every kind of produce which the soil will yield, owning a large number of horses and cattle; and in keeping with this material prosperity, ordering their households well, and bringing up their children in the fear of God, some to carry on the cultivation of the soil, others to follow the professions and trades in the neighbouring colonies.

'On the other hand, there are others who would starve were it not for getting a dinner here and a supper there because they won't work. If they did starve they would none of them be missed, but many of them have wives and little ones and for them the case is hard.'

Moreover, he said, those engaged in whaling made a 'trifling' profit, yet declined to buckle down to agricultural pursuits that offered a steady return. It was a story that would be repeated many times over the next century. However, in the late 1880s it was religion that set man against his brother and daughter against her mother. On 1 August 1888, a petition signed by 55 adult males demanded the deportation of the 49-year-old Albert Phelps and his wife. The preachers angrily rejected their marching orders; but the strain told on Albert, and two years later he died and Mrs Phelps returned to America. Nevertheless, they had planted a vigorous seed, and by 1900 more than 100 of the islanders followed the Methodist teachings.

By then yet another schism had appeared with the arrival in 1893 of two American Seventh Day Adventist pastors, E. H. Gates and A. Read – together with two visitors from Pitcairn – on an Adventist schooner named the *Pitcairn*. They had already made many converts on the 'home' island and within two months had recruited George Hunn Nobbs's fourth son Alfred, then the community's schoolteacher. When Alfred then declined to teach the Anglican catechism at school he was summarily fired, and according to Adventist Church records, 'suffered persecution such as having his water tanks drained'. This only served to enhance his resolve and in 1895 he took clerical orders in Sydney before returning to Norfolk as an elder and leader of the Adventist Church there until his death in 1906.

The civil authorities in London and Sydney were becoming increasingly concerned about the state of the island community, and in 1896 the British Government revoked the order in council setting up Norfolk as a distinct and separate settlement and moved to place it under the control of the Government of New South Wales. In February that year, the New South Wales governor, Viscount Hampden, visited the island and was shocked by the state of the place. Crops were rotting in the fields; animals roamed at will; much of the housing and all public buildings were neglected, dilapidated and unsafe; the people were ill-shod and the children seemed to be running wild. However, his principal concern was the appalling administration of justice.

He immediately appointed two commissioners, 'To make a full and complete inquiry generally into all and every aspect of the state of affairs in and the status and condition of the inhabitants of the said island, nothing excepted, and more especially into the mode of the administration of justice, the enforcement or observance of the laws or of any orders issued or proclamation made by any of my predecessors as governor of said island.' The full extent of endemic corruption would be laid bare. But whether that would lead to a sustained and worthwhile resolution was quite another matter.

CHAPTER NINETEEN

'Field-hands for the Lord'

In the 12 years between the death of George Nobbs and the arrival of Viscount Hampden there had been a complete breakdown of the island's administration. This was the inescapable conclusion of commissioners J. H. Carruthers and Charles J. Oliver, who reported their findings to the New South Wales governor at the end of March 1896.

The evidence sworn before them was damning. A Norfolk storekeeper, for example, pleaded for a law preventing cruelty to animals. Thievery was rife, he said, and cattle duffing commonplace. The acting schoolmaster Thomas Buchanan, seconded from the St Barnabas Mission, was equally blunt. He had found the school in a 'disgraceful' state. 'Every facility was given for living a life of immorality,' he said. 'Boys and girls used the same [water] closets. The school was undisciplined. The attendance was most irregular. The teacher was related to half the pupils and they were led to think that if they did anything wrong they would not be punished.[1]

'As to the morals of the girls, they were all right whilst at school,' he said, leaving the clear implication that home was another matter. 'The young men are terribly disappointing – they have little respect for God or man, and still less for women. Purity in life is little thought of. A girl who has made "a few slips" finds it no bar to getting married, and girls who are forced to get married come up to the altar without a blush of shame.'

On 14 November, Hampden returned on the HMS *Katoomba* and called a meeting of the islanders. He told them bluntly they had to become more industrious. It was 'not to their credit' that the island was overrun with wild tobacco and poison bush. 'Crime, serious and trivial, is rife; the moral tone is very low; and the administration of justice is a burlesque,' he said.[2] He then revoked all powers of governance from Norfolk Island and proclaimed new laws and regulations under the total control of the New South Wales Government. A Council of Elders set up in 1877 to regulate behaviour in the community was reconstituted as an advisory body of 12 elected annually from among all males over 25 who had lived on the island for at least six months.

He brought with him on the *Katoomba* a British Army officer, Lieutenant-Colonel William Warner Spalding, who boasted a CMG for services rendered the crown, probably in the Zulu wars, although the record is far from clear. He was sufficiently pompous and overbearing for Hampden to have chosen him as just the chap to pull the islanders into line, and the governor appointed him chief magistrate. Spalding in turn appointed his son, Lieutenant Willie Spalding, clerk of the court, and together they set about defrauding the crown by pocketing the fines and fiddling the books. They were shameless, treating Norfolk as their own private treasure chest to be raided at will. The islanders, led by Arthur Buffett, hit back with petitions and letters to the governor and open defiance towards both men. They were assisted in their campaign by the presence of Francis Nobbs as postmaster. This gave them a window into the chief magistrate's correspondence both to and from of the island.

When Buffett confronted the younger Spalding – appropriately enough at the Longridge Lawn Tennis Club – for his 'scandalous' activity, the lieutenant demanded 'a complete withdrawal and an apology in writing' otherwise he would 'immediately take proceedings against you in the Chief Magistrate's Court for libel, defamation of character and ill-treatment received at your hands, laying the damages at £20'.[3]

Since the case would be heard by Spalding Senior, Buffett knew he had been passed down the backhand line, and not only wrote the apology but paid the plaintiff a guinea for his 'legal expenses'. However, the incident would lead to the undoing of the Spalding regime when the petitions and protests brought G. E. Brodie, the New South Wales chief inspector of public accounts, to the island in May 1898. He was outraged by young Spalding's moral turpitude. 'He appears only to have learnt sufficiently of the duties of his office to enable him to act dishonestly,' he said.[4]

The Buffett case was sufficient for him to be summarily dismissed, but Brodie then discovered he had used his military title 'with a view of intimidating and extorting money' from the residents, involving 40 islanders on no fewer than 60 occasions. Clearly, Spalding Senior was totally compromised, but while the evidence against the lieutenant was damning – and he was sacked forthwith – the colonel remained at his post until the end of the year. Even then, he brazened his way out of any proceedings against him and remained on the island. He had secured a farm – Palm Glen Plantation – and a young wife who would bear him a daughter there in 1900.

By then his place at Government House had been taken by a much more congenial figure, the 76-year-old Charles Macarthur King, grandson of the man who founded the first penal colony on the island 110 years previously, Philip Gidley King. Charles had been born in England but spent much of his life in New South Wales farming and in public service. The appointment was a pleasant sinecure for his golden years, and he did little to disturb the status quo. He largely ignored Hampden's concerns about the drift in islanders' morals, particularly in their home life, where the governor had urged 'a stricter separation of the sexes'.

It was a theme that would run through public perception of the Pitcairners' relaxed attitude to intermarriage between family members and the exploitation of young girls. It would surface in the sensational trials on Pitcairn Island in 2004 when six men, all descendants of the mutineers, were found guilty of serious sexual offences against minors.

In 1898, the issue discussed by the Council of Elders concerned the age of consent set variously at 10 and 14 for consensual sex. The matter was put to the NSW crown solicitor George Colquhoun, who doubted the necessity of raising the age because, 'I should think from the origins of the people and the nature of the climate that girls in Norfolk Island would arrive at maturity earlier than in this Colony.'

On the other side of the island among the missionaries and their pupils, Norfolk was living up to its reputation as the Isle of Sodom. In the 1890s, three white missionaries had to be dismissed for their paedophilic activities with Melanesian schoolboys. Indeed, according to Hilliard, adolescent homosexuality was 'rampant' at St Barnabas during the 1890s.[5] Moreover, when they sent Melanesian missionary graduates back to the islands to proselytise, they indulged in 'adultery and fornication' to such a degree than the new bishop, Cecil Wilson, suspended no fewer than 13 teachers in 1899 alone.

When Wilson took over, aged 33, from Selwyn whose health was quite shattered, he had eight white missionaries, two Melanesian priests and seven deacons at his disposal. His see was spread over almost 3,000 kilometres of small islands containing a small and declining group of believers. Unlike his predecessors, who were Eton and Oxford graduates, Wilson went to the rather less prestigious Tonbridge School, and on a recruiting drive drew most of his missionary colleagues from his *alma mater*. But occasionally he was able to attract volunteers from the upper crust, such as Oxford graduate Guy Bury, who in 1911 arrived from his Reading curacy filled with enthusiasm. 'I have quite fallen in love with the Melanesians already,' he wrote to his family soon after his arrival. 'They seem excessively pleased to see one.' However, he differentiated between the northern and southern Melanesian, for whom he had little use. 'He is no gent,' he wrote, unlike the northerners who were 'real sportsmen'. 'Only a short time ago one of our [northern] teachers shot a man for not coming to school regularly; and if that does not show right feeling, I should like to know what does!'⁶ Bury died soon afterwards of iodine poisoning, having too liberally dosed his malignant sores.

Another Wilson innovation was the recruitment of island girls as college 'scholars', although their religious instruction was somewhat less rigorous than that of the male pupils. About 40 were continually on the island learning to read and write, cook, make and serve tea, and launder the clothes of the college. For at least three hours daily, under the watchful eye of Elizabeth Colenso, the estranged wife of a New Zealand missionary, they would sew and patch the 1,600 garments worn annually by the boys and themselves. Unfortunately, on their return home their newly acquired skills were regarded as suspicious and their superior airs led to severe beatings in a society in which a woman's status was very different from the concept so rigidly held within missionary society.

Wilson's tenure would last from 1894 to 1911, and would be marked by the need to compete for the souls of the natives with an influx of Roman Catholic missionaries as well as the evangelical Methodists and Seventh Day Adventists. The Catholics were particularly aggressive, moving into both the Solomons and the New Hebrides, where they spread the story that the Church of England had been founded by an adulterous king (Henry VIII) whose followers could never expect the kind of blissful afterlife promised by the One True Church.

The Anglicans were taken aback. Until then they had enjoyed an untrammelled access to the pagans, and it became increasingly clear that the concentration of their resources on distant Norfolk Island was putting them at a disadvantage. Wilson decided they must deploy their Christian soldiers in the field to counter the 'clever French priests'. 'We must have men settled . . . in the islands where, for 50 years we have sown the seed, or else others will gather in our harvest,' he wrote.[7]

This required even more missionaries, and Wilson redoubled his efforts to sign up 'Field-hands for the Lord' from England, Australia and New Zealand. By 1911 when he retired to become Bishop of Bunbury in Western Australia – as far as possible from Melanesia while still remaining in Australia – he left behind 29 male missionaries, including 12 university graduates, 10 of whom were from Oxford or Cambridge. Most were destined for postings to the outer islands but, alas, few would remain more than two or three years before abandoning their perilous posts for greener and more pleasant pastures. Gradually St Barnabas would begin its gentle fade from centrality to obsolescence.

The secular Norfolk Islanders too would engage the attention of the empire only fitfully as the Victorian colonial era gave way to the 20th century. The order in council promulgated by Governor Hampden in 1897 provided for the annexation of Norfolk Island to any federal body to which New South Wales might later belong. However, when the Australian Commonwealth came into being on 1 January 1901 there was no particular interest in bringing Norfolk into the fold. Indeed, there were tripartite discussions behind the scenes between Britain, Australia and New Zealand about how best to position the island within the imperial framework.

In May 1903, the New South Wales governor Sir Harry Rawson arrived on the HMS *Phoebe* for a brief tour of inspection. He was thoroughly unimpressed, and commissioned Alexander Oliver, president of the state's Land Appeal Court, to undertake 'a full inquiry' into Norfolk affairs. Oliver reported the following year that the island should be ceded to the Australian

Commonwealth. He also noted the appalling condition of the homes occupied by the islanders at Kingston and proposed new arrangements that would make them leaseholders at a nominal rental but with responsibility to keep the structures maintained.

This led to further reports from William Houston, Deputy Administrator of Norfolk Island Affairs, and John Watkins, a parliamentary draftsman who had been involved in the 1897 inquiry. They found that of the 5,000 acres (2023 hectares) of the island's arable farmland, only 350 (141.6 hectares) were being worked, and that was mostly within the mission. The former Pitcairners were more interested in the pursuit of the whales they spotted from their island lookouts, despite the precarious living gained from the sale of whale oil. Their reports also supported Oliver's suggestions regarding the squalid condition of most of the Kingston homes, and this would lead to a major crisis on the island.

After a great deal of surly negotiation, the government finally confronted the former Pitcairners in 1907 with occupation licences that required them to keep the houses in decent repair. The islanders protested. According to local historian Merval Hoare, 'A few people accepted the conditions and were left in undisturbed possession, but where the proposals were rejected the authorities decided that the houses should be vacated and possession taken by the crown. And so it came about that early in 1908 nearly all the occupants of the Kingston buildings were evicted.'

The action was deeply resented and even today it rankles with islanders. In 1948, an old resident, Gilly Baily, recalled the events clearly. 'I saw the soldiers disembark, rifles and all, as though they were going to war. They drove the old people out of their homes and, if they resisted, they carried them out. It was a cruel thing to do; I can never forget it.'

In fact, it not only improved the health and safety of the islanders; it gave the mainland a greater stake in the administration of the island, although it would be a further five years before the Minister for External Affairs, Patrick McMahon Glynn, steered the Norfolk Island Bill through the federal parliament.

In the interim, the islanders continued their obsession with the great mammals that passed by Norfolk during the migratory season from July to October each year. The whalemen would travel to the Ball Bay station by sulky or on horseback, carrying their hessian sacks containing food and tobacco. According to whaling historian Robert Graham Tofts, 'Their food was either leftovers from the night before such as Irish potatoes, sweet potatoes, pot roast or mutton which they would pool when they were ready to eat. There were also oranges, bananas and home made pies.'[8]

The pies were a legacy of decades of visits from the American wives of whaling captains who often travelled across the oceans with their husbands and were welcomed ashore by the Norfolk Island women. Sometimes the Island men would join a whaling crew and return with newfound expertise. Indeed, the island's first store, founded in 1886 by C. C. R. Nobbs, carried a wide range of whaling weapons and equipment, although it was not always of the hardiest quality. 'The whalers put their signatures on dockets [each season] when they went into the store to purchase their supplies – rope, copper nails, canvas for sails and paint were just a few things imported from New Zealand and Australia.

'Some of the ropes attached to the harpoons didn't last a full season and whales were lost. Ropes often snapped. Some of the whale boats were damaged by high tides and the waves crashing and rolling over the rocks.'[9] They hauled the great cetaceans ashore either at Cascade, Ball Bay or Kingston depending on the prevailing wind and seas. But even the best season provided more sport than commercial success; year after year whaling returned little more than a subsistence income.

When the new external affairs minister Hugh Mahon assumed control of the territory on behalf of the Commonwealth in 1914, he dispatched the head of his department, Atlee Arthur Hunt, to evaluate the island's state of development and its potential to become self-sustaining. While his time on the island was limited to only three weeks, Hunt had the benefit of two decades of policy development for the south-west Pacific and the advice of his lifelong friend, the island's administrator Michael 'Vince' Murphy, who had been closely involved in the royal commission of 1896 under Charles Oliver. Murphy enjoyed the respect and support of successive NSW and Commonwealth governments.

The resulting report to the minister would provide the foundation for Commonwealth policy for more than a generation. And it was as clear-sighted as it was devastating to the recalcitrants among the former Pitcairners, still asserting their rights to self-government.

By 1914, Hunt noted, there were fewer than 1,000 residents on Norfolk, of whom about 600 were former Pitcairners and whalers they had taken into their social network. The others were Melanesian students and missionaries, some Australian and New Zealand administrators and the small staff of the Pacific Cable Station who transmitted messages from Australia and

New Zealand via the undersea cable laid in 1902 to Canada and thence to the world.

The former Pitcairners, he found, were strong and capable 'when necessity drives or adequate incentive offers'. However, he said, 'Unfortunately, owing to generations of intermarriage of close relations, there are signs of decadence, which have become manifest in a more marked degree in regard to the intellectual faculties, though evidences of physical deterioration are not wanting.[10]

'They resemble children in many respects, they lack persistence and are easily discouraged; they lack initiative and need leaders. In manner they are courteous and affable though reluctant to disclose their real thoughts to outsiders. They are fairly truthful, but possess that weakness observable throughout the South Seas of always being ready to give such answers as they think most pleasing to their questioners.

'They have always been more or less spoon-fed and have come to look for assistance from outside as a right rather than a favour. They have scant knowledge of places outside their own Island and are ignorant of any bases of comparison and are therefore not ambitious for themselves as a community.

'Their very kind-heartedness has militated against them; lazy folk, because they are of the community and therefore closely inter-related, are always sure of their food and remain disinclined to more than the minimum of effort. No one works for the sake of wealth that constant work would bring . . . they *can* work hard and well but they need to be spurred in some way.'

Hunt rejected the charge that the islanders exhibited a 'low moral tone'. Instead, he found that 'This community will at present day bear comparison in regard to morals generally with any in the Commonwealth or the Empire'. This was probably due, he thought, 'to the supervision and careful guardianship of the excellent school teachers who have been supplied in recent years by the Education Department of NSW', though 'it is found that the children of pure Pitcairn descent are not as bright, and have not the same degree of application, as the children of outsiders.'

As a small, tight community they were 'helpful in adversity' and 'Every passer-by on the road stops to exchange friendly chat, and strangers walking, riding or driving are saluted with gracious courtesy.' Moreover, there was 'a complete absence of serious crime . . . thanks largely to the prohibition of manufacture or general sale of strong drink'.

He was unimpressed with the 'bastard jargon' they used in speaking among themselves. 'It is not picturesque nor effective,' he said, 'and justifies its description as "a barbarous attempt to garrotte the English language".'

He recommended greater powers for the administrator (who was also chief magistrate) to approve spending on public works within an annual budget and a continuing contribution from the federal government of £2,500 'for some years at least'. He poured scorn on the islanders' preferred occupation of whaling, particularly when 'In practically every occupation on the island antiquated methods and waste of effort are obvious.' He clearly drew on the experience of his old Sydney Grammar School chum 'Vince' Murphy for a vivid picture of whaling practice: 'When the cry of "fast boat" has gone through the island,' he wrote, 'and the people assemble to see the whale towed into the cobble beach at the Cascade landing, there is a scene of much animation but little method. Men set to work stripping the half-submerged body of its blubber, being assisted in this process by hordes of sharks who boldly venture into the shallow water.

'This blubber is then boiled in open cauldrons, whence the oil is ladelled into tanks, to be subsequently barrelled for export. There is no attempt at refining or grading so that consignees complain of uneven quality and bad colour; and there are no appliances for utilising the flesh or bones which elsewhere are the source of substantial profit. These are left to be eaten by the sharks, or to rot and profane the lovely natural air with the vilest of stenches.'

Not surprisingly perhaps, the Hunt Report was not released publicly, although the government of Prime Minister Andrew Fisher clearly accepted its recommendations. Murphy was given additional powers for budgetary initiatives as administrator and would remain in the post under various governments until 1920. Minister Mahon also dispatched an all-party delegation of MPs in December 1914 and they returned the following January with varied impressions of the island and its people. Most eloquent was Frank Anstey, the prominent Labor member, who was appalled at the architectural decrepitude, but especially among the convict buildings. 'Everywhere walls crumbling, roofs falling, doors hanging from their hinges,' he wrote. 'It is creepy in the daytime; at night, when the ghost birds give their cries to the wind and the desolation, you hear lost souls in their agony, the clank of chains, and you hurry by.

'It is a dead city. It once contained 2,000 men, the majority moving in manacles, the minority warders and soldiery. The humans – bond and free alike – have passed to their graves. Along Quality Row are the barracks and stores, loopholed for defence like castles of the middle ages. Further along are the houses wherein dwelt the doctors, parsons, priests and officers of convictism. The city – penal and industrial – its streets, and walks, its structures, its gardens, waterworks and sewerage system, are fast falling into decay. Today only a few families live within its boundaries.'[11]

Administrator Murphy's relations with the islanders would deteriorate over the period, particularly after 1916 when a copy of the Atlee Hunt Report came into the possession of storekeeper and community leader C. C. R. Nobbs. He and his followers protested that the island was theirs by gift of Queen Victoria and the Australian Government had no right to assume authority over their territory. During the Boer War the Norfolk Islanders had contributed their own tiny contingent. And in 1914, when the call to arms rang out through the empire, the islanders answered the imperial summons. No fewer than 77 volunteered for service. However, their numbers were insufficient for an independent unit and they fought in the New Zealand and Australian forces. Two were killed at Gallipoli and four wounded; and by the end of the war 13 young men had sacrificed their lives in the imperial cause while at least 20 others were wounded in action on the Western Front.

Atlee Hunt had recommended a form of compulsory military training so that a team of riflemen could repel an attack on the vital cable station from an invading force. But with the simmering tension between the administrator and the islanders, the matter was permitted to quietly expire of its own accord. By the end of the war there was little taste for rebellion; the returning diggers had broadened their outlook and most were content to resume the quiet life within the extended island family.

The war also had its effect on the mission. The carnage that decimated a generation of young Englishmen meant that missionary recruits virtually dried up. By 1918 there were five fewer Europeans on staff than 10 years previously; seven district stations were vacant. The workload became so great – and the support so meagre – that in October 1918 they mutinied. Eighteen clergy and lay workers passed a unanimous vote of 'dissatisfaction at the present working of the Mission'.[12]

Bishop Wilson's successor, Cecil John Wood, was mortified. A graduate of St Peter's College, Oxford, he had moved among the more socially prominent curacies of High Halden, St Marylebone and Bethnal Green before his appointment as Vicar of Wimbledon in 1906. It was a less than perfect springboard for his leap into the Anglican hierarchy as Bishop of Melanesia. And when his missionaries demanded a greater say in the operations of the diocese, he was undone. He resigned in disgust and returned to England, accepting a much lesser post as Rector of Witnesham in rural Suffolk. He would never again rise to the episcopal heights.

His departure marked the beginning of the end of the mission on Norfolk Island. His successor, John Mainwaring Steward, had spent 17 years as a missionary and would manage the closure of the St Barnabas facility in 1920. Together with the man who would become his successor, Frederick Merivale Molyneux, he would relocate their headquarters to Siota in the Solomon Islands. The Patteson memorial chapel would remain, since it was impossible to remove it, and it stands today as both a tourist attraction and a sad reminder of 50 years spent in imperial evangelical futility. Bishop Molyneux, a graduate of

Keble College, Oxford, would remain with the church on Siota until November 1931 when he resigned his diocese following a complete nervous breakdown caused by 'erotic involvements with men'.[13]

CHAPTER TWENTY

The new century

While the administrator was given increased powers, the Norfolk Island Act also provided for an Executive Council of islanders; and therein lay the seeds of endless rancorous disputation. It would be led for the most part by Charles Chase Ray ('CCR') Nobbs, the grandson of the patriarch, and son of Fletcher Christian Nobbs and Susan Quintal. Born on Norfolk only three years after the arrival of the Pitcairners, he was one of the few to receive a mainland education – at the King's School, Parramatta where in his final year he made prefect and played in both the First XI and the First XV. He then joined the Bank of New South Wales and rose to be acting accountant at Port Macquarie at 23, when he resigned to return to his island home in 1882.

The following year he was appointed manager of the Norfolk Island Cooperative Society, and when it was liquidated four years later he opened his own store. Married to New Zealand-born

Agnes Allen, he built a substantial home at Longridge, and like some other members of his family he cherished the myth of aristocratic descent, naming it *Moira* after his supposed great grandfather, Francis Rawdon-Hastings, the Earl of Moira.

The Executive Council consisted of 12 members, six nominated by the administrator and six elected annually by all adult islanders. They were essentially an advisory body, but were given some responsibilities for road maintenance, public reserves and the control of noxious weeds. Nobbs was a member almost continuously from 1917 and would be president three times. He soon became the leading commercial figure on the island and on occasion was said to hold title to a third of Norfolk's arable land as security for debts. Relations between the council and Murphy's replacement as administrator in 1920, Lieutenant-General John Parnell, were relatively peaceable. Parnell had risen through the ranks of army engineers to become commandant of the Royal Military College Duntroon. He was a radio enthusiast and on the island conducted classes in morse code and semaphore signalling. He took particular pleasure in constructing the Norfolk's first telephone line, which ran between Kingston and Cascade.[1]

However, within weeks of the arrival in 1924 of his successor Colonel Edwin T. Leane, hostilities broke out between Government House and the elected members of the council. Now 65, the prickly and outspoken CCR Nobbs saw himself as the guardian of the former Pitcairners' rights while Colonel Leane, one of Australia's most distinguished soldiers from the Great War, was determined to run the island 'by the book'. Leane at 56 had fought in the Boer War where he was commissioned in the field and enlisted in the AIF in World War I as a captain. He landed at Gallipoli and by the end of the war was in charge of all ordnance services for the entire AIF in France. He had been mentioned in dispatches five times, and was awarded the CBE and the Belgian *Croix de Guerre*. His brother, Brigadier Raymond Leane, won the Military Cross, the Distinguished Service Order and Bar and the French *Croix de Guerre*. According to official war historian Charles Bean, they were leading figures in 'the most famous family of soldiers in Australia's history'.[2]

The clash was inevitable and brought credit to neither man. They belonged to different worlds, and the most minor slights were magnified beyond measure. For example, when the administrator exhibited some of the splendid vegetables from the Government House garden in the annual agricultural show soon after his arrival, they were not entered in competition, but labelled as 'an object lesson' for the islanders. Nobbs and his cronies took this as deliberate insult. And when Leane brought an action as both prosecutor and chief magistrate against the McPhail family over goods taken from a harvest festival – and then refused an appeal – they became further incensed.

Nobbs now opposed the administrator at every turn. The situation degenerated further when the Anglican clergyman A. R. Martin joined in gestures of disrespect. Leane wrote him a sharp letter noting that, 'The rudeness shown by you to the administrator during the last few weeks culminated today [4 December] when, in the presence of two other government officials, you were guilty of not making the customary acknowledgement which is expected from a gentleman to those in authority, but which is the imperative duty of an official when the administrator enters a government office.

'Your action was studied and deliberately offensive. I have been very patient with you but will not overlook your impertinence any longer. I have decided to abolish the position you occupy with regard to the government of this island and to cease paying the emolument which is attached to it.'[3] Leane's attitude was patronising and partisan. Nor was his wife, the well-meaning but foolishly superior Katie Mary, any help in smoothing the waters. On the contrary, her message to the *Sydney Morning Herald* just before her departure for Norfolk that she proposed to bless the islanders with 'fresh interests and a wider knowledge of things musical and literary' only served to inflame the situation.

Leane pressed on conscientiously, repaired the public buildings, and for the first time began to recognise the heritage value of the prison and other structures of the convict era. Until then the islanders had appropriated the stonework as they required it for their own buildings. Leane sought to regulate the situation but approached the issue high-handedly and once again met determined resistance. Nobbs and his supporters peppered the mainland press and the federal government with protests, petitions and complaints. Finally in January 1926 the Prime Minister's Department responded and Governor-General Baron Stonehaven appointed the former New South Wales postmaster-general, Francis Whysall, to inquire into the situation and 'investigate any complaints by the residents of the Territory in regard to local conditions with a view to the suggestion of such remedial measures as may appear to you to be desirable'.

Commissioner Whysall arrived on the island the following month and was duly inundated with complaints orchestrated by Nobbs. He remained until April and took evidence from almost 100 witnesses. He published his report in July, and while he strongly supported Leane's achievements in the rehabilitation of public buildings, commercial initiatives and other duties, he was cutting in his criticism of the military man's inability to properly exercise his judicial functions as chief magistrate. While at first his approach had been 'sympathetic' to the islanders, he found this quickly changed and that he treated them as 'base and unworthy of respect'.

In a damning conclusion he wrote, 'The residents recognised the respect due to constituted authority, but their conception of the attributes of an administrator were rudely shattered by the extraordinary attitude adopted by Colonel Leane. It is manifest that in the exercise of his judicial functions his conduct was distinctly combatant [sic] and quite inconsistent with the principles of justice.' Perhaps more importantly, he was so clearly out of sympathy with the community he was called upon to administer that, 'In the interest of the Commonwealth and Norfolk Island, the present Administrator [should] be recalled without delay.' It was a resounding win for Nobbs. Colonel Leane was duly withdrawn, although it is significant that when he relieved the administrator of the Northern Territory, F. C. Urquhart, when he was on sick leave for six months, his tenure was quite uncontroversial.

On Norfolk the former administrator Vince Murphy was recalled until a new appointment could be arranged. The man chosen was a throwback to a much earlier time: Major-General V. C. M. Sellheim, the grandson of the notorious commandant James Morisset. Alas, the appointment was too much for the ailing general and he died within a year. So too did his successor, Justice Charles Edward Herbert, and for a period Norfolk had to make do with a professional public servant, H. S. Edgar, a former inspector in the Postmaster-General's Department. Mr

Edgar would remain on the island until his death, aged 90, in 1937.

In late 1929, the post was taken up by Colonel Alfred Bennett whose distinguished military career was followed by his appointment as headmaster of Waverley Public School in Sydney. He would begin his task with genuine enthusiasm, but confronted by the intractable CCR bloc on the Executive Council, he shut himself up in his residence 'seeing few people and admitting none to his confidence'.[4] And there he waited out his term until he could honourably depart in 1932, never to return.

However, later that year a new and well-connected figure arrived off Kingston in driving rain and strong wind to take over from the sad recluse. Captain Charles Robert Pinney, a Military Cross winner in the Great War, had been educated at Essendon Grammar, wounded at the battle of Lone Pine at Gallipoli and in 1918 married Mary Desmond, the only daughter of Sir Hubert Murray, who would head the Australian administration of Papua from 1908 to 1940. Pinney had served under his father-in-law as a member of the Legislative and Executive Councils and had applied for the post at Norfolk some years previously with the support of former prime minister Stanley Bruce. By 1932 the family included a daughter, 13-year-old Maura and her brother Peter, 10, who would later become the highly regarded author of a series of popular travel books.

It was too rough for them to land, but the faithful H. S. Edgar braved the seas in a whaleboat to welcome them, and as the weather calmed a little, Pinney and his small party joined them in the boat for the journey to shore and a waiting guard of honour of boy scouts and rovers.[5] They repaired immediately to Government House, which by then was in a state of serious disrepair with salt-sweating walls covered in hideous wallpaper, and in Mrs Pinney's words, 'furniture and carpets that might have graced some Transylvanian dungeon'.[6] It was, nevertheless, spotlessly clean.

Pinney set about inspecting his fiefdom. Norfolk's population remained about 1,000, the departing mission staff and scholars having been replaced by natural increase from the former Pitcairners, outside settlers (including some from Pitcairn) and additional administration staffers. At the school some 160 pupils came under the tutelage of a headmaster and four teachers, three of whom were young women.

Whaling still preoccupied many of the islanders during the season, but some progress had been made in developing the production and export of bananas and other tropical fruits. In 1932, growers shipped more than 18,000 cases of bananas to Sydney as well as a variety of vegetables and passionfruit. However, poor handling methods meant that the bananas especially failed to return an optimum price. Bean seed, another Norfolk specialty, was also found to be mouldy or infested with weevils on arrival.

Tourism briefly became the new panacea. In his 1914 report, Atlee Hunt had foreshadowed its development. 'To the Australian to whom a five days' voyage offers no terrors, Norfolk Island stands out as an ideal holiday resort,' he wrote. 'Tourists are accommodated in boarding houses about the middle of the island where, although space may be limited, no comfort that cleanliness, good cooking, and refined attention can provide is wanting to make them feel thoroughly at home. The island offers no excitement, unless for anglers who, if content to use the handline, and accept advice and assistance from local boatmen, are sure of excellent sport.'[7]

By 1932 little had changed, except that the SS *Morinda* had cut a couple of days off the round trip; but the lack of a decent harbour would be a continuing impediment both to tourism and commerce. Indeed, the unloading of *Morinda* via boatmen in lighters would be Pinney's first crisis when a dispute broke out over both payment and availability of local crews. It took firm action by the administrator to push through a resolution. But the real bane of his existence was CCR Nobbs, who by now had become so notorious a complainant to the Department of External Affairs and its subsequent incarnations that his correspondence was routinely marked by departmental officers 'Take no notice. File.'[8] The administrator on the spot had no such recourse. And as the Great Depression extended its skeletal fingers around the island's economic vitals the mood of the residents became increasingly fractious.

Nobbs's demeanour had been further aggravated by one ill-starred commercial venture after another. In the early 1920s, his cousin George Parkins Christian, who had spent many years in the American whaler *Charles W Morgan* – and, some said, in the Kanaka slave trade – persuaded Nobbs to finance the building of a substantial vessel, the *Resolution*, on the land behind Emily Bay (later the local golf course). They used Norfolk pine and followed Christian's plans to the letter. By 1925 she was ready to be launched and fitted out. The following year, with a local crew and cargo, the ship set sail for New Zealand 'with the hope of selling their produce and with great hope to export other commodities in the future'.[9]

Christian took charge as skipper. However, 'There were problems on the ship's first voyage because of lack of ventilation in the hull. The produce began to deteriorate causing a lot of the cargo to be condemned.' Christian returned to the drawing board and installed an engine to make a faster passage to markets but 'this became too costly and caused the venture to fail'.[10] The ship was later acquired by Burns Philp for trade between the islands, but in 1949 it sank mysteriously at its moorings.

This financial disaster for Nobbs followed similar setbacks when the lemon juice industry in which he had invested a small fortune collapsed from want of a secure supply chain and steady market. He opened a cinema and while it was popular with the locals it soon required an electricity subsidy to remain viable.

By 1934 the island was facing a crisis. People were departing for the mainland. Protectionism in New Zealand had closed the market for oranges and fresh vegetables, and poor banana prices in Sydney meant planters could barely feed themselves and their families. Pinney secured an advance for the growers from the federal government but it did little to ameliorate their plight. Nobbs became so obstreperous as president of the Executive Council that Pinney was forced to act against him. On 19 May he won a vote from two-thirds of the elected and appointed members of the council to remove his *bête noire*. Nobbs vacated the chair and Eustace Christian was elected in his place. However, Nobbs was by now ungovernable and sued the administrator for £3,000 for having 'wrongly and unjustly' removed him from office. A Sydney judge heard the case on Norfolk in 1935 and awarded Nobbs £2.

Nevertheless, he was an effective community organiser and was untiring as chairman of the school and hospital boards and as a patron of island sport. He had been inducted into Freemasonry on the mainland and attended meetings whenever he visited New South Wales. He was never able to satisfy the ruling body in Sydney that Norfolk merited a temple, but the former Pitcairners constituted their own closed society, albeit with frequent and quarrelsome divisions.

Nobbs was not the only infuriating individual to haunt the administrator's nights as the surf pounded endlessly on the Kingston bar. James Macarthur-Onslow, a ghost from the island's past as descendant of the man who led the New South Wales Corps in their mutiny against Captain Bligh, had arrived on the island in 1933 after a rambunctious past that had seen him disinherited and bankrupted by his father. He and his wife, Constance Herbert, a former actress, were quickly accepted into the society of those whose ancestors had also mutinied against the irascible Bligh, the more so because he shared their aristocratic pretensions, albeit of the Bunyip variety.

He pressured the government medical officer to permit him a weekly liquor permit despite the general prohibition, and he entertained flamboyantly. He disdained the administrator and became the focus of opposition to the disaffected. In May 1934, he had the gall to threaten Pinney with his recall and offered to lease his Norfolk property. Pinney fumed but there was little he could do until Macarthur-Onslow defied his orders and began to organise a local troop of light horse. At the time the radical right wing New Guard, whose Colonel de Groot had disrupted the opening of the Sydney Harbour Bridge, was giving the authorities deep concern. Macarthur-Onslow's actions could not be tolerated. The government authorised Pinney to apply the controversial Immigration Restriction Act of 1901 whereby a person could be deported if he failed a dictation test in a language of the government's choosing.

Pinney ordered a test of 50 German words, which Macarthur-Onslow failed when his only correct rendering was of 'Kamerad'. Convicted as a prohibited immigrant, he was imprisoned in one of the old convict cells. His supporters on the island responded with cables and letters to the Prime Minister Joe Lyons and Opposition Leader Jack Scullin threatening a 'breach of the peace' unless Pinney and his official secretary Captain Eric Stopp were immediately recalled. Nobbs organised a public meeting in Rawson Hall and 400 applauded Constance's appeal for support. They demanded a 'stay of execution' and recorded their 'abhorrence' at the use of the German language for the test. But all to no avail. The family, including their two-year-old son, were shipped aboard the *Morinda* on 12 July, returned to Sydney and disappeared from history until Macarthur-Onslow's death in 1959.

Pinney's father-in-law, Sir Hubert, applauded his 'very brilliant victory' and despite petitions for yet another royal commission, the administrator was reappointed in 1935 to a further one-year term. The Minister for Territories, Sir George Pearce, visited in March, and Nobbs, now president of the Norfolk Island Association, reprised his complaints from the days of Colonel Leane. However, Pearce was unimpressed and supported both Pinney and Captain Stopp ('a man of bustle and snap'). He did, however, decide to replace the Executive Council with a fully elected eight-member Advisory Council. Once again Nobbs was successful in the election and the members voted him into the presidential chair.

Pinney too was reappointed to his post for a further one-year term, although the strain was beginning to tell on his health. In June 1936, he suffered a heart attack but recovered quickly, and in his annual report was able to strike an optimistic note: 'While the force of economic circumstances during the past four or five years has caused many residents to look to the government for assistance, the spirit of self-reliance has not been destroyed, and with the growing tendency for all sections to work in harmony, future prospects are encouraging . . . the morale of the community is definitely higher than a year ago.'

In December Pinney took leave with the family after the Christmas celebrations and arrived in Sydney in time for New Year. On his return he dealt with a series of battering storms that isolated the island for long stretches. But by now the worst of the Great Depression was over and in a month nearly a ton of fish was exported to Sydney from a cold storage factory established under his jurisdiction. His appointment was due to expire on 30 June, but in May 260 residents, including 202 Pitcairn descendants and their families – led by the new Advisory Council President, Cobby Robinson – petitioned the government for a two-year extension. However, the implacable Nobbs would have none of it and forced through a motion at the next council meeting that 'The term of office of any administrator or official secretary should in no circumstances extend beyond three years unless on the express wish of at least two-thirds of the electors.' And his Norfolk Island Association supported the demand for Pinney's departure.

Pinney accepted the rebuff, and with his family finally left in sadness and regret on 4 November 1937. While he attempted to find further administrative posts, his health was broken. He moved to the Bowral district, where his condition gradually deteriorated. He died at 62 in November 1945. It was of scant consolation that his nemesis, Nobbs, had passed away, aged 89, eight months after Pinney had left the island.

The new administrator, Sir Charles 'Rosie' Rosenthal, a remarkable character – distinguished architect, brilliant military commander and an accomplished musician with a rousing baritone – would head the island's administration for a record nine years. He would organise a volunteer infantry unit at the outbreak of World War II and manage the influx of several thousand servicemen from Australia, New Zealand and the United States. Once again Norfolk Islanders enlisted in the Australian services, and of the 80 who volunteered, nine made the ultimate sacrifice.

In August 1942, American and Australian engineers arrived to survey a suitable site for an airstrip. They chose the plateau of Longridge, where an avenue of 500 pines had stood since convict days. There followed a massive building effort, and the aerodrome was completed in only three months. On Christmas Day 1942, New Zealand Air Force planes flew in Christmas cheer for the Kiwi troops stationed at strategic points around the island. Shortly afterwards, a squadron of Hudson bombers began dawn to dusk patrols from their Norfolk base. The following year, a radar station was established. However, no contact was made with the enemy, and the island's main function was as a staging base for aircraft heading to and from Australia and the United States.

Nevertheless, the war brought some important changes to the island. The village of Burnt Pine, adjacent to the airport, was developed and expanded; a twenty-bed hospital was built;

the prohibition on alcohol went out the window; and some new blood entered the communal arteries – either by accident or design. But it was the airport that would bring about the transformation of the island's economy. From 1948, when control passed to the Federal Department of Civil Aviation and both Qantas and New Zealand National Airways began operating regular services, mainland tourists began discovering the calm beauty and historic significance of the island. Sir Charles Rosenthal, who had remained on the island following his retirement in 1946, had developed a program to preserve and protect the convict buildings from further dismantling by the islanders. And he vigorously encouraged the development of a tourist industry.

Alas, on both counts, the former Pitcairners were reluctant starters. They had no connection with – or interest in – the terrible convict saga; its partially ruined buildings were alien grotesques or free supplies for their own building projects; and they had no particular desire to encourage hordes of 'outsiders' to interfere with the languid routines of their insular lives. So while tourism boomed briefly, with Qantas planes on a weekly schedule until 1955, the following year the service was halved to one flight a fortnight.

For the islanders of Pitcairn descent, 1956 was a momentous year: the centenary of their arrival on the land they believed had been gifted to them by Queen Victoria. They devoted countless hours organising a week's festivities beginning on 8 June – Bounty Day. The administrator of the day was yet another military man, Brigadier Colin Norman, one of the Rats of Tobruk who had earned both a DSO and an MC in North Africa and New Guinea. He formed a committee of residents to develop plans for the occasion and Governor-General Sir William Slim headed a guest list of federal government dignitaries.

More than 900 Pitcairn descendants re-enacted the landing at Kingston Pier in traditional costume, picnicked beside the ancient prison walls and made merry for the rest of the week. It was an occasion that drew public attention from across the world. But then, instead of opening their arms in an expansive gesture to the wider community, the islanders returned to their favoured endeavour: the pursuit of the leviathans of the deep with harpoon poised to strike. Whaling was back with a vengeance.

In the first year of hunting – 1956 – the islanders scored their full quota of 150 whales, and over the next five years they even increased their catch, but by 1962 their predation had produced the inevitable result – their chaser captured only four whales. The game was up. This coincided with a downturn on the mainland, which slashed the tourist trade and Norfolk's economic refugees packed up and made for Australia or New Zealand. The population fell from a high of more than 1,200 to little over 800. And with hardship came the usual dissension in the ranks.

The Minister for Territories, Paul Hasluck, had been among the guests at the centenary celebrations, and as a keen historian he was greatly taken with the heritage values of the penal colony ruins. He instituted three separate studies and developed a pres-ervation program at the Commonwealth's expense. Moreover, he ordered his department to prepare plans to transform the Advisory Council to a legislative body that would have real powers and responsibilities. In May 1959, Hasluck travelled to the island and offered to hand over to the council all Norfolk revenue from liquor excise, motor vehicle registrations and other similar Commonwealth sources; to maintain the airport at Australia's expense; to pay the administrator's salary and upkeep; to transfer the ownership of all Commonwealth plant and equipment without charge; and to continue the annual grant of at least £32,000.

However, he raised the prospect that the island would also need to raise funds from its own population. And while the council willingly accepted the deal, when elections were held in 1960 the newly constituted legislature reneged. In a roar of resentment against perfidious Australia, the establishing ordinance 'was literally torn to shreds and thrown to the floor of the Council Chamber'. And while the council remained in place, its powers were largely in abeyance, and the gremlin of mutiny was again loose among the former Pitcairners.

In 1963, Hasluck responded with another Norfolk Island Bill in line with their demands, saying, 'The people have preferred . . . reliance on the [Australian] Government rather than accept responsibility in large measure for raising their own revenues and administering their own affairs.' The Labor opposition spokesman, Kim Beazley Sr, said, 'While supporting the Bill, I think we should take this opportunity to express disappointment that a group of people should not wish to govern themselves, and also surprise that the descendants of the *Bounty* mutineers should not want to govern themselves. I hope that in the near future there will be a change of view . . .'

It was a vain hope. Resentment continued to simmer, and in 1964 their cause was taken up by a long-time resident, H. S. Newbery, who had persuaded himself that the territory was 'a distinct and separate dominion' and all the legislation imposed by Australia since 1856 was invalid and unconstitutional. As a test case he refused to enrol for a council election as required by ordinance, and when convicted appealed to the ACT Supreme Court. Newbery conducted his own defence in the case heard before Justice Eggleston, who summarily dismissed his claims. However, the islanders continued to agitate with petitions to the United Nations and demands for royal commissions. Administrators from the retired ranks of the Australian military came and went in short order, often at a cost to their health, until in 1964 a New South Wales farmer turned politician, Roger Bede Nott, took up the post following a successful term as administrator of the Northern Territory.

Nott was determined to make the island self-sufficient in food and he imported seed wheat from his own farm, which he made available to Norfolk landholders. The following year, 66 acres of top quality wheat – the largest crop since convict days – was harvested from several farms. Nott also imported sorghum and other grain seed as well as new breeds of livestock, particularly Landrace pigs, which thrived in their new home.

But with the mid-1960s upturn in the Australian economy, tourists were returning and the council, which by this time had become monumentally recalcitrant, was 'far more interested in tourism than agriculture'. The island's agriculture officer departed in frustration, and it was several years before a replacement was appointed. Nott himself left in 1966.

The councillors did, however, take time out to offer a haven from the French nuclear tests on Mururoa to their relatives on Pitcairn, where numbers were declining. The response from the Pitcairn leader, John Lorenzo Christian, was gracious and expressed 'deep thanks for the invitation to settle on your beautiful Norfolk Island, subject to the French tests . . . we shall be happy to accept your invitation if urgent exigency requires . . .' In the event, the Pitcairners remained on their tiny rock, although there were mutual visits between the islanders and a steady stream of correspondence.

By the end of the decade, tourism had reached unprecedented heights, with almost 10,000 visitors annually. Norfolk Island struck its own commemorative postage stamps, which became a big money-spinner; tax avoidance schemes were attracting mainland clients; and Commonwealth grants totalled more than $66,000. A wave of prosperity swept over the island. But instead of assuaging the perennial discontent it only encouraged the islanders to greater excess, and in 1972 they petitioned the Queen to save them from Australia's unfeeling grasp.

Buckingham Palace let that one pass through to the 'keeper. But two years later Queen Elizabeth, Prince Phillip, Princess Anne and Lord Louis Mountbatten visited on the Royal yacht *Britannia*. Though the royal party spent only 12 hours ashore, the visit would no doubt have left an indelible impression. They travelled to a favoured lookout – thereafter named in honour of the Queen – that gave a panoramic view of the prison ruins where the victims of her predecessors' governments had suffered so egregiously. But the highlight of the afternoon's entertainment was a burlesque performed in skimpy tutus by four of the hairiest and burliest men among the Pitcairner descendants.

As the report of the day recorded, 'It must have been a unique experience for Her Majesty to see classical dance performed by burly men dressed as ballerinas in tutus, singlets, wigs, socks and ballet shoes. Prince Phillip grins widely as he turns to see the reaction of the Queen who appears to be stifling much more than a smile. The rest of the royal party looks on in disbelief before also laughing at the sight in front of them. Perhaps nowhere else but on Norfolk Island with its laid back nature and unique humour would this performance ever have been considered as a suitable inclusion in a royal performance.'

More seriously, the visit added fuel to the constitutional fire. The islanders agitated remorselessly for change. Finally, in 1975, the federal government commissioned Justice Sir John Nimmo to report on 'the future status of Norfolk Island and its constitutional relationship to Australia; and the most appropriate form of administration if its constitutional position were changed'. The result was the most thorough and judicious appreciation of all the elements at play. His description of the population was devastating. He had unearthed, he said, a faction-riven community, of 'Pitcairn descendants, traders, operators of tax avoidance schemes, retired people and new farmers, all constituting divergent interests. A superficial friendliness and conviviality masks a deal of resentment and dislike among some of the groups.'

His recommendations, which incorporated a High Cou decision that refuted island claims to independence, we unequivocal: Australia should either abandon the isla completely or accept responsibility for maintaining it as a via community. If they chose the latter, then it should becom territory of the Commonwealth and the residents Austra citizens. As there were far too few to constitute a sep electorate, the voters should be included in the electora Canberra to give them representation in the federal parlia The Pitcairn descendants would lose their special statu council would be abolished and replaced by a Norfolk Territory Assembly with powers to raise revenue and an annual grant from the Commonwealth. Most importantly, the islanders would henceforth pay income tax.

The day after the news broke on Norfolk, about 24 Pitcairner descendants (and one former mainlander) conducted a house-to-house poll asking residents to choose between Nimmo's recommendations or for Norfolk Island to remain a '*distinct and separate* Territory of Australia with its own system of laws, benefits and taxes'. The result was 36 for Nimmo and 467 for the Pitcairner-backed alternative. There followed months of bickering before yet another Norfolk Island Act passed through the parliament in 1979. The council became the Legislative Assembly, consisting of nine seats. Electors would cast nine equal votes, of which no more than four could be given to any individual candidate. Four of the members of the assembly formed the Executive Council, led by a chief minister. This group would devise policy and act as an advisory body to the administrator. Residents were entitled to enrol in a mainland electorate where they had family connections, or in the seats of Canberra in the ACT or Solomon in the Northern Territory. Enrolment was not compulsory, but once enrolled they had to vote.

Since the 1979 arrangement, successive federal governments have sought to reconcile continuing Pitcairner demands with their obligations to racial discrimination laws, and to responsible budgeting versus the sense of entitlement that still actuates many of the descendants of the *Bounty* mutineers. One parliamentary report has followed another, and in 2003 the External Territories Committee chaired by Senator Ross Lightfoot made disturbing findings.

They reported that 'the majority of the community are peaceful and law-abiding, hardworking, conscientious, possessing a strong sense of civic duty and with an inherent ethic of supporting those in the community who may be less well off. Yet evidence available to the committee points to the fact that elements within the community are able to exploit the current governance system, with its lack of effective checks and balances, for their own ends. It has become increasingly clear that beneath the surface informal mechanisms can and do operate with relative impunity. The committee has grave concerns that a culture of fear and intimidation has taken root on the island to the detriment of the majority of the community.' Senator Lightfoot cited acts of arson and physical assault to pressure some residents to leave the island; misuse and abuse of political power; interference with mail, email, the monitoring of telephones and 'other more subtle forms of intimidation'.

CHAPTER TWENTY-ONE

'Fascinate and horrify'

Lightfoot's findings took on a darker shade than the usual revelations of favouritism and self-seeking among the highly complex family relationships because at the time the Australian Federal Police were investigating the first reported murder on the island since 1893.

On 31 March 2002 – Easter Sunday – the body of 29-year-old Janelle Patton was found, wrapped roughly in black plastic, at the Cockpit Waterfall Reserve, adjacent to the abandoned Cascade whaling station.

She had been beaten with a blunt object and had several defence wounds to her hands and arms. She had suffered a fractured skull, broken pelvis and broken ankle. She died from a stab wound to the chest that punctured her lung.

In a heart-breaking coincidence, Janelle's parents, Ron and Carol, who had honeymooned on the island 34 years previously, had flown in from Sydney the day before to join her for a short, sentimental holiday. That evening she had treated them to fish and chips at the Castaway Hotel, where she ran the dining room, before they returned to their nearby Panorama Gardens resort. They arranged to meet for a tour of the island at lunchtime the next day.

In the morning, petite but well muscled, and wearing her dark hair in a ponytail, Janelle worked her usual breakfast shift at the Castaway before driving herself back to the cottage she rented from 'Foxy' McCoy and his wife Ruth. On the way she stopped off at the Foodland supermarket, where unexpectedly she met the elderly Ruth and gave her four Easter eggs for her young relatives.

When she reached home she changed into a singlet and shorts for her usual vigorous late morning walk. She headed along Rooty Hill Road to Queen Elizabeth Lookout, where she was seen 'chatting to one or maybe two people who were sitting in a car'.[1] That was the last sighting from a witness who knew her. By now it was somewhere between 11.30 and 11.45 a.m. About that time, golfers playing in the Kingston area beneath the lookout later reported hearing a blood-curdling scream. Then silence.

In the early evening at Cascade on the northern side of the island, two New Zealand tourists out for a stroll came upon Janelle's body. Shortly before 6.30 p.m. they called the police, who hurried to the site and established a crime scene. By now the Pattons had reported their daughter missing and were on the way to the police station. Detective Sergeant Brendan Lindsay had the unenviable duty of breaking the crushing news. While Ruth McCoy accompanied the police to identify the body, a local GP admitted the Pattons to the island hospital, where they remained in gentle care for several days.

Sergeant Lindsay reported to Australian Federal Police Headquarters in Canberra, and by Tuesday a charter plane had delivered a forensic team and a pathologist to the island. The following day, Detective Sergeant Bob Peters arrived to take charge. He would remain with the case for the next five years until a New Zealander, Glenn McNeill, was convicted of the murder by a Norfolk Island jury. McNeill was sentenced to 24 years, which he is currently serving in Australia at Lithgow Correctional Centre. McNeill pleaded not guilty at his trial, but following his conviction admitted some involvement in the crime. However, he now claims – in phone and personal interviews with the author – that two others killed Janelle and that his only part in the tragic events of Easter Sunday was to dispose of the body. McNeill's revelations would reveal much about Norfolk Island today.

Peters's investigation revealed that in the two years Janelle spent on the island she found herself in a unique milieu, very different from the moral norms she had known in her previous 27 years under the roof of her parents' home in the leafy northern Sydney suburb of Pennant Hills. She had matriculated from the local high school, where she was academically above average but where she also displayed a character trait that would become more apparent later – a self-assertiveness that sometimes brought her into conflict with friends and associates. She dropped out of university in her first year to join a major bank, and over the next few years gained further experience in both Australian and international banking houses. Her last job on the mainland – from 1997 to 1999 – was as a junior executive with IBM. She had an active social life and two serious relationships, the second in Sydney with Rick Battersby, a seaman in the Royal Australian Navy. It was this volatile – and at times physically abusive – love affair that triggered her decision to leave Australia for Norfolk Island and its emotional tranquillity . . . or so she believed.

Soon after her arrival she took up with a Canadian, Larry Perrett, and they lived together in Dead Rat Lane in Burnt Pine. The relationship quickly ran into difficulties and at the urging of a workmate at Foodland supermarket, Susan Fieldes, she moved into a room in the home of long-time resident Charlie 'Spindles' Menghetti. However, when she learned that Fieldes, a married woman, was having an affair with Menghetti, she confronted her and this would lead to a physical brawl in a pub bar.

Menghetti also took issue with her attitudes and Janelle moved into the home of his brother Paul, nicknamed 'Jap', a middle-aged widower who lived with his children on a farm in the west of the island. They cohabited for nine months before conflict with the eldest children led to her departure to Foxy and Ruth McCoy's cottage. She later discovered that while she was living with him, Jap had been having an affair with Robyn Murdoch, then chief executive of the Norfolk Island Administration, who lived in Quality Row. (They would later marry.)

She then took up with Laurence 'Bucket' Quintal, who worked in the building industry, but the relationship quickly descended into mutual physical abuse. Other lovers – most relatively brief affairs – included barman Shane Warmington, tourist Brent Wilson, and a one-sided (on his part) romance with 38-year-old carpenter Raymond 'Tugger' Yager.

Detective Peters interviewed them all, and gradually eliminated each from his list of 'persons of interest'. He was assisted by the discovery of Janelle's diary, which portrayed in graphic terms her social life with the islanders. It also revealed the distance she had travelled from her days as a rising young bank executive in Sydney's northern suburbs. For example on Tuesday 29 January 2002, '. . . Saw Bucket at Foodies – invited me out to tea (Chicken and salad) Basically only wanted a root so I left . . .'

One of the more interesting aspects of the diaries is the absence of any mention of Glenn McNeill who, according to the prosecution case, would commit a crime of uncontrolled and passionate rage against her person. Yet for almost all of her two years on the small island McNeill was involved in the same tight-knit hospitality industry.

Glenn McNeill was born in Christchurch in 1978, the youngest of three children. His parents, Peter and Lynne, moved the family to Nelson on the northern tip of New Zealand's South Island when he was a youngster. According to his mother, he was 'a peace-loving child without an ounce of violence in his body'.[2] He particularly enjoyed school holidays with his grandmother in the coastal resort of Mouteka. According to his sister Erica, 'Glenn was not a great scholar; none of us were, but he was always active and played cricket and then lawn bowls with our grandparents. He attended Nelson Polytech and got his first two bars in chefing then moved to Omaru when he was about sixteen.' There he boarded with relatives, returning to Nelson when he was 18 and scoring a position as trainee chef at Seifried's Vineyard Restaurant in the picturesque Appleby district on the outskirts of the town.

Erica says, 'He was a drifter and also a ladies' man, which did cause some upsets with Scott, his older brother.' He moved to the Quayside Restaurant and Convention Centre in the heart of

Nelson the following year. It was there he met Aliesha Taylor, who worked in the Carter Holt Harvey sawmill as a wood planer in the mill as well as taking a turn at the reception desk.[3]

Glenn and Aliesha moved to Norfolk Island in June 2000 and both quickly gained jobs in the hospitality industry. They lived in a flat in a small dead-end street, Little Cutters Corn. Glenn became a chef at the Mariah Restaurant of the Hillcrest Hotel, one of several tourist resorts in the area, while Aliesha worked in the hotel's reception. They kept to themselves and in January 2002 they returned briefly to New Zealand to be married at her parents' Mouteka deer farm.

Two months later Janelle Patton was murdered.

Detective Peters's investigation quickly ran into trouble. His case had all the elements of a murder mystery novel – the suspects limited to the 2,771 people on the island at the time, and a series of forensic clues, including unidentified female DNA on the victim's clothing. Janelle's shorts and underwear had been slashed, yet there was no indication of sexual abuse.

The response of the islanders to his questioning ranged from a cacophony of gossip to sullen taciturnity. It was almost impossible to chart a course between the two. Peters, who at 56 had led a team of 'cold case' detectives, was the possessor of a bulldog persistence. But every line of enquiry ran up against unshakeable alibis or simply petered out. Eventually he would organise a mass fingerprinting – a total of 1,632 individuals would volunteer – but without result. And to the growing frustration of all involved, the exercise would produce even greater ferment on the island as fingers were pointed at the 23 per cent of locals who declined to cooperate.

Meantime, Glenn McNeill departed in May to attend his brother Scott's wedding in New Zealand, and because his own marriage was, he says, going through a 'rough patch', he did not return. Erica says, 'Glen was quiet and there were rumours in the family that something had happened on the island.'[4] Aliesha remained on Norfolk until December, serving out her contract with the hotel, before returning to New Zealand and shortly afterwards departing for London.

By then McNeill, a solid, good-looking man in his late 20s, had found a new job as a chef at Café Affair run by his old boss Derrick Harding. He soon had a new partner, Shelley Hooper, a dental assistant, and together they started a family with a daughter, Paige, followed by a baby boy they named Connor. However, Glenn was using drugs and was having trouble meeting the demands of his job. Erica says, 'I was living in Christchurch when I was asked to come up to Nelson as Glenn had admitted himself to the drug rehab unit and wanted to see me. Over this time I asked Glenn to talk to me and he let me in, but he was scared and kept telling me it was better I not know.'

Back on Norfolk, by 2004 the investigation seemed to be no nearer a resolution. Then suddenly another murder rocked the community when the local Lands and Environment Minister, Ivens 'Toon' Buffett, was found shot dead in his Quality Row office on 19 July.

He was also known to Janelle Patton. Her parents, leafing through her photo album on hearing the news, found pictures of him. Ron Patton says his immediate thought was that there might be a connection. Toon was a gregarious character with a larrikin streak.[5] However, it soon became clear that the killer was Toon's 25-year-old son, Leith, who had come to believe his father was 'The Evil Prophet'.

In a hearing it was decided Leith was incompetent to stand trial and he was transferred to the Long Bay prison hospital. The cause of his mental state, whether congenital or drug induced, was not determined but the editor of the *Norfolk Islander* told the ABC's *World Today* that 'Both his parents had been most perturbed about the boy's mental condition over the last few months. They had been desperately trying to seek some sort of counselling that the boy could undertake.'

By then another scandal close to the hearts of the Pitcairner descendants was occupying the world's news media. On Pitcairn itself, the morning of 29 September ushered in one of the more distasteful trials in British colonial history. Shortly after 9 a.m. a group of distinguished legal practitioners led by Chief Justice Charles Blackie made their way from the mission house to a dilapidated timber courthouse for the trial of Steven Raymond Christian, the island's 53-year-old mayor. Christian's was the first of seven trials at which he and his co-defendants – Randy Christian, Dennis Christian, Terry Young, Jay Warren, Len Brown and Dave Brown – would be charged with rape and sexual assault. All the victims, most of whom were close relatives, were under 16. Also charged but not present were Shawn and Trent Christian. Two months later in an Auckland court another 32 charges, including 10 counts of rape, would be preferred against four men who had relocated to New Zealand, including a former teacher on the island.

The trials on Pitcairn would fascinate and horrify. They would end forever the romantic notions so conscientiously fostered for more than 150 years of an idyllic South Seas arcadia of gentle and devout Christians. Devout they may have been, but these Christians were made of tougher stuff. The island trials lasted a month and, in the end, three generations of Pitcairners from Len Brown, 78 years old and half deaf, to Randy Christian, 30 and brimming with vigour, were found guilty of a total of 35 offences. The men were all descendants of the *Bounty* mutineers, and so were the women whose lives they had blighted.[6] The curtain finally fell on the purblind British fantasy.

Further charges of possession of child pornography would be brought in 2010 against the then mayor, Michael Warren. Despite the charges, Mr Warren – a senior figure in the locally powerful Seventh Day Adventist Church – was convincingly re-elected as mayor shortly after his arrest.

This is not to suggest that the Pitcairner relatives on Norfolk Island – or indeed other Norfolk residents – indulged in similar illegal and disgraceful behaviour, although there have been significant exceptions. In 2001, for example, the Norfolk Supreme Court convicted 69-year-old Stephen Nobbs, the Seventh Day Adventist deacon, of assault and acts of indecency against children. Two of the girls were from the Christian family and one a Nobbs. But because there was no 'penetration' the assaults were classified at the lower end of the sexual assault scale. Justice Wilcox found Nobbs was a man 'used to getting his way', and that 'no remorse had been shown' and sentenced him to 48 weekends of periodic detention.[7]

Also in the recent court files are assault cases, apprehended violence orders, two rape cases, and an arson case involving someone attempting to burn down the local RSL club while people were drinking inside. All were acquitted by island juries.

In 1994, members of the Australian Law Reform Commission travelled to the island to investigate the extent of domestic violence in the community. Commissioner Chris Sidoti said later that local women were afraid to talk to the commissioners during the day lest they be observed.

'They were extremely busy at night,' he said, 'as women beat a path to their door . . . under cover of darkness. The stories these women told was one of widespread domestic violence . . . that was largely swept under the carpet. There were even some locals who were driven off the island because of their opposition, their stand at what was going on.'[9]

But when Detective Bob Peters finally made his arrest in the Janelle Patton case, no former Pitcairner would be implicated. As far as the prosecution was concerned, Glenn McNeill, the New Zealand chef from a good family, who had never shown the slightest inclination to violence, committed the horrendous crime of murder alone and unaided. Moreover, they would contend that he wrapped his victim in a large sheet of black plastic and drove her in his car to the Cockpit area of Cascade, where he left her body to be discovered by the next passer-by.

CHAPTER TWENTY-TWO

'To serve thee better'

Detective Peters's big break came late in 2004 when a 70-year-old aircraft refueller, Dudley Hudson, who lived in Little Cutters Corn, called the police station to report an abandoned white Honda. In fact, it had been abandoned for no less than two years in the narrow road. At one stage Hudson had tried to dump it at the airport where there was a facility for destroying wrecked vehicles, but he found the gates closed and returned it to his backyard. There he exchanged a seat cover for one on his own well-worn Prelude. Two years later he just happened to hear that the police were looking for a white car because one had been seen in the area where Janelle Patton had taken her final, fateful walk.

The local police arrived 30 minutes later. It was 2.30 p.m. on Tuesday 21 December 2004. Hudson recalled a Sunday in March or April 2002 hearing a screech and a thud, and when he looked out he saw the car, driven by his neighbour Glenn

McNeill, being towed by a black sedan with Aliesha Taylor at the wheel. Hudson thought the Honda must have bumped into the back of the other car. Later he saw the couple drive away in the black sedan.

The police removed the car to the police station and sealed it off. And there it remained until February 2005 when an AFP forensic team finally turned their attention to its contents. Their investigation yielded fragments of glass that were similar to those found in Janelle's hair. There were also several strands of hair that an American DNA analysis would later find 'could not be excluded' as having come from Janelle or her maternal relatives. They then searched Glenn McNeill's former flat and in the backyard discovered a sheet of builders' black plastic similar to that wrapped around the victim's body. While this proved to be unconnected with the crime, on the actual wrapping they were able to match a partial handprint or fingerprint with a sample of McNeill's prints taken when he'd been questioned (and cleared) about a break-in at Bounty Centre, a Burnt Pine tourist store.

These were thin pickings, but by now the investigators were getting desperate. They had testimony from Aliesha Taylor, taken by an AFP officer in London, that on Easter Sunday 2002, on three occasions around the time Janelle was murdered McNeill phoned his wife at the Hillcrest from their flat in Little Cutters Corn. The calls were timed at 12.40 p.m., about an hour after Janelle was last seen on Rooty Hill Road heading for the Queen Elizabeth Lookout, then at 1.10 p.m. and 2.05 p.m. Aliesha told detectives he had called her first to offer her a toasted sandwich. She had called him back to say, 'Yes, thanks,' and after he had delivered it to the Hillcrest he had rung to see if she'd enjoyed it.

The AFP decided there was enough evidence to justify a plane trip to New Zealand for Bob Peters and his partner, Detective Senior Constable Tony Edmonson, to confront the suspect. They alerted the Nelson police to keep him under surveillance until they arrived. By now Glenn McNeill had been discharged from the drug rehabilitation clinic, had returned to work as a chef and was living in the Nelson suburb of Stoke. On Wednesday 1 February 2006, Peters and Edmonson, accompanied by New Zealand Detective Sergeant Chris Roberts, knocked on the door of his Orchard Street house. Their arrival was not entirely unexpected. After talking to the detective in London, Aliesha had called McNeill at his work to tell him he was a suspect in the murder.

Roberts made the arrest 'in relation to the murder of Janelle Patton'. Shelley Hooper and the children looked on bewildered as McNeill changed his clothes and was led away. Later she said, 'He's not a violent man; he never loses his temper . . . he's just a very loving, smoochy kind of character.'[1]

At the Nelson police station – with the video recording equipment switched off – Peters warned him that he did not have to say anything but that anything he did say might be used in evidence. He then laid out the evidence of the fingerprints on the plastic, the DNA test result on the hairs and the glass fragments. He said nothing about the female DNA found on Janelle's clothes, and nor was he obliged to. According to Detective Roberts, at this point McNeill suddenly confessed that he had accidentally run into Janelle while driving the Honda under the influence of cannabis.

Hastily the police turned on the video recorder and over the next two hours – with one break during which McNeill was unsuccessful in contacting his lawyer and a second for coffee and a cigarette – he elaborated his story, claiming that 'I pulled her out [from beneath the car] and put her in the boot because I thought she was dead. I drove back home and I just sat at home for about, oh, an hour or two and then grabbed a knife, and I, I think I stabbed her.' The killing was over quickly. 'Three or four stab wounds, just like that.'[2]

The police forensic pathologist would provide expert testimony that Janelle's injuries were not consistent with her being struck by a car. On the other hand, the judge – Chief Justice Mark Weinberg – would rule that the DNA test on the hairs was inadmissible. And despite extensive testing there was no murder weapon and nothing to connect McNeill's flat with the crime. So the forensic evidence hung by a thread.

However, the accused man would change his story radically. During his 2007 trial, in an unsworn statement from the dock, McNeill said that on the day of the killing he had been sick. 'Sometime between 11.30 a.m. and 12.00 midday, as best I can recall – I'm not too sure – I made a toasted sandwich for Aliesha's lunch before the luncheon rush hour started.

'I suppose it took me a couple of minutes to get ready and five minutes or so to make it. I then got in the car and drove down to Hillcrest.

'I sat with Aliesha as she ate her sandwich during her break. I cannot recall what we talked about. As best I can recall I was there for about 20 minutes. I then drove home. I recall I telephoned Aliesha once or twice in the afternoon. Because it was five years ago I can't recall what was said. I stayed at home that afternoon, watched TV or played PlayStation until about 4 p.m. when Aliesha arrived home from work.

'I didn't see Janelle Patton that day. I didn't drive along Rooty Hill Road that day. I didn't abduct or murder Janelle Patton that day. Aliesha and I went for a long drive. We drove along Prince Phillip Drive as well as many other roads on the island.

'People had all sorts of theories and talked about the case. I recalled that it was said she was found under black plastic at Cockpit, that she had been run over in a hit-and-run and that she had been stabbed. It was impossible to go anywhere on the island without hearing talk about what had occurred.

'I was booked to return to New Zealand in May 2002 to attend my brother's wedding. While I was there I took up an offer of a job by a friend. I spoke with Aliesha about it and we agreed that I should take it rather than return to Norfolk Island . . . We spoke regularly but our relationship was rocky at the time.

'In September 2002 something happened which I didn't plan or expect. I met Shelley my partner now and I fell in love with her. From this time my life started to get complicated. I had the stress of trying to resolve my relationship difficulties and periods of unemployment. I became in debt and people were demanding payments from me.

'Shelley and I had two children, adding to my responsibilities. My life started to spin out of control from them on. My drug-taking got worse as the pressure increased. It all came to a head in November 2005 when I cut my wrists. My life was hopeless and no longer in my control. I got a booking for a drug and alcohol treatment clinic in February 2006. I was dark and numb. I was running on autopilot. This period of my life is just a blur to me.

'I was arrested on my first day back at work. I spoke with them [the police]. I don't recall now what I told them. I would have admitted to anything due to my mental health problems at the time. I have seen the tape and say what I told the police was complete rubbish. It sounds like it was what I thought they wanted to hear. I am shocked by what I said. I didn't kill Janelle Patton. I didn't abduct her. She never went to Little Cutters Corn when I was living there.

'I have been told about the glass in the boot of the Honda. I used this car to take rubbish to the tip. It was dirty and not much more than a wreck when I got it and had no carpet in it whatsoever. It was just a cheap vehicle and I was not worried about the rubbish leaking in the boot. I have also been told about the fingerprints on the black plastic. I do not know how they got on to it. I may have touched the black plastic when I was on Norfolk Island at some time. I am not too sure.

'I feel very sorry for the Patton family. Their loss is enormous, but I didn't murder Janelle Patton. Thank you for listening to me.'

No doubt they listened closely. Certainly Detective Peters did. He told a journalist covering the trial, 'He was our best witness.'[3] Despite the outstanding efforts of McNeill's counsel, Peter Garling SC, the Norfolk Island jury took less than 24 hours deliberation to return a verdict of 'Guilty as charged'.

McNeill was sentenced to 24 years imprisonment with a non-parole period of 18 years. Paradoxically, the island whose entire *raison d'etre* had once been as a prison no longer had the facilities to house a single inmate. But as McNeill was taken away in chains, the islanders breathed a collective sigh of relief. At the 2004 coronial inquiry before Canberra magistrate Ron Cahill, the police had named 16 'persons of interest' – mostly long-time island residents – and the rumour mills had roared into overdrive. Reputations were trashed; old scores were settled. Now they could return to their casual and unhurried lifestyle with the tragedy safely behind them.

It was not to be. In the years since, doubts have arisen about what really happened on that tragic Easter Sunday. Despite the rejection of his legal appeals, from his prison cell in Australia Glenn McNeill began a determined effort to revisit the events surrounding the case. In July 2011, he made the stunning claim to New Zealand documentary film-maker Bryan Bruce that a man and a women who sold marijuana on the island had stabbed Janelle to death. While admitting he disposed of the body, McNeill said he had kept the identity of the killers a secret because the couple 'made violent threats to Aliesha and myself'.

'He [the dealer] said, "I know that you're the one that's ripped my pot plants off . . . you've been to my house a few times taking my pot." He said, "You're gonna dump this body," then he threatened my partner at the time, Aleisha, that if you don't do it we're gonna get rid of her."

Bruce said the woman involved could be the source of the unknown female DNA found on Janelle's clothes. The pathology and telephone records backed up McNeill's claim, and what he had uncovered proved it was not possible for Glenn to have acted alone. Pathologist Timothy Koelmeyer, interviewed in the documentary, also supported the finding. 'This woman has been attacked by more than one person . . . [she] has been restrained,' Dr Koelmeyer said. Bruce then lodged a sworn statement with the AFP giving the names of the couple as supplied by McNeill. The AFP agreed to investigate McNeill's allegations.

His efforts were supported by his partner Shelley Hooper, who told journalists, 'There was no way that Janelle was attacked by one person, the whole case was stuffed. The evidence states that more than one person was involved in the murder and I just cannot see how this can be ignored.'[4]

In another surprise development, in December 2011, the Sydney *Sunday Telegraph* reported that within hours of the conviction a juror had told a 'legal source' that 'his fate was sealed' even before the trial began. The juror told their source, 'We know he didn't do it, but [he] know[s] who did. He wouldn't tell us, so we decided to slot him.'

In September 2012, I arranged through prison authorities and McNeill's sister Erica to interview him at Lithgow Correctional Centre. In preparation I read two books and all media reporting of the case. We met in a special secure area of the visitors' block set aside for maximum security inmates.

At 34 and with a short prison haircut, he is a lithe figure of medium height, with a lean face, a fair complexion, an engaging smile and a grip powered by his devotion to weightlifting. 'I work on it in my cell,' he says. 'That's about all I can do here.' It is not a new activity. When he was on Norfolk Island prior to the murder, he worked out at a Burnt Pine gym at least three or four times a week.

We talk for more than an hour.

He is willing to discuss many of the elements of the case but backs away from others. However, it is soon clear that underlying the tragedy is a drug culture that enveloped McNeill almost from the time of his arrival on Norfolk. He had experimented with drugs in New Zealand but nothing like this. 'Everyone on the island grew pot and smoked it,' he says. To a 26-year-old chef it was like some kind of dark paradise. 'It was an island,' he says. 'It was like a holiday. Lots of drugs. It got to the stage where it was the first thing I did when I woke up in the morning.'

And it was cheap — about $150 would buy half a bag of cannabis. 'They grew it in the middle of other crops, like sugar cane,' he says. 'That way it couldn't be spotted by the cops. But they also rigged up booby traps in the fields to stop others from pinching the plants.'

He describes a barbed noose that snaps on to an intruder's wrist. And 'they', he says, (he refuses to name them) also grow a lot indoors using a hydroponic system. This is known as 'skunk' and is much stronger than regular cannabis. According to authorities 'skunk' combined with other drugs — from steroids to LSD to methamphetamine, all of which, McNeill says, were imported to Norfolk — could produce a virtual schizophrenic state. He becomes a regular user. Indeed, he frequently calls in sick and moves from one job to another.

By Easter Sunday 2002 he is out of work.

He starts smoking pot at 6 a.m., he says. Aliesha goes to work at the Hillcrest Hotel. He continues to smoke . . . and now his story becomes as cloudy as the living room must have been in the flat on Little Cutters Corn. But at some stage, even by his own admission, he comes in contact with Janelle Patton. At first he tells me that he doesn't know her, had never met her on the island despite the tight-knit hospitality community and his frequent change of jobs. He and Aliesha, he says, kept to themselves, although he insists she resists all drugs. But a little later says he might have seen Janelle 'in the supermarket', although he is not necessarily referring to the fatal day.

By now he has completely abandoned his original story to the police and his unsworn statement to the court, which he says, 'was what the legal team suggested; I knew it wasn't true when I was saying it.'

So, what did happen?

'Why should I tell you? What's in it for me?'

The question surprises me. If I were in his position, I say, and the true story would help to secure an earlier release, I would tell anyone and everyone who would listen.

He is unimpressed.

I ask him to name the 'real' killers. He declines. 'You couldn't put them in the book. They would sue.'

If they really did it, I say, there's no way they would sue. Oscar Wilde tried that and went to gaol himself.

We change the subject.

On that day of the murder, does he go out to the gym or to shop?

No.

We bat the evidence back and forth. If the murderers forced him to dispose of the body, I ask, why not cast it from a cliff into the sea? Why leave it in such a public place?

'She deserved to be found,' he says.

There are only two points on which we are in total agreement: if he had kept his mouth shut, he would never have been convicted; and without the island's drug culture Janelle Patton, who detested drugs and made her feelings plain, would be alive today.

In the end, he says, 'Only I know what really happened that day.' He also says he wishes 'with all my heart' that he had never gone to Norfolk in the first place. That I believe.

Whatever the extent of his guilt, either as the murderer who in a frenzied, drug-induced haze plunged the knife into her chest, or as the accessory charged with disposing of Janelle's body, there is one aspect of the case that troubles me. The authorities decided that he should serve his sentence at Lithgow, despite the fact that the crime was committed on Norfolk, his family lived in New Zealand and visiting him would not only be expensive but extraordinarily complex. It would involve a drive from Nelson to Christchurch, a flight to Sydney, a bus or hire car to the remote NSW coal town and a further bus to the prison at Marangaroo, 7 kilometres from town.

Given the difficulties of their remaining in touch, the relationship with Shelley Hooper has broken down. According to his sister Erica, 'Glenn has no support from his mother or our father. This is due to matters after his trial and at Glenn's request. He has had no contact from our brother since the trial on Norfolk.

'I have been to visit him once and our grandmother has been over twice but she is at the age where she will not be able to go back. Glenn has not seen his kids in about three years, though Glenn and I talk most weekends. Glenn was in the wrong place at the wrong time and knew the wrong people!'[5]

A guard at the prison told me McNeill was a model prisoner. 'He's very quiet, keeps to himself, no trouble to anyone.' He telephones his children once a week. Yet because he is a Norfolk prisoner, which has no legal relationship to New Zealand, he remains banished across the sea. It is an additional punishment, one that no other Lithgow prison family is forced to endure. And one may ask what effect this isolation will have on the man who, with continued good behaviour, will be released in 11 years aged only 46.

A more humane and sensible alternative would be a New Zealand facility or even Canberra with its frequent direct charter flights from Christchurch. There would be a remarkable irony in the latter, as the Canberra gaol is named the Alexander Maconochie Centre in honour of the only figure from the island's convict past who would have approved the transfer.

Meantime, as Glenn McNeill began his sentence, Norfolk Island's fortunes took a turn for the worse. By 2007 its economy was almost totally dependent on tourism from Australia and New Zealand. But no real attempt had been made then or since to exploit the obvious potential of its long and colourful history. There is a regular, if grindingly amateur, re-enactment of the mutiny on the *Bounty*, in which Captain Bligh is portrayed as the unmitigated villain. There are over-priced 'ghost walks' where a crude dinner is served in one of the convict buildings at Kingston while a woman with acting ambitions tells unlikely stories of ghostly visitations. And there are guided tours of the cemetery, in which the graves of the convict era are distinctly separated from those of the Pitcairn descendants.

The restaurants are few, the service ordinary and the food no better. The tourist shops are expensive, the souvenirs tasteless and the roads in a state of dangerous disrepair. Domestic fowls have run wild in their thousands, although the locals say the Fijian maids who work in the hotels for a pittance are starting to make a hole in their numbers. Not surprisingly, the tourist trade has fallen each year since 2005, when it was estimated that to break even they needed 100,000 visitors annually. At that time they reached 32,000; by 2012 the figure was less than 27,000.

A 2006 Australian Government review proposed that the island's Legislative Assembly, unchanged since 1979, be reduced to the status of a local council. However, later that year citing the 'significant disruption' that changes to the governance would impose on the island's economy, the Howard Government ended the review and retained the status quo.

By 2010 Norfolk was insolvent, and in an outburst that surprised many islanders, Chief Minister David 'the Colonel' Buffett suggested on 6 November that the island would voluntarily surrender its self-governing status in return for a financial bailout from the federal government. The Minister for External Territories Simon Crean, ordered yet another review and in March 2012 released a report revealing that the government had pumped emergency aid of $37 million into the island's economy – more than $20,000 per person – to prevent it going bankrupt. The governmental status quo remained and the islanders showed 'little evidence of a clear vision or sustainable long-term plan'.

Nevertheless, on 8 June 2012 – Bounty Day – the Pitcairner descendants assembled in a show of triumphalism to mark the 156th anniversary of their landing on Norfolk's shores. The seas were too rough for a seagoing re-enactment so they all walked down to the Kingston Pier – at least 300 of them dressed like their ancestors – where they were 'received' by the administrator, Neil Pope, who had been appointed nine weeks previously. A friend of Simon Crean, Pope had been a Labor member of the Victorian Parliament and subsequently ran his own engineering consultancy. According to Mrs Pope, the appointment came as 'a pleasant surprise'.

The short, bearded Administrator stepped up on Bounty Day looking suitably Victorian in an attenuated stovepipe hat and black suit. He was pretending to be the island's 1856 commissariat storekeeper, Stewart, who looked after the place after the last of the convicts left in 1854. He was accompanied by David Buffett dressed in knee breeches, black shoes, white socks, black waistcoat and cutaway black tails adorned with a Royal Navy captain's gold epaulettes; and atop his bearded grey head was a plumed three-cornered hat. He was pretending to be Captain Denham, who had arrived a few weeks before to see that everything went off tickety-boo.

The original Pitcairners had come ashore in heavy rain, and on this occasion the weather cooperated to provide a watery verisimilitude. But then, as they left the pier in their remarkably authentic 19th century costumery, the clouds cleared. They strolled past the gates to the gaol ruins, up to the cenotaph, while on the sidelines a few tourists took photos, especially of the golden-haired moppets who romped along with their elders and then climbed over the memorial to the 13 lost in the Great War, nine in World War II and one in Korea. While Mr Pope laid his wreath and doffed his ancient hat, they sang *God Save The Queen*, since they refuse to recognise the Australian National Anthem.

On a whistle they resumed their stroll along Quality Row, which now houses the island's administration in buildings converted from barracks built by Major Anderson in 1835; past the old officers' baths incorporating spring water that bubbles down the hill towards the gaol; past the renovated houses; past Government House and then to the cemetery on a gentle slope down to the dunes of Slaughter Bay.

At the gates they struck up a hymn, *In The Sweet Bye and Bye*, with its prospect of a heavenly reunion 'on that beautiful shore'. Then Joe Adams in costume read the prayer of his ancestor John Adams, the lone male survivor of the mutineers' murderous early years on Pitcairn. It was a plea to the Lord 'to serve thee better than ever I have done before, that I may be fitter to dwell in heaven'. This was followed by the Pitcairn Anthem, a mournful repetition of the maritime theme to 'hoist the sail and catch the breeze' on the ship that 'will land you safe at last on Canaan's happy shore'.

By now the skies had cleared to a perfect blue and the Pitcairners headed into the cemetery to lay flowers and pay respect to their relatives buried in the foreground; beyond, the graves of the soldiers and their families, the convicts and their gaolers lay bare and neglected in the winter sun. Another whistle called them back to the gates, this time for a strolling return to Government House for 'a cup of tea' with the Popes. Non-Pitcairners were barred from this event, which was held in the spacious and beautifully maintained grounds. However, we had wandered through its restored high-ceilinged rooms two days before. We had found Mrs Pope sitting at the magnificent mahogany table that could easily have seated 20 guests in the splendid dining room.

'It's wonderful,' she said, still thrilled at the posting, which had come from the blue. 'And the people are so friendly.'

It is a common misconception. The hearty greetings and affectionate expressions are no more than a colourful carapace, an impenetrable barrier to genuine friendship which is reserved for their own kind. Outsiders are mistrusted and resisted, except on their terms. These require an acceptance of the Pitcairners' illusion of their exceptionality, the mirage of their Christian righteousness, and the charm of the pidgin that passes for their so-called dialect: 'Norf'k'. Even then, according to long-term residents, 'outsiders' are kept at arm's length unless they can be manipulated to serve the Pitcairners' cause. At present it is raw survival and it is becoming more urgent by the day as they seek to negotiate yet another financial bailout from the federal government, while retaining their control over the island's affairs (and funds).

The Australian Government maintains a splendid scenic lookout and monument to Captain Cook on the point where he landed several centuries ago to begin the island's imperial history. It is a fine place for a monument. The eminence of Mt Pitt is at your back and the boundless sea before. The blue–green rollers sweep across the seascape to smash themselves on the rocks below. The wind blows into your face and you cannot help but imagine yourself standing there, watching, like some time travelling sentinel, as the billowing sails of the *Resolution* carry the Great Navigator ever closer to that fateful landfall.

And you cannot help but wonder if James Cook, that paragon of empire, knew what a dark shadow of the human spirit would enfold and envelop this little piece of paradise, whether he would choose another course and leave Norfolk to the unkempt squalls of nature and to the Birds of Providence.

Epilogue

There is hope for the island's future – that day is almost upon us.

In March 2011, David Buffett and Simon Crean signed a 10-page 'Road Map' that would rescue Norfolk from bankruptcy and place it on a firm economic footing. Starting immediately, responsibility for the island's governance would travel in ordered array from the Legislative Assembly at Kingston to the Australian Parliament in Canberra. And along the way it would pass a series of markers that signalled the progress of mutual cooperation. At the end of the journey, Norfolk Island would be fully incorporated into the Australian polity.

By 2015, the islanders would enjoy the protection and stability of Australia's education, health, pension, business, industry, tourism, immigration and defence provisions. In return – for the first time – they would pay the same taxes as the rest of the country.

But that, not surprisingly, is where the legendary Pitcairn cussedness kicked in. Despite the Australian Government's injection of $29 million emergency aid to keep the process moving, on 13 March 2013 David Buffett was dumped as Chief Minister, and replaced with Lisle Snell, descendant of a whaling family on one side and the Quintals on the other.

Administrator Pope went on radio to warn the islanders: 'In no way can we walk away from the reform process,' he said. 'I now need to know from the nine Members of the Assembly whether they indeed are going to continue with that reform. Because if they are not, I have to let Canberra know that the appetite is no longer here.' He then confronted the newly elected assembly, telling them he had been in touch with Minister Crean. 'Pie in the sky solutions that are unachievable or, worse still, no solutions at all, will only condemn this island to a state of dependency, scrambling for the next handout,' Pope said.

Within a week, word reached Canberra that the Administrator was no longer welcome and should be withdrawn. Three days later Crean himself departed, after the farcical attempt to topple Prime Minister Julia Gillard, and replace her with Kevin Rudd (a descendant of Norfolk Islander, Mary Wade).

By now the 'Road Map' was heading for a cliff. The one saving grace was that financial reality awaited the downward plunge. Businesses were closing in record numbers, people were leaving for the mainland to find work.

And it really didn't need to be that way. For Norfolk is a treasure trove of colonial history in all its fascinating horror. Its convict past with the stark ruins of Kingston and Arthur's Vale is a potential tourist bonanza. So too the tale of mutiny on the *Bounty* and its murderous aftermath. So too the missionary martyrs, and their gunboat proselytising.

So too the vistas, the fishing, the botanical wonders.

Both sides of the Australian Parliament agree: incorporation *will happen*; and when it does the island will be transformed. Investment will flow; tourists will follow. Immigration will break the back of Pitcairn privilege. The howls of resistance will fade. The sinister cloak of centuries will finally be ripped away.

The long, long nightmare will be over.

Author's note

Some places on this earth are redolent of a terrible evil, from Auschwitz, to Srebrenica, to the killing fields of Cambodia. They are dark places, bred of shadows, obscenities, and wrongful death. The world knows them well. There is another. It is brilliantly disguised in the garments of paradise in the South Pacific. It is Norfolk Island.

On a chance visit there I hire a bicycle and begin to tour the island. I find the Bounty Folk Museum and discover its extraordinary archive of Norfolk's history. I'm plunged into the past . . . It is 1825 and the sadistic commandants of the second convict settlement appear. I seem to see them as ghosts on street corners, ridiculous but threatening in their blood-spattered uniforms, their sneering floggers by their side . . .

I visit the RSL Club – it is a scene from a Hogarth painting, of drunken men and women, drugs on special, screaming music. They barely pause for the remembrance pledge. It feels almost as though they nurse a guilty fear, a dread that some outsider will expose a terrible secret. The stampede to intoxication is their escape hatch.

As the days pass I become ever more entangled in the past and present life of the place . . . It is 1865 and the High Anglican Mission arrives on the heels of the Pitcairners to make their headquarters on the best land. And the missionaries tempt the boys to come from their Melanesian homes for religious instruction, only to seduce and assault their lithe young bodies . . .

On one starry night at Kingston among the convict ruins, suddenly it is 1908 and the NSW Government has lost all patience with the former Pitcairners who are living in squalor. They send soldiers to evict them from the homes they have occupied and trashed on Quality Row . . .

I read a report to the Federal Parliament in 2003 that the claims the island was 'ceded' to the Pitcairners in 1856 is 'a myth perpetuated by a minority of Pitcairn descendants and other more recent, often wealthy, arrivals motivated by self-interest to resist the imposition of income tax.'

I learn of the Janelle Patton murder in March 2002. I visit the places where she worked and where her body was found. I hear whispers about the island jury who, five years later, convict a New Zealand chef, Glenn McNeill. Something about the case doesn't ring true . . .

—

Many of those who assisted my subsequent research on the island and elsewhere would prefer not to be publicly identified for fear of retribution. I respect their concerns. I am also aware that some authors whose work is quoted would prefer not to have their contribution acknowledged. I must, though, pay tribute to historians Anne Salmond, Margaret Hazzard, David Hilliard and Raymond Nobbs whose dedication to the truth overrode any temptation to gild the lily. Thanks also to Kathy Marks, Tim Latham and Roger Maynard whose books on the Pitcairn trials and the sad case of Janelle Patton's murder were essential reading.

Special thanks as usual to my best researcher and loving companion Wendy Macklin, to my lifelong friend Peter Thompson, whose wise counsel was vital, and to my publisher Matthew Kelly, whose support and creative judgement was always helpful.

Robert Macklin, Canberra, 2013
www.robertmacklin.com

Endnotes

Chapter One

1 Cook's Journal, 22 April 1770.
2 Gammage, Bill, *The Biggest Estate on Earth*, Allen & Unwin, 2011.
3 It would also begin the production of carbon dioxide that would in time imperil human life on the planet.
4 The two ships lost contact in a storm off New Zealand and missed a prearranged rendezvous at Queen Charlotte Sound by four days, and by the time Cook left Norfolk Furneaux was almost back in England.
5 Captain John Walker, a Whitby ship owner.
6 Gilbert, George, (Holmes, C. ed.), *Captain Cook's Final Voyage: The Journal of Midshipman George Gilbert Holmes*, 1982, pp. 33–4.
7 Salmond, Anne, *Bligh: William Bligh in the South Seas*, Penguin, 2011, p. 99.
8 ibid., p. 75.
9 ibid., pp. 78–9.
10 His half-sister had married the naval surgeon John Bond, but he was without influence in the Admiralty hierarchy.
11 ibid., p. 105.
12 ibid.

Chapter Two

1 Edwards, 'Early Writings', CMP, p. 102.
2 Coincidentally, the *Swallow* had recently returned from a voyage to the South Pacific under Captain Philip Carteret who in 1767 had discovered and named Pitcairn Island after the midshipman who first sighted it.
3 She would later become a prison hulk.
4 Originally 'New Wales' in Cook's Journal, and later corrected by him to 'New South Wales'.
5 No relation.
6 Anderson, Atholl, Smith, Ian and White, Peter (eds), *Prehistoric Archaeology of Norfolk Island, Southwest Pacific*, Australian Museum, 2001.
7 King's dispatches to Arthur Phillip, 1788.
8 King's Journal, p. 55.
9 ibid.
10 King, Letter-book, Mitchell Library, quoted in Hazzard, Margaret, *Punishment Short of Death: A History of the Penal Settlement at Norfolk Island*, Hyland House, 1984, p. 21.
11 Collins, Lt David, *An Account of the English Colony in New South Wales*, p. 50.
12 King, Letter-book, quoted in Hazzard, Margaret, *Punishment Short of Death*, p. 41.

Chapter Three

1 Banks in Beaglehole, C. (ed.), *The Endeavour Journal of Joseph Banks*, 1962, vol. I, p. 341.
2 Christian, Charles, quoted in Salmond, Anne, *Bligh*, p. 121.
3 ibid., p. 128.
4 Nicholson, Harold, Diaries, 17 August 1950.
5 Bligh's report to the Admiralty following the mutiny.
6 Salmond, Anne, *Bligh*, p. 178.
7 ibid., p. 206.
8 ibid., p. 209.
9 Testimony at the trial of the mutineers.

Chapter Four

1 Clark, Ralph. Journal, 26 May 1790.
2 Clark, Ralph. Journal, 21 June 1790.

Chapter Five

1 King, letter to Nepean, 1792.
2 Hazzard, Margaret, *Punishment Short of Death*, pp. 37–8.
3 King to Dundas, 10 March 1794.
4 ibid.
5 Hazzard, Margaret, *Punishment Short of Death*, pp. 50–1.

6 Mundle, Rob, *Bligh: Master Mariner*, Hachette, 2010, pp. 256–7.
7 Lummis, Trevor, *Pitcairn Island: Life and Death in Eden*, Ashgate, 1997, p. 58.

Chapter Six

1 Lummis, Trevor, *Pitcairn Island*, p. 66.
2 ibid., p. 87.

Chapter Seven

1 Hazzard, Margaret, *Punishment Short of Death*, pp. 54–5.
2 Recollections.
3 ibid.

Chapter Eight

1 King to Home Office, quoted in Salmond, Anne, *Bligh*, p. 460.
2 ibid., p. 461.
3 Folger's log, quoted in Young, Rosalind, *Mutiny of the Bounty and the Story of Pitcairn Island, 1790–1894*, Pacific Press, 1894, pp. 38–40.
4 Marks, Kathy, *Pitcairn: Paradise Lost*, HarperCollins, 2008, p. 214.
5 Hazzard, Margaret, *Punishment Short of Death*, p. 107.

Chapter Nine

1 Holt, Joseph, *Memoirs*, 1838.
2 *Historical Records of Australia*, series 1, vol. 11, p. 322, quoted in Hazzard, Margaret, *Punishment Short of Death*, p. 109.
3 *Historical Records of Australia*, series 1, vol. 11, p. 604.
4 Duffield, Ian, 'The life and death of "Black" John Goff', *Australian Journal of Politics & History*, vol. 33, issue 1, April 1987, pp. 30–44.

Chapter Ten

1 Brown, p. L. (ed.), Memoirs recorded at Geelong, Victoria, Australia by Captain Foster Fyans (1790–1870), 1962.
2 ibid.

3 ibid.
4 Darling to Bathurst, December 1826.
5 *Historical Records of Australia*, series 1, vol. 13, Hay to Darling, 20 May 1827, p. 315, quoted in Hazzard, Margaret, *Punishment Short of Death*, p. 122.
6 Memoirs of Norfolk Island, Frayne's undated ms, transcribed and quoted by Robert Hughes in *The Fatal Shore*, Vintage Books, p. 462.
7 ibid.
8 ibid., p. 463.
9 ibid.
10 Hall to Goderich, 9 February 1832.
11 Brown, p. L. (ed.), Memoirs recorded at Geelong, p. 92.
12 Fyans, F., 'Autobiography to 1843', State Library of Victoria, p. 96.
13 Hazzard, Margaret, *Punishment Short of Death*, p. 128.
14 Fyans, F., 'Autobiography to 1843', p. 109.

Chapter Eleven

1 Young, Rosalind, *Mutiny of the Bounty and the Story of Pitcairn Island, 1790–1894*, pp. 55–6.
2 ibid.
3 Barrow, John, *A Description of Pitcairn*, London, 1845, quoted in Nobbs, Raymond, *George Hunn Nobbs, 1799–1884: Chaplain on Pitcairn and Norfolk Island*, Pitcairn Descendants Society, 1984, p. 19.
4 Lummis, Trevor, *Pitcairn Island*, p. 137.
5 Nobbs, Raymond, *George Hunn Nobbs, 1799–1884*.
6 Young, Rosalind, *Mutiny of the Bounty and the Story of Pitcairn Island, 1790–1894*, p. 68.
7 Nobbs, Raymond, *George Hunn Nobbs, 1799–1884*, pp. 12–13.
8 Young, Rosalind, *Mutiny of the Bounty and the Story of Pitcairn Island, 1790–1894*, p. 60.
9 Report by Sandilands to Rear Admiral Sir E. Owen, 26 May 1831.
10 ibid.
11 Lummis, Trevor, *Pitcairn Island*, p. 142.
12 ibid, p. 144.

Chapter Twelve

1 Burton, *Religion and Education*, p. 154, quoted in Hughes, *The Fatal Shore*, p. 477.
2 *Sydney Gazette and NSW Advertiser*, 3 October 1834.
3 Anderson, J., *Recollections of a Peninsular Veteran*, 1843, pp. 152–4.
4 Hughes, *The Fatal Shore*, p. 480.
5 Bunbury, Thomas, *Recollections of a Veteran: Being Personal and Military Adventures in Portugal, Spain, France, Malta, New South Wales, Norfolk Island, New Zealand, Andaman Islands, and India*, vol. 2, p. 320.
6 ibid.

Chapter Thirteen

1 Young, Rosalind, *Mutiny of the Bounty and the Story of Pitcairn Island, 1790–1894*, p. 92.
2 Kent, Graeme, *Company of Heaven: Early Missionaries in the South Seas*, Reed, 1972, pp. 84–5.
3 Lummis, Trevor, *Pitcairn Island*, p. 157.
4 Hilliard, David, *God's Gentlemen: A History of the Melanesian Mission 1849–1942*, UQP, 1978, pp. 1–2.
5 ibid.
6 ibid., p. 103.
7 Barry, J.V., *Alexander Maconochie of Norfolk Island*, Oxford University Press, 1958, pp. 6–7.
8 ibid.
9 ibid.
10 Maconochie, Alexander, *Supplement to Thoughts on Convict Management*, 1839.
11 Maconochie, Alexander, *Report to London Society for the Improvement of Prison Discipline*, 1837.
12 Barry, J.V., *Alexander Maconochie of Norfolk Island*, pp. 67–70.
13 ibid.
14 ibid.

Chapter Fourteen

1 Hazzard, Margaret, *Punishment Short of Death*, p. 156.
2 Maconochie, Alexander, *Norfolk Island*, p. 5.
3 Correspondence re Convict Discipline, 1846, p. 61.
4 Hazzard, Margaret, *Punishment Short of Death*, p. 169.
5 *History of Tasmania*, 1852, vol. 1, p. 67.
6 Barry, J.V., *Alexander Maconochie of Norfolk Island*, p. 130.
7 Gipps, Correspondence, 25 February 1840.
8 Gipps to Stanley, April 1843.
9 Morris, Norval, *Maconochie's Gentlemen*, Oxford University Press, 2002, p. 99.
10 Rogers, Thomas, Correspondence, p. 144, quoted in Hughes, *The Fatal Shore*, p. 535.
11 *Secondary Punishment in the Penal Period in Australia 1788–1850*, 1977, p. 7.

Chapter Fifteen

1 Deposition taken before John Price, 4 December 1846.
2 Deposition taken before John Price, 26 November 1846.
3 Cash, Martin, *Martin Cash: The Bushranger of Van Diemen's Land, in 1843–4: A Personal Narrative of His Exploits in the Bush and His Experiences at Port Arthur and Norfolk Island, 1870*, p. 154.
4 ibid.
5 Barry, John Vincent, *The Life and Death of John Price: A Study of the Exercise of Naked Power*, p. 60.
6 Eardley-Wilmot to Gladstone, 6 July 1846, quoted in Hazzard, Margaret, *Punishment Short of Death*, p. 215.
7 Jeffrey, Mark, *A Burglar's Life*, 1893, p. 90, quoted in Hazzard, Margaret, *Punishment Short of Death*, p. 236.
8 ibid.
9 Correspondence, Wilton to Denison, 22 May 1852.
10 Barry, *The Life and Death of John Price*, MUP, 1964, p. 16.

Chapter Sixteen

1 Nobbs, Raymond, *George Hunn Nobbs, 1799–1884*, p. 37.

2 Young, Rosalind, *Mutiny of the Bounty and the Story of Pitcairn Island, 1790–1894*, p. 107.
3 ibid.
4 McFarland, Alfred, *Mutiny in the Bounty and Story of the Pitcairn Islanders*, 1884, p. 190.
5 Nobbs, Raymond, *George Hunn Nobbs, 1799–1884*, p. 43.
6 Young, Rosalind, *Mutiny of the Bounty and the Story of Pitcairn Island, 1790–1894*, p. 113.
7 Sarah Nobbs, diary, quoted in Nobbs, Raymond, *George Hunn Nobbs, 1799–1884*, p. 51.
8 Nobbs, Raymond, *George Hunn Nobbs, 1799–1884*, p. 50.
9 ibid., p. 76.
10 Young, Rosalind, *Mutiny of the Bounty and the Story of Pitcairn Island, 1790–1894*, p. 156.
11 *Pitcairn News*, vol. 2, no. 7, July 2008.

Chapter Seventeen

1 Hilliard, David, *God's Gentlemen*, UQP, 1978, p. 20.
2 ibid.
3 *Pitcairn: The Island the People and the Pastor*, 1854.
4 Prebble, A. E., MA Thesis, Uni of NZ, pp. 58–61, quoted in Hilliard, David, *God's Gentlemen*.
5 ibid.
6 Nobbs, Raymond, *George Hunn Nobbs, 1799–1884*, p. 82.
7 ibid.
8 ibid., p. 84.
9 ibid.
10 Young to Secretary of State Lord Newcastle, May 1862, quoted in Nobbs, Raymond, *George Hunn Nobbs, 1799–1884*, p. 86.
11 Young, Rosalind, *Mutiny of the Bounty and the Story of Pitcairn Island, 1790–1894*, pp. 160–1.
12 *Sketches of the Life of Bishop Patteson in Melanesia*, Society for Promoting Christian Knowledge, pp. 86–95.
13 Belcher, pp. 354–5, quoted in Nobbs, Raymond, *George Hunn Nobbs, 1799–1884*, p. 89.

Chapter Eighteen

1 Fox, Charles E., *Kakamora*, Hodder & Stoughton, 1962, pp. 13–18.
2 ibid.
3 ibid.
4 Hilliard, David, *God's Gentlemen*, p. 43.
5 Fox, Charles E., *Kakamora*, p. 17.
6 Hilliard, David, *God's Gentlemen*, p. 37.
7 ibid.
8 ibid., p. 64.
9 Kent, Graeme, *Company of Heaven*, pp. 152–5.
10 ibid.
11 Hilliard, David, *God's Gentlemen*, p. 67.
12 ibid., p. 80.
13 Nobbs, Raymond, *George Hunn Nobbs, 1799–1884*, p. 95.
14 Hilliard, David, *God's Gentlemen*, p. 91.
15 Penny, Alfred, *Ten Years in Melanesia*, 1888, pp. 17–18.

Chapter Nineteen

1 Tiakihana, Tamati, *Norfolk Island*, 1948, p. 34.
2 ibid.
3 Correspondence, Lt W. E. Spalding to Arthur Buffett, Norfolk Museum, p. 3.
4 ibid.
5 Hilliard, David, *God's Gentlemen*, p. 155.
6 ibid., pp. 144–5.
7 ibid., p. 143.
8 ibid., p. 28.
9 Tofts, R. G., *Norfolk Island Whaling Days*, 1977, p. 23.
10 Report to Minister, Atlee Hunt, National Archives of Australia, CP697/14, 262089.
11 'Report of Visit of MPs – Their Views about the Island', Government Printer, 1915.
12 Hilliard, David, *God's Gentlemen*, p. 209.
13 *Blain Clergy Directory*.

Chapter Twenty

1 Hoare, Merval, *Norfolk Island: An Outline of its History 1774–1968*, p. 122.
2 *Australian Dictionary of Biography*, vol. 10, 1986.

3 Nobbs, Raymond, *Norfolk Island and its Third Settlement, 1856–1956*, pp. 174–5.
4 ibid., p. 177.
5 Hoare, Merval, *Norfolk Island in the 1930s*, p. 1.
6 ibid.
7 Hunt, Atlee, Report to the Minister, 1914.
8 Hoare, Merval, *Norfolk Island in the 1930s*, p. 24.
9 Tofts, R. G., *Norfolk Island Whaling Days*, p. 26.
10 ibid.

Chapter Twenty-one

1 Nobbs, Raymond, *Norfolk Island and its Third Settlement, 1856–1956*, p. 222.
2 Hoare, Merval, *Norfolk Island 1950–1982*, p. 19.

3 Richards, Lisa, 'A lovely day', *Your World*, 2012, p. 23.
4 Nimmo Report, p. 46.
5 Maynard, Roger, *The Fatal Flaw*, Random House, 2007, p. 5.
6 ibid., p. 154.
7 ibid., p. 151.
8 Latham, Tim, *Norfolk: Island of Secrets*, p. 19.
9 Marks, Kathy, *Pitcairn: Paradise Lost*, HarperCollins, 2008, pp. 170–1.

Chapter Twenty-two

1 Maynard, Roger, *The Fatal Flaw*, p. 155.
2 ibid., p. 145.
3 ibid., p. 247.
4 *Sunday Telegraph*, Sydney, 12 June 2011.
5 Interview with the author, August 2012.

Index

Pitcairn, Robert 55
Pitcairn Fund Committee 231, 238
Pitcairn Island trials (2004) 272, 313–314
Pitt, William 123
Pitt the Younger 102
Plaistowe, John 163
Pomare, Queen 157, 158
Pomare II, King 155, 156
Pope, Neil 328–330
Portland, Lord 70, 88
Portlock, Nathaniel 71
Pratt, Charles 102
Price, Aaron 138–139, 144–146, 171, 216, 227
Price, John Giles
    background 218
    commander of Norfolk Island 214–215, 220–224
    Pentridge stockade 224–225
    Van Diemen's Land 219–220
Price, Sir Rose 218
Pringle Stuart, Robert 201, 209–211, 215
Pritt, Lonsdale 256
Prudence (Tahitian on Pitcairn Island) 75, 76
Puarai 74–75
Purcell, William 36, 41
Putland, Lieutenant John 106–107

Q
Qantas 298
Quintal, Arthur 232, 266
Quintal, Edward 89, 153, 177–178-9, 232
Quintal, John 233, 242–243
Quintal, Laurence ('Bucket') 309
Quintal, Matthew
    Bounty expedition to Tahiti 35, 43–45, 54, 55–56
    on Pitcairn Island 75, 80, 82–86, 88–90
Quintal family 158, 159, 160

R
Raniani 179
Rawdon-Hastings, Francis 153, 286
Rawson, Sir Henry 275
Read, A. 267–268
Reid, James 194
Rice, John 30
Rice, Richard 119
Richards (convict) 94–95, 99
Richardson, Sir John 122
Richardson, Sarah 122
Riley, Patrick 138
Riley, William 167–168
Roberts, Detective Sergeant Chris 318
Roberts, Henry 12
Robertson, Gilbert 220
Robinson, Cobby 296
Robinson, Joseph 62
Rogers (couple) 235
Rogers, Reverend Thomas 204, 212, 215, 216, 220, 221
Rosenthal, Sir Charles 297, 298
Ross, Major Robert 49–50, 51, 59–61
Rossiter, Thomas 238, 251
Rowley, Captain Thomas 93
Royal Geographical Society 155, 188
Rum Corps see New South Wales Corps
Russell, Lord John 183, 199
Russell, Simon 225
Ryan, Major Thomas 176, 195

S
Samson (Samoan teacher) 182
Samuel, John 44
Samwell, David 11
Sandilands, Captain Alexander 156–157
Sapimbuana, Charles 265
Sarah (Tahitian on Pitcairn Island) 75, 83, 84, 89
Scullin, Jack 295

Sellheim, Major-General V. C. M. 289
Selwyn, Bishop George Augustus
    appointed to Australian diocese 181–183
    background 122
    Bishop of Lichfield 258–259
    Melanesian Mission on Norfolk Island 240–242, 245–246, 249
    Nobbs 244–245
    Pitcairn Islanders 241–243
Selwyn, John 263, 266
Selwyn, Mrs 243–244
Shears, James and Mary 103
Shears, Mary Ann 103, 116
Sherwin, Ann 97–99, 115
Short, Captain Joseph 106–107
Sidoti, Chris 315
Simm, John 194
Skinner, Richard 45
Slim, Governor-General Sir William 299
Smith, Alexander (also John Adams) see Adams, John
Smith, Christopher 71
Smith, J. W. 200
Smith, Stephen 213
Spalding, William Warner 270–272
Spalding, Willie (son) 270–272
St Barnabas see Melanesian Mission on Norfolk Island
Staines, Captain 114–115
Stanley, Lord 202, 204, 205
Stavars, Captain 160
Steward, John Mainwaring 283
Stewart, George
    Bounty expedition to Tahiti 37–39, 51–52, 54, 57, 59
    mutiny on Bounty 42, 44